Practical Sustainability

Practical Sustainability

From Grounded Theory to Emerging Strategies

Nasrin R. Khalili

palgrave
macmillan

PRACTICAL SUSTAINABILITY

Softcover reprint of the hardcover 1st edition 2011 978-0-230-10452-5
MyCopy version of the original edition 2011

First published in 2011 by
PALGRAVE MACMILLAN®
in the United States—a division of St. Martin's Press LLC,
175 Fifth Avenue, New York, NY 10010.

Where this book is distributed in the UK, Europe and the rest of the world, this is by Palgrave Macmillan, a division of Macmillan Publishers Limited, registered in England, company number 785998, of Houndmills, Basingstoke, Hampshire RG21 6XS.

Palgrave Macmillan is the global academic imprint of the above companies and has companies and representatives throughout the world.

DOI 10.1057/9780230116368

Library of Congress Cataloging-in-Publication Data

Khalili, Nasrin R., 1955–
Practical sustainability / Nasrin R. Khalili.
p. cm.

1. Sustainable development. 2. Management—Environmental aspects. 3. Corporations—Environmental aspects. 4. Social responsibility of business. I. Title.

HC79.E5K445 2011
658.4'083—dc22 2010025269

A catalogue record of the book is available from the British Library.

Design by Newgen Imaging Systems (P) Ltd., Chennai, India.

First edition: January 2011

Springer.com/mycopy

To my sons, Parham and Parsa,
for their love, support, and encouragement.

CONTENTS

ILLUSTRATIONS

Tables

Figures

ACKNOWLEDGMENT

I wish to thank Ms. Margaret M. Murphy for her editorial assistance and contribution to this book. Margaret is Assistant Director of the Wanger Institute for Sustainable Energy Research (WISER) at the Illinois Institute of Technology. Ms. Murphy holds a B.A. degree from Northwestern University and an M.S. degree in Technical Communications and Information Design from IIT.

CHAPTER 1

Theory and Concept of Sustainability and Sustainable Development

NASRIN R. KHALILI

This chapter provides an overview of the theories and concepts of sustainability and sustainable development and their anticipated links to global environmental, economic, and social crises. The theory of climate change and its likely impact on natural resources and their capacity for supporting sustainable economic development are discussed, and a comprehensive analysis of the concepts of sustainability (definition and types) and the sustainable development paradigm is provided. Due to its relevance to the topic of environmental sustainability, an overview of the Natural Capital, Natural Steps, and Factor X rules and definitions are also provided. Scenario-based analysis that has been used successfully in the development of strategic planning exercises and sustainability-related policies, rules, and regulations is discussed. The core thrust of economic, social, and environmental sustainability, emerging strategies, and developing praxis presented in this chapter and throughout the book support the concept of *practical sustainability* defined here as an integrated approach to long-term environmental sustainability.

Introduction

The *Random House Webster's College Dictionary* defines "environment" as the aggregate of surrounding things, conditions, or influences. The surroundings include the air, water, minerals, organisms, and all other external factors surrounding and affecting a given organism, as well as social and cultural forces. The term "ecology" is characterized as the branch of biology dealing with the relationships and interactions between organisms and their natural environment. Both environment and ecology have the potential to change according to external and internal, and natural and man-made forces, such as severe air and water pollution, drought, floods, deforestation, and land degradation due to natural disasters, wars, or political and social transformations. For example, heavy metal pollution, especially lead pollution, is considered to be one of the major factors that contributed to the fall of Rome.[1]

The industrial revolution and economic growth have also been linked to the observed environmental and ecological changes and transformations. The rate and the characteristics of the changes, however, vary according to the biophysical, geographical, social, cultural, and economic conditions and the intensity with which materials and energy are used and industrial pollutants are discharged to the environment.[2]

Economic growth, as expected, results in increases in both production and consumption of goods and services, and also generation of different types of pollution, waste, and by-products over a wide range of scales. Two important dimensions of the interaction between natural environmental resources and pollution are the "pollution patterns" and the "nature of variation" in the characteristics, health, and environment's absorptive capacity for emissions. The dynamics of such interactions change according to the natural resource endowment and the environmental space. As a result, if the mechanisms of economic growth are not controlled or altered, they could severely impact the environment via overexploitation of natural resources and degradation and loss of environmental utility (physical, chemical, and biological conditions), space, and adsorptive capacity.[3,4]

The most discussed, publicized, and politicized impact of economic growth and industrialization on the natural environment is, however, the theory of the "climate change" phenomenon. Climate can be defined by patterns of temperature, precipitation, humidity, wind, and seasons, or the average weather over a longer period of time. Climate change, therefore, is explained by the change in the statistical distribution of weather over given periods of time that could range from decades to millions of years. As a normal and expected phenomenon, climate has been changing throughout geological history, and as such, current climate changes can also be attributed to the natural variability. However, recent strong observational evidence and modeling studies suggest that human activities and industrial growth, especially during the last five decades, have significantly impacted the characteristics and dynamics of such a change, particularly with regard to the climate temperature profile and sea levels. Climate change is no longer perceived as the normal fluctuations of the weather; rather, it is identified as the factor that is altering the nature and rate of those changes.[5]

The *International Panel on Climate Change (IPCC)* refers to climate change as a change in the state of the climate that can be identified by changes in the mean or the variability of its properties over decades or longer. The *United Nations Framework Convention on Climate Change (UNFCCC)* has also identified climate change as a change of climate attributed directly or indirectly to human activity that alters the composition of the global atmosphere and is, in addition to natural climate variability, observed over comparable time periods.[6,7]

What Causes Climate Change and Global Warming?

The main effect of the industrial process is attributed to the air emissions that result in changes in the concentration of certain trace gases such as carbon dioxide, chlorofluorocarbons, methane, nitrous oxide, ozone, and water vapor, known collectively as greenhouse gases (GHGs), in the atmosphere. Global GHG emissions due to industrial activities and human behavior have grown consistently since preindustrial times, resulting in a 70% increase between 1970 and 2004. The annual emission of carbon dioxide (CO_2), the most important anthropogenic GHG, alone has grown during this period by about 80%, from 21 to 38 gigatons (Gt), accounting for 77% of the total anthropogenic GHG emissions in 2004.

These results and other theoretical estimations suggest that carbon dioxide emissions alone account for about half of the human-induced GHG contribution to global warming since the late 1800s, with increases in the other GHGs accounting for the rest.[8]

Having strong potential for trapping heat, GHGs are accumulating in the troposphere, the earth's lower atmosphere. Acting as a blanket, these gases reduce the outgoing infrared radiation emitted by the earth and its atmosphere, resulting in an increase in the surface and atmospheric temperature and changes in the global temperature profile.

GHGs, however, differ in their warming influence, or radiative forcing, on the global climate system due to their different radiative properties and lifetimes in the atmosphere. The warming influence of GHGs may be expressed through a common metric based on the radiative forcing of CO_2, defined as "CO_2 equivalent" emission. Equivalent CO_2 emission is a standard and useful metric for comparing emissions of different GHGs. The equivalent CO_2 emission is obtained by multiplying the emission of a GHG by its Global Warming Potential (GWP) for a given time horizon. For a mix of GHGs, warming influence is then obtained by summing the equivalent CO_2 emissions of each gas. The CO_2-equivalent "concentration" is defined as the "concentration" of CO_2 that would cause the same amount of radiative forcing as a given mixture of CO_2 and other forcing components.[9]

The severity of the impacts of climate change, however, is subject to the circumstances of the exposure, geographical conditions, lifestyle, culture, social and technical resources, and the economic and concurrent health status of the exposed populations.[10]

The Potential Impacts of Climate Change

With *a high level of confidence*, IPCC studies suggest that recent regional changes in temperature have had discernible impacts on the earth's physical and biological systems. Examples of such impacts include the enlargement and increased numbers of glacial lakes, increased ground instability in permafrost regions, rock avalanches in mountain regions, changes in some Arctic and Antarctic ecosystems including those in sea-ice biomes, increased runoff and earlier spring peak discharge in many glacier and snow-fed rivers, and warming of lakes and rivers in many regions that affected thermal structure and water quality.

Other effects of temperature increases that have been documented with *a medium confidence level* are in agricultural and forestry management in the higher latitudes of the Northern Hemisphere. Examples of such changes are earlier spring planting of crops and alterations in disturbances of forests due to fires and pests. Some aspects of human health, such as excess-heat-related mortality, changes in infectious disease vectors in parts of Europe, and earlier onset of and increase in seasonal production of allergenic pollen in Northern Hemisphere high and mid-latitudes are also attributed to the unexpected rate of global warming.[11]

Although debatable, it is logical to assume that the economies of all regions or nations would be damaged by an increase in global temperature, and as such we would face a global economy that is affected by this phenomenon.[12] The 2009 report "Shaping Climate-Resilient

Development," by the Economics of Climate Adaptation Working Group, estimated that climate risks could cost nations up to 19% of their GDP by 2030, with the highest impact being observed in developing countries. For example, in Florida, under a high climate change scenario, the report estimates an annual expected loss of $33 billion from hurricanes, more than 10% of GDP.

Even though the impacts of future ecological and climate changes can be spatially and socially differentiated and resource-dependent communities are expected to be impacted the most according to their natural and social systems, upon analysis of eight separate cases in China, the United States, Guyana, Mali, the United Kingdom, Samoa, India, and Tanzania, the report concluded that cost-effective adaptation measures to climate change already exist and, if used properly, could prevent between 40% and 68% of the expected global economic loss.[13,14]

Managing Climate Change Risk

The IPCC has used socioeconomic information and emissions data to predict climatic change by characterizing anthropogenic drivers, impacts, responses to climate change, and their linkages. With an increased understanding of these linkages, it is now possible to evaluate potential development pathways and global emissions constraints that would reduce the risk of future impacts that society may wish to avoid. The 2009 report suggests a methodology for determining risks that climate change imposes on the economy and a set of decision-making tools for a tailored approach to estimating impacts based on local climate conditions.

Despite much uncertainty, "economic growth" has been identified as the main driver of biodiversity losses related to climate change. The main challenge today is how to configure economic growth in an ethical manner and address the rules of ethics/social behavior, atmospheric space for safe levels of GHG emissions, ecological space for socially beneficial economic growth, ecological and economic carrying capacities, development options, and economic growth space of the planet.[15] The core thrust of future economic developments should be satisfaction of the basic economic, social, and security needs now and in the future without undermining the natural resource base and environmental quality on which life depends. Under proper financial, social, and environmental policies and programs, climate change could move from *speculation* to a *strategic opportunity* for economic, environmental, and societal development.

Climate change looms large on the sustainability agenda for economic development and business practices and models for a sustainable future. It is no longer considered simply an environmental issue. Societies can respond to climate change by adapting to its impacts and by reducing GHG emissions, thereby reducing the rate and magnitude of change. This requires design, development, adaptation, and mitigation options supported by well-designed policies, programs, and strategies for "sustainable development." The capacity to adapt and mitigate is, however, dependent on socioeconomic and environmental circumstances, in addition to the availability of information, education, communication, and technology innovations.[16] The following sections discuss the concept of "sustainability" and the "sustainable development paradigm," which emphasizes addressing climate change.

What Is Sustainability?

The basic underlying concept behind most notions of sustainability in the literature appears to be the implicit measure of the economy's generalized capacity to produce economic well-being over time.[17] The impacts of economic development and industrial growth on the existing physical, institutional, and intellectual structure of society and its natural systems are, however, well documented. Sustainability, by definition, addresses these impacts by defining and formulating the relationship between dynamic human economic systems and slower-changing ecological systems, in which human life can continue indefinitely, human individuals can flourish, and human cultures can develop, while the diversity, complexity, and function of the ecological life-support system are protected. Sustainability is also an economic state in which the demands placed upon the environment and natural resources by people and commerce can be met without reducing the capacity of the environment to provide for future generations.[18]

Economics Nobelist Sir John Hicks conceptualized sustainability in 1946 when he defined income as the amount, whether natural or financial capital, one could consume during a period and still be as well-off at the end of the period. The concept became global after Brundtland and the United Nations Commission announced in 1987 the urgent need for sustainability. Since then, many nations and institutions have been trying to define the concept of "sustainability" and its relevance to their operations, values, and functionality. In 1991, Solow defined sustainability as "an obligation or injunction to conduct ourselves so that we leave to the future the options and the capacity to be as well-off as we are, not to satisfy ourselves by impoverishing our successors."[19]

The concept of sustainability, however, is still evolving as we learn more about its multi-faceted, complex nature. Most efforts toward defining sustainability to date have focused on the interdisciplinary theoretical issues and the empirical understanding of economic aspects, ecological conditions, and social values of sustainability, or the *economy-ecology-social* nexus.[20] The need for defining and pursuing sustainability has become increasingly evident as the ecological crisis has been further linked to human activities and, similarly, the environmental crisis was clearly correlated with the economic, social, political, and cultural crises. Because natural, economic, and social systems are all interdependent, it is logical that they must all be addressed when creating sustainable solutions to the environmental crisis.[21] Due to its integrated nature, sustainability has been classified into three systems: *economic*, *social*, and *environmental*.[22] Following is a brief introduction to the three systems of sustainability:

Economic sustainability. Economic sustainability focuses on the portion of the natural resource base that provides physical input, both renewable and exhaustible, into the production process. In economic terms, sustainability can be described as the "maintenance of the capital" or "nondeclining capital" in which capital is referred to as man-made capital.[23]

Environmental sustainability. Environmental sustainability adds consideration of the physical input into the production process, emphasizing environmental life-support systems such as atmosphere, water, and soil. According to environmental sustainability, environmental service capacity must be maintained in order to support economic and social sustainability; accordingly, continuous depletion and damage by human activities to irreversible and nonsubstitutable environmental services would be incompatible with the thrust of environmental sustainability.

Social sustainability. Social sustainability addresses poverty and human development. Poverty reduction, as presented in the next section, is the primary goal of sustainable development. Environmental sustainability, or the maintenance of the life-support system, is the predominant prerequisite for social sustainability.[24]

While there is some overlap among the three core thrusts of sustainability, and certainly linkages, they are commonly disaggregated and addressed separately by different disciplines. However, environmental sustainability, as defined today, addresses protection of the *natural environment* and the *social systems*, and as such also speaks to welfare and economic growth. A more detailed review of environmental sustainability and its principles are provided in the following sections in order to describe what environmental sustainability is, what it stands for, and how and at what capacity it can be associated with the sustainable development paradigm.

Environmental Sustainability

The scientific revolution of the seventeenth century led to the development of such environmental-ecological-social theories as "technocentrism" (*also labeled as cornucopianism, expansionism, growthmania, shallow environmentalism*, or *weak sustainability*) and "ecocentrism" (*referred to as neo-Malthusianism, preservation, steady-stateness, deep ecology*, or *strong sustainability*) in an attempt to understand the human-environment relationship. The "sustaincentric" science and technology theory was then developed in an effort to define the extent to which natural systems can absorb and equilibrate human-caused disruptions in their autonomous processes. This theory also suggested that the global ecosystem is finite, non growing, materially closed, vulnerable to human interference, and limited in its regenerative and assimilative capacities, and as such recommended that an economic system to provide humanity with its material goods must sustain ecological systems since changes in one affect the other significantly.[25]

In the 1960s and 1970s, it was well recognized that human activities have potentially disastrous impacts on the natural environment. In 1977, when concern was high over the consequences of fossil fuel depletion, John Hartwick published the Hartwick Rule, which stated, "To sustain consumption/utility in the face of declining resource stocks requires maintaining the total capital stock constant, which means investing all resource rents in reproducible capital." Decades later, environmental sustainability was defined in response to the concern over the sustainability of consumption as the result of increasing evidence of long-term damage being done to the global natural environment.[26]

In 1977, the term "natural capital" was introduced for the aggregate of natural resource stocks. The World Bank defined natural capital as the sum of nonrenewable resources (including oil, natural gas, coal, and mineral resources), cropland, pastureland, forested areas (including areas used for timber extraction and nontimber forest products), and protected areas.[27]

The main focus of the natural capital approach is management of renewable (and, to some extent, nonrenewable) resources via aggregation using a certain set of prices. According to Stern, 1997, the issue with the natural capital approach is that, even if the assumed prices of natural capital are the "correct" sustainability prices, they do not reflect opportunity costs and preferences that result from the distribution of wealth endowments among individuals and organizations. The risk, therefore, is that it might not always be possible to define and process compensation for irreversible environmental changes resulting from uncontrolled use of resources.[28] Consequently, moving from the current economic system to natural capitalism would require a dramatic increase in productivity of natural resources by implementing whole system design, adopting innovative technologies, using biologically inspired production models (*closed-loop manufacturing, elimination of use of toxics in production*), developing solutions-based business models (*service leasing, not product selling*), and finally reinvesting in natural capital to protect and replenish our natural resources.[29]

Natural Steps. The Natural Steps approach introduced the foundation for the *paradigm shift to sustainable development*. According to this approach, in a sustainable society nature should not be overexploited, extraction of substances from the earth's crust must be restricted, concentrations of substances produced by society must be controlled, and people and society as a whole should not be compromised and subjected to conditions that systemically undermine their capacity to meet their needs. In translating these to sustainability, four principles can be created to directly eliminate (a) our contribution to the progressive buildup of substances extracted from the earth, (b) progressive buildup of chemicals and compounds produced by society, (c) progressive physical degradation and destruction of nature and natural processes, and (d) conditions that undermine people's capacity to meet their basic human needs (for example, unsafe working conditions and insufficient pay).[30]

Factor X (factor 4/factor 10). One of the emergent ideas in the 1990s relevant to reducing the environmental impact of economic activities is the factor *X* reduction in resource use, with *X* being between 4 and 50. The factor *X* is a quantitative measure that is qualitatively similar to the concepts of "dematerialization," "eco-efficiency," and "increased natural resource productivity." Given technological constraints, achievable values for *X* may vary widely among different economic activities. In practice, it is likely that government-driven technology-based programs could assist in achieving a desired value for factor *X*. The factor *X*, as it is used in practice, may relate to a product, a service, an area of specific need, a sector of the economy, or the economy as a whole. The lower values proposed for *X* (a multiple of four) relate to near-term possibilities for environmental improvements, while the higher values indicate longer-term improvement potential.[31]

The factor *X* is also related to the theory of *IPAT*, which defines relative contributions of *population*, *affluence*, and *technology* to the environmental impact of the economies. In this context, the following formula is often used to estimate environmental impact as a function of population, affluence, and factor of technology:

$$I(\text{environmental impact}) = P(\text{population}) \times A(\text{affluence}) \times T(\text{technology})$$

$$I = P \times A \times T$$

$$I = P \times \frac{Y}{P} \times \frac{I}{Y}$$

$$A = \frac{Y}{P} = \text{Output } Y \text{ per Capita}$$

$$\frac{I}{Y} = \text{Environmental Impact Per Unit of Output}$$

Similar formulas may be used to characterize resource or material flows in the economy. The factor *X* debate concentrates largely on the technology factor and puts forward that improvements in technology may be counterbalanced by increases in affluence or population. For example, this model suggests that one dollar's worth of solar heating stresses the environment less than one dollar's worth of heat from a lignite-fired thermal power plant. According to the IPAT model, environmental sustainability could be achieved via investing in environmental production (for the amenity value) and reducing the environmental impact of human activities by changing three main variables: P, A, and T (*limiting population growth, limiting affluence,* and *improving technology to reduce throughput intensity of production*).[32,33]

The Four Degrees of Environmental Sustainability

In economic terms, sustainability is defined as nondeclining utility that provides life opportunities with specific endowments of reproduced capital, technological capacity, natural resources, and environmental quality. The capital resource substitutions then are acceptable if they benefit both present and future generations. The four degrees of sustainability concept defines capital as (a) man-made, which is commonly considered in financial and economic accounts; (b) natural; (c) human, which refers to education, health, capability, and nutrition of individual; and (d) social, which is the institutional and cultural basis needed for a society to function. Depending on the degree of impact on these types of capital, sustainability can be defined as *weak*, *intermediate*, *strong*, or *absurdly strong*. The difference between them is dependent on how substitutable and interchangeable the four types of man-made, natural, human, and social capital are. Figure 1.1 illustrates and explains the four degrees of environmental sustainability. As shown, intermediate sustainability represents a significant improvement over weak sustainability, but at defined limit(s), intermediate sustainability approaches strong sustainability. When dealing with strong sustainability, efforts to define sustainability in the context of economic theory could face firm criticism. For example, given the spirit of sustainability, it is not acceptable that sustainability criteria impose constraints on policy choices and the conception of social welfare via economic development. The choice between intermediate and strong sustainability highlights the trade-offs between human-made capital and natural capital.

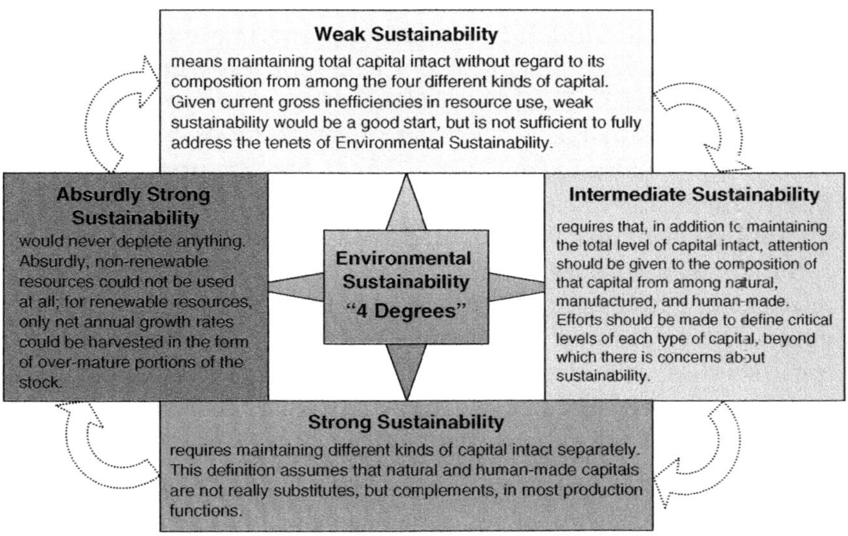

Figure 1.1 The four degrees of environmental sustainability.

The sustainable paths should endorse efficiency and equity as ethical axioms and address those axioms in economic analyses with policies designed to achieve them. Sustainable paths should also invest substantially in sustainable development limiting factors such as growth and maintenance of natural capital, relief of pressure on natural capital stocks and increase in efficiency of products, infrastructure services, and life-style. If economic sustainability is a social goal, the task in the twenty-first century will be to define practical strategies to achieve it.[34]

Environmental sustainability has been branded as the primary approach to sustainable development due to its focus and emphasis on social and economic sustainability such as maintenance of per capita manufactured capital (artifacts, infrastructure), maintenance of renewable natural capital (healthy air, soil, ocean fish stock, natural forests), maintenance of per capita nonrenewable substitutable natural capital, and maintenance of nonrenewable, nonsubstitutable natural resources (e.g., waste absorption by environmental sink services).

Sustainable Development

Sustainability, at its core, means maintaining a sustainable economy that can prevent liquidation of natural capital. Under this condition, sustainable development can be warranted and social sustainability can be linked to environmental sustainability and sustained economic growth.[35]

The concept of sustainable development can be traced back at least as far as the mid-1960s, when "appropriate technology" was promoted as the sustainable way to develop growing nations and evolving countries. The historical and conceptual precursors of the concept of sustainable development have been evolving since and were formally addressed during the famous Stockholm Conference on Environment and Development in 1972 and the World Commission on Environment and Development (WCED) in 1987.[36]

Sustainable development is a vision that is structured around the relationships among economical, social, and environmental phenomena. A wide range of nongovernmental as well as governmental organizations have embraced it as the new paradigm of development[37] and have identified different drivers, solution epicenters/platforms, and leadership instruments for sustainability:

- The Brundtland Commission, through its report *Our Common Future* (1987), initiated the most current discussions on the concept of sustainable development and its geopolitical significance.

Since the definition and subsequent popularization of the term by WCED in 1987, numerous efforts have been made to capture the meaning of the concept of sustainable development. In broad terms, the existing variety of definitions of "sustainable development" are categorized, depending on the constituent, into three major groups: institutional, ideological, and academic. All of these definitions acknowledge that the world is faced with an environmental crisis, and therefore a fundamental change must be made in the way economic development is pursued to overcome this crisis.

- Committed to the sustainable development paradigm, the International Institute for Environment and Development (IIED) called for objectives of any process of development to be centered on maximizing the biological or ecological resource system, the economic system, the social system, and all these three systems at one time through an adaptive process of trade-offs.
- The United Nations Conference on Environment and Development (UNCED) Rio Conference (also known as the Rio Summit) led to the production of major international documents such as the Rio Declaration, Agenda 21, and conventions on desertification, biodiversity, and climate change in its effort to lead the world toward sustainable economic development.
- The World Business Council on Sustainable Development (WBCSD) has firmly committed to the concept of sustainable development and has recognized that economic growth and environmental protection are inextricably linked, and that the quality of present and future life rests on meeting basic human needs without destroying the environment upon which all life depends. The charter of WBCSD states: "Business leaders are committed to sustainable development, to meeting the needs of the present without compromising the welfare of future generations."[38]

In addition to establishing an ecologically and environmentally desired or target value, sustainable development objectives must be set according to the economic and social values through a societal negotiating process, and strategies and models that can be formulated according to the welfare economics and societal cost-benefit analysis.[39] In the quest to find a single concept to sum up the business approach to sustainable development, most firms have opted for eco-efficiency as their guiding principle. Eco-efficiency is serving as a valuable part of corporate strategies toward sustainable development. It is, however, important to treat eco-efficiency as only one part of the corporate sustainability criteria.[40,41]

Global Sustainable Development Scenarios

The pursuit of sustainable development requires an understanding of the present situation, a vision for future economic development, and the formulation of policies that can support it according to the limitations and constraints of natural systems, environmental carrying capacity, and climate change. The projected levels and types of economic growth can also be influenced by cultural distinctions, international governance, geopolitical conflict, migration, and global warming.[42] Among other strategies, scenario-based analysis has been used successfully in the strategic planning exercises summarized in the most recent assessment report of the Intergovernmental Panel on Climate Change. Scenario-based analysis is a strong strategic planning tool used to develop conceptual frameworks for the analysis of sustainable development scenarios and the quantification of economic, social, technological, and environmental drivers of sustainability.

Worldviews or scenarios built according to economic measures and capability analysis would assist governments with their policy decisions and analysis of the risks and opportunities associated with sustainable development scenarios and alternatives. Focusing on economic growth, a precondition for the continuation and improvement of the quality of life, de Vries and Petersen (2009) showed how "worldviews" can shape sustainability scenarios. In a participatory setting, with stakeholder involvements, they have identified four dimensions of global logics for sustainable development: Market Force Logic, Fortress World Logic, Global Governance Logic, and Civic Society Logic.[43] As shown in Figure 1.2, for example, *Market Force Logic* predicts a market-oriented world that can be developed according to the economic and wealth measure. In this world material wealth is essential to a high quality of life and can only be acquired using a specialized skill set in a free market. Growth and development are ensured by market driven economic efficiency, and minimal government regulation and barriers to trade goods, services, capital, labor, and allocation of resources are allowed. In contrast, *Civic Society Logic* refers to development that is rooted in small-scale enterprises, social and cultural traditions, the community, and nature. The focus of this development is on local needs and livelihoods to which technology

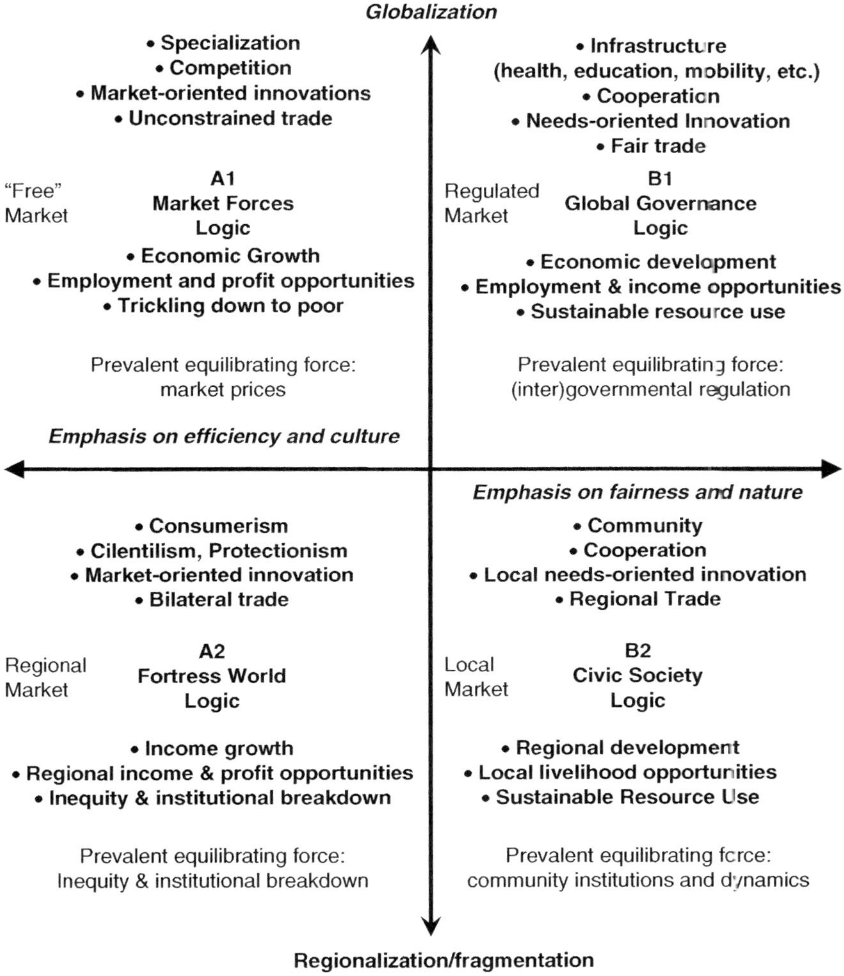

Figure 1.2 Scenario logic in the four IPCC-SRES quadrants: economic growth (with permission from de Vries and Petersen 2009, p. 1012).

and governance should be geared. The *Global Governance Logic* identifies international cooperation and solidarity as the core for solving large-scale and long-term social and environmental problems that the world is facing today. This scenario requires a strong governmental and institutional commitment to the provision of basic needs in health and education, aid, and fair trade based on institutions and the diplomacy of the European Union and the United Nations. The *Fortress World Logic* primarily focuses on regional market growth and profit opportunities. The prevalent equilibrating force for this logic is inequity and institutional breakdown.

Sustainability-Related Policies, Rules, and Regulations

Recognition of the social and financial risks associated with uncontrolled release of industrial emissions and resulting environmental damages spawned environmentally thoughtful stewardship and development of environmentally focused programs and specific laws and regulations enforcing pollution control and abatements in the early 1970s. A decade later, the concepts of pollution prevention and cleaner production emerged and were enforced in order to minimize the release of pollutants at their sources. Into the 1990s, regulatory and enforcement agencies, and corporations and business communities began ruminating on environmental sustainability as a contributing component to protecting the environment while maintaining business sustainability.[44] The corporate approach to environmental sustainability, however, has been gloomy and uncertain. In the mid-1990s, it was recognized that environmental sustainability is unlikely to be achievable without addressing the companion issues of economic and social sustainability. Accordingly, the World Bank expanded the sustainability formula and included traditional investments in human capital, concerns with governance and promotion of the civil society (investment in social capital), and growing concern with natural capital and its maintenance.[45]

Impact of Environmental Policies

Economic growth and industrialization result in significant societal and structural changes. For example, growth results in negative externalities due to the emission of pollutants and waste resulting from both production and use of goods and services. A wide variety of policy initiatives, such as pollution control law and regulations, and pollution prevention programs have been developed and aimed at the abatement and reduction or elimination of those emissions. Abatement, however, can be pursued by political "technology forcing" through command and control policies. While still in practice, this approach requires significant investment and commonly results in the generation of different types of secondary emissions (for example, the generation of wastewater from the treatment of polluted air emissions). The pollution control and abatement approach is fast and effective, but it is not fully efficient and is limited in its scope. Avoiding emissions at their source can be achieved via programs such as USEPA pollution prevention or UN cleaner production programs, by substitution, by throughput reduction, or a combination of all of these.[46] These methods, however, are costly and are constrained by the availability of technologies and financial resources.

Environmental policy instruments are classified as those focused on legislation, education, and information to consumers. Market-based instruments such as subsidies, taxes, and pricing have been emerging and are proven to be successful for fighting pollution and environmental externalities. Policy instruments are also used to design free market allocation of resources, niche or green marketing, and incentives for long-term investments in the market.[47]

Climate Change Policies

Economics has played a visible role in climate policy debates in the United States and elsewhere—a more prominent role than it has played in some other environmental problems. Dimensions of the economic approach to analyzing, understanding, and developing solutions to the problem of climate change are complex, technology-constrained, and predominantly involve, among others, the identification and assessment of physical and technological dimensions of the problem and possible solutions; estimates of the costs and benefits of controlling the emissions leading to climate change; review of the fundamental economics of the problem; development of an example analytic model that captures the economic approach to the problem; design of climate policy instruments; and formulation of viable international climate agreements.[48]

Governments may have different sets of criteria for assessing international and domestic greenhouse policy instruments. Among these criteria are efficiency and cost-effectiveness; competence in achieving stated environmental targets; distributional (including intergenerational) equity; flexibility in the face of new knowledge; understandability to the general public; and consistency with national priorities, policies, institutions, and traditions. The choice of instruments may also partly reflect a desire on the part of governments to achieve other objectives, such as sustainable economic development, meeting social development goals and fiscal targets, or influencing pollution levels that are indirectly related to greenhouse gas emissions. A further concern of governments may lie in the effect of policies on competitiveness.[49]

Different scenarios can be assumed while a climate change policy is discussed. The scenario-based approach defines the best scenarios, given the availability of certain policies, for meeting the policy objectives. The first best scenario assumes the availability of a policy mechanism that can target R&D efforts either through a tax or a subsidy. In the absence of such a mechanism, a higher initial carbon tax to spur R&D expenditures can be suggested indirectly by increasing abatement costs. These scenarios are more effective when environmental damage is certain or reasonably quantifiable. Under uncertainty of environmental damage, achieving environmental goals must be pursued at the least monetary cost to industry. All of the proposed policy scenarios assign a cost or provide a benefit if a subsidy is used to fund R&D activities.[50]

Summary

The Industrial Revolution and resulting economic growth have also resulted in dramatic ecological changes and environmental adversities and degradation. The rate and the characteristics of the environmental and ecological transformation vary according to social, economic, and technological changes; cultural diversity; and the intensity with which material and energy are used and pollutants are discharged. Due to its nature and distinctiveness, environmental crises such as climate change and global warming are attributed to the pattern of human activities, particularly industrialization. Although it is difficult to recognize and measure these changes during an individual lifespan, they are indeed occurring, according to the observational studies and global trajectory models.

The impacts of economic development and resulting industrial growth on the existing physical, institutional, and intellectual structures of society and its natural systems are well documented. Sustainability, by definition, addresses these impacts by defining and formulating the relationship between dynamic human economic systems and slower-changing ecological systems, in which human life can continue indefinitely, human individuals can flourish, and human cultures can develop, while diversity, complexity, and function of the ecological life-support system are protected. Sustainability is also an economic state in which the demands placed upon the environment and natural resources by people and commerce can be met without reducing the capacity of the environment to provide for future generations. Human society applies a set of goals to economic, social, and environmental systems of sustainability, each with its own hierarchy of subgoals and targets.

We must learn to manage renewable resources for the long term; to reduce waste and pollution; to use energy and materials with scrupulous efficiency; to use energy economically and, more importantly, to invest in repairing the damage to portions of the natural capital stock that are deemed nonsubstitutable by man-made alternatives. Sustainability demands such critical natural capital to remain intact or preserved by setting preventive constraints on resources. Other less critical natural capital, however, can be converted into man-made capital possessing equivalent welfare-generating capacity. Using various scenarios, sustainability studies attempt to understand how global development could evolve during the coming decades; what the critical uncertainties are; how environmental, social, and economic processes could interact; and what direction policies and programs should take to best assist in the quest for a sustainable world. The maximization of present value should then be constrained in an economic and practical manner by the well-being of future generations.

From a business perspective, the goal of sustainability is to increase long-term shareholder and social value, while decreasing industry's use of materials and reducing negative impacts on the environment. Polices specific to sustainable development must be developed in support of a growing economy that aims at reducing the social and environmental costs of economic growth. Accordingly, sustainable development must foster policies that integrate environmental, economic, and social values in all facets of decision making. From a business perspective, *sustainable development* favors an approach based on capturing system dynamics, building resilient and adaptive systems, anticipating and managing variability and risk, and earning a profit. Sustainable development is a *reflection of the synergy* between business and the environment, *not the trade-off* between them.

Case Study

Global Warming Effect on Midwestern Heat Waves

In coming decades heat waves in the Midwest are likely to become more frequent, longer, and hotter than cities in the region have experienced in the past. This trend will result from a combination of general warming, which will raise temperatures more frequently above thresholds to which people have adapted, and more frequent and intense weather patterns that produce heat waves. Examples of heat wave impacts due to global warming include *health risks* and *impact on wildfire.*

Studies projecting future mortality from heat anticipate a substantial increase in health risks from heat waves. Several factors contribute to increasing risk in Midwestern cities, including demographic shifts to more vulnerable populations and an infrastructure originally designed to withstand the less severe heat extremes of the past. The elderly living in inner cities are particularly vulnerable to stronger heat waves; other groups, including children and the infirm, are vulnerable as well. Adaptations of infrastructure and public health systems will be required to cope with increased heat stress in a warmer climate.

Wildfire is a natural part of the Western landscape and is very sensitive to climate variability. In recent decades, a trend toward earlier spring snowmelt and hotter, drier summers has already increased the number and duration of large wildfires in the West. Although total annual precipitation may increase in the Northwest, climate projections generally foresee less precipitation throughout the West during the summer when risk of fire is greatest. In Alaska and Canada, warming has accelerated the reproduction of insect pests and increased the winter survival and geographic range, which may make forests more vulnerable to fire by killing more trees. Development in the West has placed more people and assets in fire-prone areas, increasing the need to suppress wildfires. Ironically, suppression increases the risk of catastrophic fire by allowing vegetation to build up, providing more fuel for fires when they ignite. Humans have also introduced invasive plant species that consume limited soil moisture and burn readily. Careful attention to development decisions and human-induced ecosystem stressors may help with adapting to increased risk from fire in the West resulting from climate change.[51]

Notes

1. Desta Mebratu, "Sustainability and Sustainable Development: Historical and Conceptual Review," *Environmental Impact Assessment Review* 18 (1988): 493–520.
2. Jean Garner Stead and Edward Stead, "Eco-Enterprise Strategy: Standing for Sustainability," *Journal of Business Ethics* 24 (April 2000): 313–29.
3. Richard M. Auty, "Pollution Patterns during the Industrial Transition," *The Geographical Journal* 163 (1997): 206–15.
4. Joachim H. Spangenberg, "The Environmental Kuznets Curve: A Methodological Artefact?" *Population and Environment* 23 (2001): 175–91.
5. Charles D. Kolstad and Michael Toman, "The Economics of Climate Policy," *Resources for the Future* (June 2001). http://ageconsearch.umn.edu/bitstream/10783/1/dp000040.pdf.
6. "Intergovernmental Panel on Climate Change Report," Nov. 12–17, 2007, Valencia, Spain, report assessment.
7. Resources for the Future. The Economics of Climate Policy, June 2007, http://ageconsearch.umn.edu/bitstream/10783/1/dp000040.pdf.
8. "American Meteorological Society: An Information Statement," *Climate Change*, February 2007, http://www.ametsoc.org/policy/2007climatechange.pdf.

9. "Intergovernmental Panel on Climate Change Report," Nov. 12–17, 2007, Valencia, Spain, report assessment.
10. Anthony J. McMichael and Andrew Haines, "Global Climate Change: The Potential Effects on Health Source," *British Medical Journal* 315 (Sept. 27, 1997): 805–9.
11. "Intergovernmental Panel on Climate Change Report," Nov. 12–17, 2007, Valencia, Spain, report assessment.
12. Kenneth R. Stollery, "Constant Utility Paths and Irreversible Global Warming," *The Canadian Journal of Economics* 31 (1998): 730–42.
13. Neil W. Adger, "Social Capital, Collective Action, and Adaptation to Climate Change," *Economic Geography* 79 (2003): 387–404.
14. Shaping Climate-Resilient Development: A Framework for Decision-Making", 2009, A Report of the Economics of Climate Adaptation Working Group, http://www.swissre.com/resources, (accessed September 2, 2010) (http://www.swissre.com/resources/387fd3804f928069929e92b3151d9332-ECA_Shaping_Climate_Resilent_Development.pdf) (Swiss re).
15. Jon Rosales, "Economic Growth, Climate Change, Biodiversity Loss: Distributive Justice for the Global North and South," *Conservation Biology* 22 (2008): 1409–17.
16. Neil Adger, "Social Capital, Collective Action, and Adaptation to Climate Change," *Economic Geography* 79 (2003): 387–404.
17. Martin L. Weitzman, "Sustainability and Technical Progress," *The Scandinavian Journal of Economics* 99 (1997): 1–13.
18. Thomas N. Gladwin, James J. Kennelly, and Tara-Shelomith Krause, "Shifting Paradigms for Sustainable Development: Implications for Management Theory and Research," *The Academy of Management Review* 20 (1993): 874–907.
19. Robert Goodland and Daly Herman, "Environmental Sustainability: Universal and Non-Negotiable," *Ecological Applications* 6 (1996): 1002–17.
20. Michael A. Toman, "Economics and Sustainability: Balancing Trade-Offs and Imperatives," *Land Economics* 70 (1994): 399–413.
21. Desta Mebratu, "Sustainability and Sustainable Development: Historical and Conceptual Review," *Environmental Impact Assessment Review* 18 (1998): 493–520.
22. Richard Peet and Michael Watts, *Liberation Ecologies: Environment, Development, Social Movements* (London: Routledge, 1996), page 1–5.
23. Robert Goodland and Daly Herman, "Environmental Sustainability: Universal and Non-Negotiable," *Ecological Applications* 6 (1996): 1002–17.
24. Robert Goodland, "The Concept of Environmental Sustainability," *Annual Review of Ecology and Systematics* 26 (1995): 1–24.
25. Thomas N. Gladwin, James J. Kennelly, and Tara-Shelomith Krause, "Shifting Paradigms for Sustainable Development: Implications for Management Theory and Research," *The Academy of Management Review* 20 (1993): 874–907.
26. Kenneth R. Stollery, "Constant Utility Paths and Irreversible Global Warming," *The Canadian Journal of Economics* 31 (1998): 730–42.
27. Kirk Hamilton, *Where Is the Wealth of Nations? Measuring Capital for the 21st Century*, (Washington, DC: The World Bank, 2006), page 13. http://siteresources.worldbank.org/INTEEI/214578-1110886258964/20748034/All.pdf.
28. David I. Stern, "The Capital Theory Approach to Sustainability: A Critical Appraisal," *Journal of Economic Issues* 31 (1997): 145–73.
29. Amory B. Lovins, L. Hunter Lovins, and Paul Hawken, "A Road Map for Natural Capitalism," *Harvard Business Review* 85 (1997): 172–83.
30. Timothy Forsyth, "Environmental Responsibility and Business Regulation: The Case of Sustainable Tourism," *The Geographical Journal* 163 (1997): 270–80.

31. Lucas Reijnders, "The Factor X Debate: Setting Targets for Eco-Efficiency," *Journal of Industrial Ecology* 2 (2008): 13–22.
32. Robert Goodland and Daly Herman, "Environmental Sustainability: Universal and Non-Negotiable," *Ecological Applications* 6 (1996): 1002–17.
33. Richard B. Howarth, "Sustainability as Opportunity," *Land Economics* 73 (1997): 569–79.
34. Alistair Ulph and David Ulph, "Global Warming, Irreversibility and Learning," *The Economic Journal* 107 (1997): 636–50.
35. Robert Goodland, "The Concept of Environmental Sustainability," *Annual Review of Ecology and Systematics* 26 (1995): 1–24.
36. Desta Mebratu, "Sustainability and Sustainable Development: Historical and Conceptual Review," *Environmental Impact Assessment Review* 18 (1998): 493–520.
37. Sharachchandra M. Lele, "Sustainable Development: A Critical Review," *World Development* 19 (1991): 607–21.
38. Desta Mebratu, "Sustainability and Sustainable Development: Historical and Conceptual Review," *Environmental Impact Assessment Review* 18 (1998): 493–520.
39. Arthur C. Petersen and Bert J.M. de Vries, "Conceptualizing Sustainable Development: An Assessment Methodology Connecting Values, Knowledge, Worldviews, and Scenarios," *Ecological Economics* 68 (2009): 1006–19.
40. Thomas Dyllick and Kai Hockerts, Beyond the Business Case for Corporate Sustainability *Business Strategy and the Environment* 11 (2002): 403–520.
41. Desta Mebratu, "Sustainability and Sustainable Development: Historical and Conceptual Review," *Environmental Impact Assessment Review* 18 (1998): 493–520.
42. Paul D. Raskin, "Global Scenarios: Background Review for the Millennium Ecosystem Assessment," *Ecosystems* 8 (2005): 133–42.
43. Arthur C. Petersen and Bert J.M. de Vries, "Conceptualizing Sustainable Development: An Assessment Methodology Connecting Values, Knowledge, Worldviews, and Scenarios," *Ecological Economics* 68 (2009): 1006–19.
44. Darrell Brown, Jesse Dillard, and R. Scott Marshall, "Triple Bottom Line: A Business Metaphor for a Social Construct," Departament d'Economia de l'Empresa (March 3, 2006), page 20. http://www.recercat.net/bitstream/2072/2223/1/UABDT06-2.pdf.
45. Robert Goodland and Daly Herman, "Environmental Sustainability: Universal and Non-Negotiable," *Ecological Applications* 6 (1996): 1002–17.
46. Joachim H. Spangenberg, "The Environmental Kuznets Curve: A Methodological Artefact?" *Population and Environment* 23 (2001): 175–91.
47. Timothy Forsyth, "Environmental Responsibility and Business Regulation: The Case of Sustainable Tourism," *The Geographical Journal* 163 (1997): 270–80.
48. Resources for the Future. The Economics of Climate Policy, 2000. http://ageconsearch.umn.edu/bitstream/10783/1/dp000040.pdf.
49. IPCC working group III, Summary for Policymakers: The Economic and Social Dimensions of Climate, 1995. http://www.ipcc.ch/pdf/climate-changes-1995/spm-economic-social-dimensions.pdf.
50. Reyer Gerlagh, Snorre Kverndokk, and Knut Einar Rosendahl, "Optimal Timing of Climate Change Policy: Interaction Between Carbon Taxes and Innovation Externalities," *Environmental and Resource Economics* 43 (2009): 369–90.
51. Kristie L. Ebi, Gerald A. Meehl, Dominique Bachelet, Robert R. Twilley, Donald F. Boesch, et al. "Regional Impacts of Climate Change: Four Case Studies in the United States," Pew Center on Global Climate Change (December 2007): 22. http://www.pewclimate.org/docUploads/Regional-Impacts-Full Report.pdf.

CHAPTER TWO

Strategic Tools for Achieving Long-Term Sustainability

NASRIN R. KHALILI AND WHYNDE MELAFAGNO

This chapter aims at the strategic tools for achieving sustainability. For methodological and pedagogical convenience a global perspective is employed here, spanning multiple approaches to integrate the core values of sustainability in business decisions and strategic planning. The development of strategic tools that are rooted in sustainability core values assists organizations in reaching their overall sustainability goals without compromising any long-term financial viability. Strategy is subsequently characterized as the process of positioning the sustainability concepts within business goals and objectives; developing guidelines that can delineate how specific tools, techniques, and business models can identify environmental sustainability-related issues, and instituting mechanisms to gather data and formulate economically and socially acceptable solutions. Business drivers for sustainability are identified and discussed in addition to providing a framework for the development and implementation of business models, strategies, programs, and systems rooted in core sustainability values. Case studies are utilized to illustrate the utility of corporate social responsibility, environmental management systems, Occupational Health and Safety Management Systems (OHSMS), Life Cycle Assessment (LCA) and management, product stewardship, and the Practical Sustainability System (Stakeholder, Externality, and Asset [SEA] framework) in assisting organizations to meet their business sustainability goals.

Introduction

For certain organizations, such as governmental and nongovernmental institutions, a global strategy may be required. The influence of the concept of sustainable development has increased significantly in national and international policy development, making it the core element of the policy documents of governments, international agencies, and business organizations. During the last century, economic and industrial growth created an unprecedented myriad of systemic dysfunction, each with its own ecological, economic, and social dimensions. This has led to the evolution of new concepts, including that of sustainable development as a basis for overcoming the environmental challenges. It has been nearly two decades since the terms "sustainable development" and "sustainability" were proposed following the 1987 publication of the UN-sponsored World Commission on Environment and Development (WCED) report, Our Common Future.[1]

Transforming management theory and practice so that they positively contribute to sustainable development is the greatest challenge facing industry. There is a general consciousness among industries that a transition to sustainable business practices is necessary to ensure business sustainability and economic viability in the next low-carbon economy. Those organization that anticipate the risks associated with climate change and the opportunities of pursuing sustainability could turn their social, economic, and environmental expertise into competitive advantages. Strategies presented in this chapter describe how to handle environmental issues in a company and reach overall sustainability goals without compromising long-term financial viability. Also presented are outlines for how environmental management tools, techniques, and methods can be integrated and practically used.

Strategies for Sustainability

When selecting or developing strategies and management tools, organizations should be able to simultaneously address business goals and drivers, and also sustainability goals and objectives.
There are three categories of reasons to embed sustainability into an organization's business strategy:

1. The potential for upside benefits
2. The management of downside risks
3. A values-based concern for environmental stewardship[2]

One or more of these categories may apply to an organization. Sustainable organizations do not just improve the state of the environment and society, but also obtain real business benefits at the same time.

For example, since 1997, Interface, Inc. (a manufacturer of modular carpet), led by CEO Ray Anderson, decided to produce zero waste and to not only become the first sustainable corporation in the world, but following that, become the first "restorative company." These goals have not only significantly reduced the organization's environmental impact, but also enabled it to become the number one company in modular carpet worldwide and achieve significant cost savings.

The business drivers for sustainability could be opportunities to take advantage of the "potential upside."[3] Examples of such opportunities are:

- Achieving competitive advantage by providing innovative products or delivering them more efficiently than competitors
- Providing the impetus or framework for innovation
- Creating new markets for new products or services that do not currently exist
- Creating new markets for exemplary environmentally and socially-conscious consumers
- Increasing revenue through increased sales of new or enhanced products or services
- Attracting and retaining employees who want to work for a responsible organization, which is becoming increasingly important, especially to younger generations

The business drivers for "managing the downside" are those that help an organization to increase efficiency or reduce risks, including:

- Meeting compliance requirements by saving cost of fees or lawsuits from not being in compliance with environmental regulations
- Mitigating risks, such as those posed by climate change
- Saving costs through reduced consumption of energy or materials
- Saving time or increasing efficiency through reducing transportation
- Ensuring long-term business security and viability for organizations that depend upon natural resources such as water and trees

The business driver resulting from a "values-based concern for environmental stewardship" is typically the intangible benefit of a *positive*

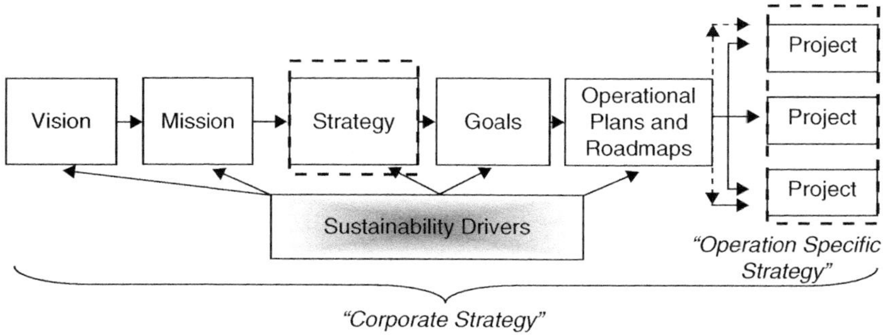

Figure 2.1 Steps involved in sustainability strategic planning.

brand image. A positive image can prove invaluable as customers, investors, governmental organizations, or nongovernmental organizations make choices and interact with an organization.[4] Figure 2.1 presents example steps involved with developing a sustainability strategy:

- Defining sustainability vision, mission, and drivers
- Developing strategies to achieve sustainability
- Defining sustainability goals and objectives, operational plans, and roadmaps
- Planning resources, operation-specific strategies, projects, and activities specific to sustainability goals, objectives, and values

Some organizations begin moving towards sustainability by taking small steps, such as implementing pilot projects, to prove its business value and gain experience with it. However, to embed sustainability in an organization and its culture, sustainability needs to be incorporated into the business strategy and goals during the strategic planning process, just like any other business idea or influence. In fact, many organizations revisit their vision and mission and revise them to align with sustainability values. Once sustainability has been incorporated in the business strategy, it should be implemented in a coordinated way across the organization through operational plans and roadmaps.

There are many approaches to strategic planning, but typically a three-step process is used to evaluate the:

1. Current situation or current state
2. Target situation, which is goals and objectives development for the ideal state
3. Path, which can be defined as a possible route to meet the goals and objectives

Current situation analysis could include analysis of the markets (customers), competition, technology, supplier markets, labor markets, the economy, and the regulatory environment.

Similar to the development or refinement of any corporate business strategy, when addressing sustainability, organizations must evaluate (a) the "external environment" for an organization, which includes factors that influence the future of the organization; (b) the "industry environment," which is a set of factors that directly influence an organization's competitive actions and competitive responses; and (c) the "competitor environment," in which the dynamics of competitors' actions, responses, and intentions are predicted.[5] The perspectives of all internal and external stakeholders should be considered as well. More specifically, as shown in Figure 2.2, the external environment factors are economic, sociocultural, global, technological, political/legal, and demographic. The industry environment factors, however, are identified to be the threat of new entrants, power of suppliers, power of buyers, product substitutes, and intensity of rivalry (also known as Porter's Five Forces).

An organization's culture should also be considered when developing or refining strategy; an organization with a highly conservative culture may not be well suited to position itself as a sustainability leader in its industry or attention by advertising this fact. Rather, it may prefer to simply keep up with competitors, comply with applicable regulations, manage costs, and maintain its reputation.

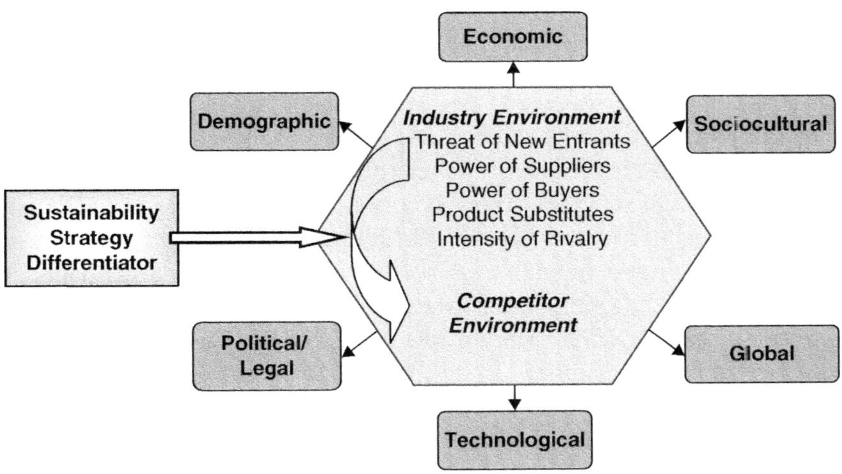

Figure 2.2 The Strategic Management Framework (inspired by Hitt et al. 2009).

Organizations may develop a comprehensive sustainability strategy separate from the overall or corporate business strategy or revise the business strategy to incorporate sustainability values. However, the best approach is the latter: to make sustainability the foundation of operations, business planning, and decision making. Organizations that start with a separate sustainability strategy, for example, a set of strategic statements or goals focused only on sustainability, should eventually incorporate it directly into the overall business strategy. Over time, sustainable thinking should fully permeate the organizational culture and become simply the way that business is conducted. Sustainability can and should touch every part of an organization. Its implications and opportunities should be considered for all activities from the design of new products/services and production processes to building a new facility to ordering paper and office supplies.

Sustainability strategies must rest on unique activities, defined methods, and models that are different from competitors'; support customers' needs; provide customers accessibility; create choices; establish strong and competitive value for individual activities; and have a horizon of decades, not a single planning cycle.

The example below illustrates how Interface, Inc., incorporated sustainability into its organization and some of the results it has achieved.[6] The company's vision was reformulated and defined as follows: "To be the first company that, by its deeds, shows the entire industrial world what sustainability is in all its dimensions: People, process, product, place and profit by 2020, and in doing so become restorative through the power of influence."

The company's mission statement was defined as "making Interface the first name in commercial and institutional interiors worldwide through its commitment to people, process, product, place and profits; to create an organization wherein all people are accorded unconditional respect and dignity; to be the one that allows each person to continuously learn and develop; to focus on product (which includes service) through constant emphasis on process quality and engineering, which we will combine with careful attention to our customers' needs so as to always deliver superior value to our customers, thereby maximizing all stakeholders' satisfaction; to honor the places where they do business by endeavoring to become the first name in industrial ecology; to be a corporation that cherishes nature and restores the environment; and to lead by example and validate by results, including profits, leaving the world a better place than when we began, and we will be restorative through the power of our influence in the world."

Although Interface did not present or disclose its specific strategy, it identified its specific goals contained within its "Mission Zero commitment" to eliminate any negative impact Interface has on the environment by 2020. Example sustainability goals identified for the company were to become a carbon neutral company by measuring, reducing, and offsetting its carbon impacts and ensuring that 100% of the fuel and electricity required to operate manufacturing, sales, and office facilities will be from renewable sources by 2020. Examples of disclosed benefits by the company include continued savings that has netted $433 million in cumulative and avoided costs since 1995 and waste minimization and management improvements as result of the 400 million pounds of raw materials purchased in 2009: 3.4 million pounds of waste was landfilled, 6.9 million pounds of raw material were recycled to be used again, and 9.6 million pounds of waste was sent to energy recovery as a use of last resort.

Other Methods for Incorporating Sustainability into Business Strategies

Traditional disciplines and jurisdictions of actors in the social world must be reexamined in response to normative definitions of sustainability that call for integration approaches in seeking solutions to environmental crises. An example of such an approach is the inclusion of sustainability goals and objectives in business planning and corporate strategies.[7] The "scenario-based" and "eco-enterprise" strategic planning methods and their application in the development of sustainability strategies are presented in the following sections. Due to its importance, also provided is the concept of "conflict management strategy" that is commonly used by firms to address diversity issues and cultural differences affecting the sustainability movement within organizations.

Scenario-based strategic planning. Scenarios draw from the human imagination as well as science to provide an account of the flow of events leading to a vision of the future. In essence, scenarios are usually stories about how the future might unfold from existing patterns, new factors, and alternative human choices. Scenario-based strategic planning has been effectively used to assess the need for, and the impact of, pursuing sustainability. As expected, this approach utilizes both qualitative narratives and scientific quantitative models to translate empirical and theoretical insight into the worldviews of individual people, the building blocks for sustainable development paths, and the models for their implementation. This approach is primarily used to develop sustainability goals and objectives, design a set of actions to support it, quantify the pathways for important system variables, and as a tool to assess sustainability.[8] Recent advances in scenario analysis have addressed the dual methodological challenge of exploring uncertainties, associated alternatives, and assumptions that are commonly made for the technological, economic, demographic, geopolitical, and social aspects of development.[9]

Eco-enterprise strategy. Within the framework of enterprise strategy, a value system (network) based on sustainability can provide a sound ethical basis for developing ecologically sensitive strategic management systems that allow organizations to satisfy the demands of stakeholders such as government, employees, customers, and shareholders. Managing in ecologically sensitive ways has emerged as a major strategic thrust in business organizations that will carry well into the twenty-first century.

The sustainability-centered values network consists of a central core sustainability value that is supported by a set of instrumental values. This network of values serves as the basis for an eco-enterprise strategy. The instrumental values are identified as wholeness, diversity, posterity, smallness, quality, community, dialogue, and human spirituality. Effectively managing ecological issues requires finding a balance between economic success and ecological protection—a divergent problem that needs to be addressed when developing or redefining business goals.[10]

Conflict management strategy. Environmental management, and especially management aimed at securing or increasing sustainability as an exercise, may be perceived as a "conflict management" situation that requires the collection of information specific to the nature of the conflicts and the use of analytical techniques such as multicriteria analysis, multiple criteria of valuation, and explicit value statements that can provide information on conflicting objectives and the consequences of their application. Collaboration among five different conflict management strategies (forcing, accommodating, avoiding, compromising, and collaborating) is the preferred method here since it promotes creative problem solving and fosters mutual respect and affinity, although it may require time and is a gradual process.[11]

Strategic Tools and Techniques for Achieving Sustainability

Operational-Level Strategies

Once the direction has been set to move towards sustainability, operational-level strategies need to be selected, which help an organization to actually accomplish its goals. The number of "strategies," tools, and techniques available to help organizations become sustainable can be overwhelming. Organizations should select management tools carefully based upon the problem that they are trying to solve, business culture, values, activities, products, and sustainability goals and objectives. As these tools are utilized, results should be measured and, if applicable, additional or different tools should be selected. A sample of the range of tools and techniques that may be selected are shown in Table 2.1. The following sections describe a few key strategies in detail.

Corporate Social Responsibility

Corporations are beginning to apply the concept of sustainability at a practical level in terms of corporate citizenship or Corporate Social Responsibility (CSR). CSR refers to the responsibility enterprises can assume in order to contribute to sustainable development. Strategies and tools for assisting organizations, a set of important values, related policies, and business strategy guidelines, have been developed to lead management and production processes toward CSR. Primarily, CSR focuses on the enterprise and the supply chains. Various definitions of CSR are provided by organizations such as the European Commission, the World Business Council for Sustainable Development, United Nations Environment Programme (UNEP), and ISO 26000:

The European Commission. A concept whereby enterprises integrate social and environmental concerns in their business operations and in their interaction with their stakeholders on a voluntary basis.

The World Business Council for Sustainable Development. CSR is the continuing commitment by businesses to contribute to economic development while improving the quality of life of the workforce and their families as well as of the community and society at large.

UNEP. A values-based way of conducting business in a manner that advances sustainable development, seeking positive impact between

Table 2.1 Operational Boundary, Tools and Techniques, and Potential Application of Strategic Tools and Techniques for Achieving Sustainability

Operational Boundary	*Tool/Technique*	*Potential Application*
Organization	Environmental Management System (EMS)	Reduce an organization's emissions and environmental impacts via increasing process and operation efficiency
Organization and Supply Chain	Corporate Social Responsibility (CSR)	Provide a framework to guide the management and the production processes toward CSR through related policies and business strategies
Employees	Occupational Health and Safety Management Systems (OHSMS)	Eliminate the possibility of accident, illness, injury, or fatality in the workplace by ensuring that hazards are eliminated or controlled in a systematic manner
Products	Life Cycle Analysis (LCA)	Identify potential environmental aspects and impacts of a product (goods or services) during its life cycle
Products	Life Cycle Costing (LCC)	Calculate the total cost of a product generated throughout its life cycle from its acquisition to its disposal
Products	Life Cycle Engineering (LCE)	Determine engineering requirements, goals, and specifications based upon performance, cost, and environmental implications
Products	Environmental Product Declaration (EPD)	Provide easily accessible, quality assured, and comparable information regarding environmental performance of products such as raw material acquisition; energy use and efficiency; content of materials and chemical substances; emissions to air, soil, and water; and waste generation
Products	Product Stewardship	Provide responsible and ethical management of the health, safety, and environmental aspects of a product throughout its total life cycle
Projects	SEA Framework Project Assessment	Provide a global framework capable of integrating three constituencies of sustainability in the course of planning actions needed to ensure business sustainability and economic viability

business operations and society, and is aware of the close interrelation between business and society as well as of enterprises.

ISO 26000 Guidelines on Social Responsibility. The responsibility of an organization for the impacts of its decisions and activities on society and the environment through transparent and ethical behavior that contributes to sustainable development, including health and the welfare of society; takes into account the expectations of stakeholders; is in compliance with applicable law and is consistent with international norms of behavior; and is integrated throughout the organization and practiced in its relationships.

Triple Bottom Line (TBL) Accounting. One of the possibilities for companies to report on their sustainability performance is triple bottom line (TBL) accounting. TBL is a term, originally used by John Elkington, to describe corporations moving from reporting only on their financial "bottom line" to assessing and reporting the three key elements of environmental, social, and financial bottom lines. The corporate sustainability TBL accordingly illustrates integration of the economic, ecological, and social capitals being satisfied simultaneously.[12]

Taking on a TBL perspective requires a focused commitment to long-term strategic thinking, planning, and action. Implementing change means facing new obstacles and challenges. An organization's culture and systems must accept the challenges and support these changes before strategies are implemented (see chapter 3 for cultural shift). The three most critical organizational supports necessary for adopting TBL approaches are integration of TBL into long-term strategies, goals, and measures; employee training on TBL concepts, measures, and challenges; and leaders within the organization modeling TBL behaviors, both professionally and personally.[13] Three international initiatives—the *Global Compact*, the *Global Reporting Initiative (GRI)*, and the *Organization fro Economic Co-operation and Development (OECD) Guidelines for Multinational Enterprises*—have contributed to the CSR movement:

The Global Compact is a CSR initiative started in 1999 by Kofi Annan, former Secretary-General of the United Nations. The Compact is "a framework for businesses that are committed to aligning their operations and strategies with ten universally accepted principles in the areas of human rights, labor, the environment, and anticorruption. As the world's largest global corporate citizenship initiative, the Global Compact is first and foremost concerned with exhibiting and building the social legitimacy of business and markets." The Global Compact is a network of businesses that have committed to respecting the ten principles and work extensively on capacity building among the enterprises.

The Global Reporting Initiative (GRI) is a multistakeholder initiative that was launched in 1997 by Coalition for Environmentally Responsible Economies (Ceres) and UNEP. It acts as a network of thousands of experts in dozens of countries worldwide who participate in the GRI's working groups and governance bodies. These entities use the GRI Guidelines to report, access information in GRI-based reports, or contribute to developing the reporting framework in other ways, both formally and informally. The GRI develops a sustainability reporting framework that standardizes organizations reports on environmental, social, and economic aspects.

The OECD guidelines for multinational enterprises is one part of the OECD Declaration on International Investment and Multinational Enterprises, which is a broad political commitment adopted by the OECD governments in 1976 to facilitate direct investment among OECD members. In addition, a social and socioeconomic Life Cycle Assessment (S-LCA) provides interesting and relevant information that brings a new life cycle perspective to CSR. S-LCA may inform and influence CSR in the future, especially in the way the concept is being operationalized.[14]

Environmental Management Systems as a Strategic Roadmap to Sustainability

A step-by-step "Sustainability Roadmap" is presented here as an approach that an organization may follow to implement its sustainability strategy and meet its goals. The roadmap is intended to be a generic framework that organizations may adapt and customize as needed.

The methodology proposed in the Sustainability Roadmap was inspired by techniques/methods used to design an Environmental Management System (EMS) for organizations. An EMS is a set of processes and practices that enable an organization to reduce its emissions and environmental impacts via increasing process and operation efficiency. EMSs are designed based on the Plan-Do-Check-Act (PDCA) methodology presented in ISO 14000 standards that has been widely accepted and used at many national and international companies. Therefore, it is an accepted environmental strategy for companies to follow.

EMSs have become a common tool that companies use to help them achieve their sustainability goals. EMSs place structure and formality around the process and lay out the detailed steps and procedures that should be taken, which is especially helpful for companies that are making an initial move towards sustainability. Executing the Sustainability Roadmap within the context of an EMS is recommended for any company, as it serves as a valuable tool to enable it. The sustainability roadmap is presented in Figure 2.3. Each step is described below.

Step 1: Develop sustainability strategy. This step was described earlier in this chapter. Steps 4–7 may also be performed at a higher

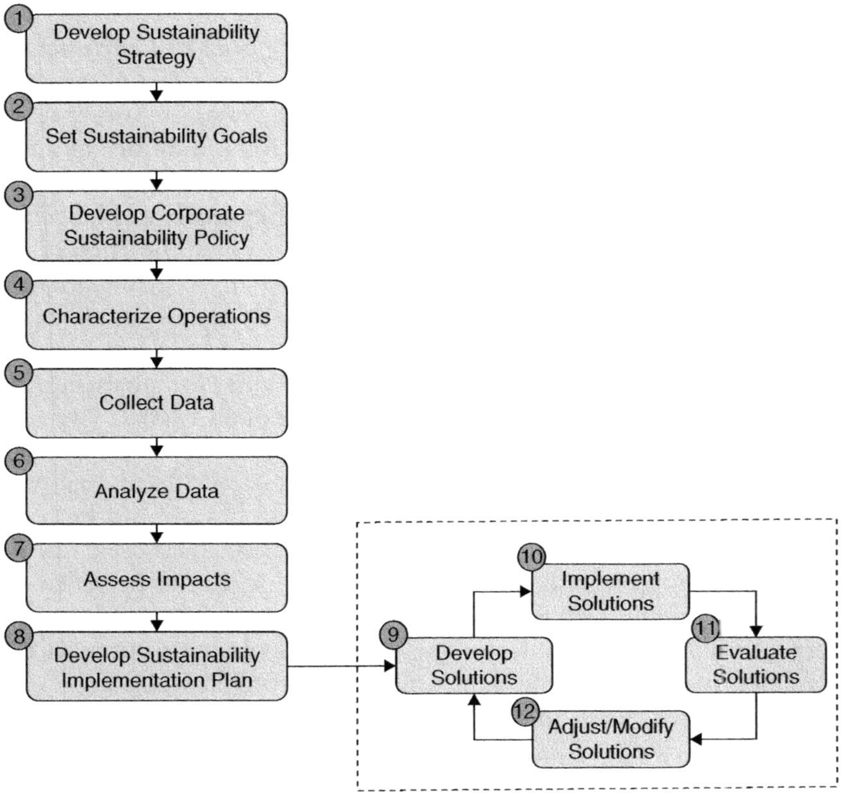

Figure 2.3 Roadmap to sustainability.

level of detail at this point to provide an analysis of the current state, which is input to the sustainability strategy developed in Step 1.

Step 2: Set sustainability goals. The objective of this step is to develop a set of measurable goals based upon the sustainability strategy, which can be used to lead an organization towards the ultimate goal of sustainability. This step is crucial as it provides direction, focus, and priority for all sustainability efforts. The remaining steps in the Sustainability Roadmap must be defined and carried out within the context of the sustainability goals and the time scale defined during goal setting.

When setting sustainability goals, an organization must decide what it wants to accomplish and how aggressive it wants to be. A best practice is to start with small, accomplishable goals and increase their scope and magnitude over time. If goals are set too aggressively to start, they may not be reached, resulting in low morale and a loss of momentum for environmental efforts. The goal of achieving an ultimate sustainability goal of "zero waste" may be a final target to which to aspire, but becomes more challenging and costly the closer one gets to it. Smaller, incremental goals, typically stated in percentage reductions, may be set along the way.

Step 3: Develop corporate sustainability policy. The objective of this step is to develop a "corporate sustainability policy" or an "environmental policy" that states the company's commitment to identify environmental and social attributes associated with its operations and pursue reducing those impacts to protect the environment and society. The policy is the main framework for planning and action and therefore serves as the foundation of an EMS.[15] The policy ensures leadership/corporate commitment to sustainability and therefore opens the door for the implementation of sustainability-based projects. The corporate sustainability policy should be based upon the sustainability goals from Step 2 and describe more tactically what the company will do to achieve them. It should be reflective of and congruent with the company's values and culture. The policy serves as a visible reminder of the environmental commitment that has been made. It may be shared across the company and even with external stakeholders and the public.

The ideas within a corporate sustainability policy may be generated by collecting input from a variety of perspectives, both internally (e.g., representatives from departments such as Engineering, Sales and Marketing, Facilities, Human Resources, Legal, Public Relations, etc.) and externally (e.g., representatives from government, nongovernmental organizations, industry organizations, customer focus groups, etc.). Best practices for policy content may be gathered by researching what other organizations have done, especially those within the same industry. At a minimum, the policy should include three key commitments: continual improvement, pollution prevention, and compliance with applicable laws and regulations.[16]

Step 4: Characterize operations and waste streams (input-output model). The objective of this step is to comprehensively identify and document the inputs (e.g., materials and energy) and outputs (e.g., waste) within the scope of operations. First, the scope of analysis must be clearly defined. There are two key boundaries to consider when defining the scope for characterizing environmental attributes: organizational and operational boundaries for which waste streams can be identified (see chapters 5 and 11 for techniques on selecting boundaries). Input-output analysis and waste characterization are both critical to sustainable operations so that effective solutions can be developed to conserve resources and prevent environmental damage. Energy usage may result from the types of technology used in operations, the hours and places of operation, company culture and education (e.g., employees do not turn off lights and equipment after use), regulations, and financial incentives (taxes or subsidies). Energy can be also produced internally (using landfill gas, boilers, solar, or wind) or purchased from the grid. The total emissions associated with energy use can be estimated according to the input-output models utilizing information gathered from processes.

Schematics such as the one shown in Figure 2.4 may be used to represent the information collected during this step. It illustrates inputs, outputs, and the disposition of waste (e.g., recycle, recovery, disposal, discharge, etc.). In addition, detailed process maps may be helpful to show the detailed sequence and flow of activities performed to accomplish a specific objective or task. Process models may uncover various types of inefficiencies such as with the usage

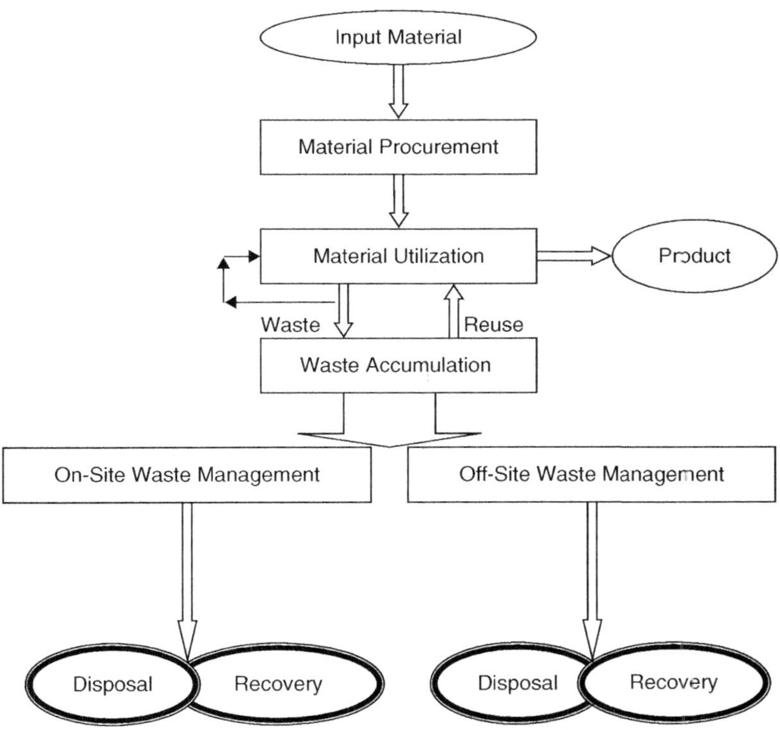

Figure 2.4 Example waste management model.

of materials, energy, and transportation. The diagrams produced in Step 4 can be used during the following steps to set scope, categorize and represent data, and organize work efforts.

Step 5: Collect data. The objective of this step is to collect detailed data *in the context of the sustainability goals defined in Step 2* for the inputs and outputs within the scope identified in Step 4. For example, if a sustainability goal was to reduce carbon emissions by a certain percentage, and if the scope only included direct emissions, then the only data that would be collected would pertain to the emissions of carbon dioxide generated from sources owned by the company from on-site production processes, from the direct combustion of fossil fuels in boilers and furnaces, and from on-site power generation.[17]

Although collecting data is often a labor-intensive activity, the results are crucial to achieving sustainability goals. Incorrect or missing data could skew the results of the data analysis and impact assessment (Steps 6 and 7), which in a worst-case scenario could lead to the wrong sustainability implementation plan (Step 8) and resulting solutions (Step 9). This not only would cause an organization to fail to reach its goals, but could prove to be an extremely costly mistake. A detailed understanding of current operations is also necessary to maintain control and uncover any business risks or exposure. The old management adage "you can't manage what you can't measure" certainly applies in this case. The critical importance of data to achieving sustainability goals also requires a well-designed quality assurance (QA)/quality control (QC) document for data collection, analysis, and reporting. The types of tools vary across companies in their platform, sophistication, and integration with other business functions (e.g., procurement or accounting).

Step 6: Analyze data. The objective of this step is to analyze the input and output data that were collected in Step 5 and organize them into metrics that may be used for decision making and reporting. For example, if a sustainability goal (from Step 2) was to reduce carbon emissions by a certain percentage, a set of common metrics may be used to analyze the data such as Total Tons of Carbon Dioxide Equivalents, Tons of Carbon Dioxide Equivalents per Unit of Product, British Thermal Unit (BTU) (Energy Consumed) per Unit of Product, and Total BTUs. (See chapter 11 for more information on greenhouse gas management strategies.)

Additional data may need to be collected after performing the analysis in order to collect more detailed information or explain certain patterns or results. For example, upon investigating a peak

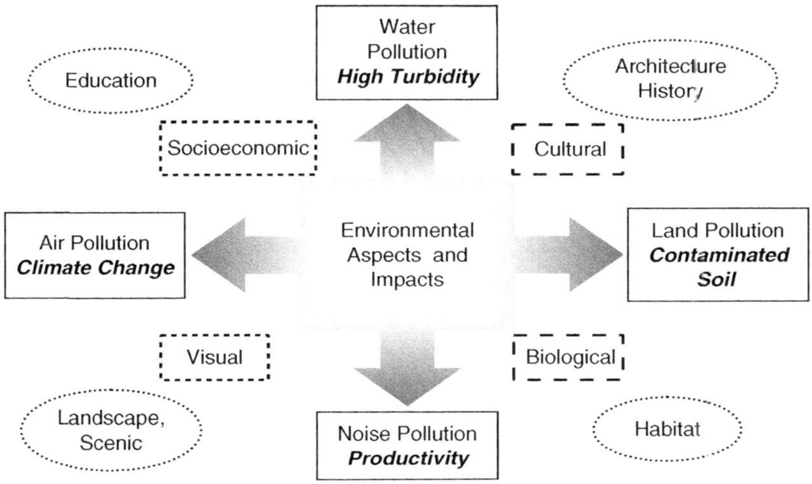

Figure 2.5 Environmental aspects and impacts.

in energy usage during the day, it may be determined that it is due to running an energy-intensive piece of equipment. During solution development (Step 9), this may lead to the identification of an option to reduce energy costs by running the equipment during off hours because the rate is lower.

Step 7: Assess environmental aspects and impact. The purpose of this step is to assess the environmental impact of the data analyzed in Step 6. Some potential categories of environmental aspects to consider (if applicable) are shown in Figure 2.5. Each aspect results in an environmental impact assessment. For example, energy usage has primary aspects such as "air pollution" and "climate change" and secondary impacts that could include habitat change or loss of visual beauty and scenic.

Step 8: Develop sustainability implementation plan. The purpose of this step is to develop and document a comprehensive, cross-departmental plan for implementing sustainability efforts over time. This plan takes into account the data analyzed in Step 6 as well as estimated environmental impact from Step 7. It must clearly identify the problems that are to be addressed by the solutions developed in Step 9 as well as the priority for each and a tentative time frame for when they will be addressed. When setting priorities, companies should forecast what the expected impacts may be, not just in the short term, but in the long term due to volatility in the price of materials and labor and the need for more reduction in emissions due to legislation and other factors. The plan may also specify an approach for environmental management efforts to further guide solution selection and development.

Step 9: Develop solutions. The purpose of this step is to develop solutions to meet the sustainability goals, guided by the priorities and approach defined in the sustainability implementation plan from Step 8.

A significant element in the selection of a solution is economic factors. Organizations should explore a number of solution options and select the one that is the most cost-effective for them. This is necessary to motivate an organization to reach its sustainability goals and ensure that it remains profitable. The economic feasibility of solutions may be determined using common financial analysis metrics such as Payback Period, Internal Rate of Return (also referred to as Return on Investment), Benefits-Cost Ratio, and Present Value of Net Benefits. For a solution that is large in scope and cost, it may be more tolerable to a company to break it into shorter, implementable pieces that can demonstrate a payback within two or three years. If a project is too expensive, it will not be sustained, even if the results produce a sustainable process or product!

In some cases, organizations may want to provide forums for employees and other stakeholders to provide solution ideas and feedback. This may be accomplished in a number of ways, such as through special interest group meetings, discussion boards, and various other methods of submitting ideas (e.g., through a general e-mail address). Pursuing this level of engagement will not only generate innovative ideas for solutions, but also increase involvement and buy-in for sustainability efforts across the organization.

Step 10: Implement solutions. The purpose of this step is to put in place (or "roll out") the solutions that were developed in Step 9. Organizations that are new to sustainability should implement solutions on a small scale as pilot projects in the beginning. This enables the organization to obtain experience and buy-in from the rest of the organization, as well as minimize risks. Some key characteristics to look for in a pilot project include having leadership interest and support (e.g., pertains to a topic related to other business goals such as reducing costs or increasing customer loyalty), visible leadership support, open-minded (and even enthusiastic) participants, the ability to demonstrate economic and other planned benefits, and a small, accomplishable scope (but not too small that it is insignificant or can't illustrate benefits).

Education and communication may be an important component of implementing solutions (which should have been planned for as part of solution development in Step 9). Anyone who will be affected by the implementation of a solution should be aware and receive the appropriate education. This includes senior leadership. The type of education provided will vary greatly depending upon a company's industry and the solutions being implemented. For example, technical engineer training may be required for solutions that involve product or production changes. On the other hand, training to change behavior or manual processes may be required for solutions that aim to improve housekeeping practices. Education and communication may be provided by the environmental management function or other departments as applicable (e.g., Engineering, Legal, etc.).

Step 11: Evaluate solutions. The purpose of this step is to review the results of the solutions that were implemented or piloted in Step 10. The evaluation should include measurement of quantitative results that can be compared to the sustainability goals. For example, if a solution was implemented to modify a production process in order to meet the goal of reducing carbon emissions, the amount of emissions produced after the process change was made must be measured to determine if it met the expected reduction. The evaluation should also include more subjective measurements such as an analysis of what went well and what could be improved. This type of feedback may be obtained by conducting interviews or having a facilitated discussion with the people involved in the solution implementation. When solutions achieve their desired result, a "success story" may be created to summarize the effort. Documented success stories are an effective method for building awareness and buy-in for sustainability goals across the company.

Step 12: Adjust/modify solutions. The purpose of this step is to make any adjustments or modifications to the implemented solutions, based upon the evaluation conducted in Step 11. The cycle of solution development and continuous improvement (represented by Steps 9 through 12) is where the majority of the work occurs to transform a company to meet its sustainability goals. The experience and buy-in that is gained over time serves as critical input into Step 2 to both refine the sustainability goals and prepare a company to increase the magnitude of the goals.

Applying the Sustainability Roadmap

The Sustainability Roadmap describes the steps to be taken in the most logical and efficient order. However, organizations may perform them in parallel or even out of sequence in some cases. For example, in organizations that are new to the concepts of environmental management and sustainability (e.g., those in service industries), sometimes individual business departments begin putting environmental solutions in place (Steps 9–12) before the organization has formally set its sustainability strategy, goals, or policy (Steps 1–3). In this case, once the goals and policy have been set, any existing efforts should be reevaluated and realigned (if applicable) to the organizational direction. Following the exact order of the steps as they are shown in the roadmap is less important than ensuring that the function of each is performed at some point, and that the resulting sequence still allows a company to meet its sustainability goals.

The ultimate goal of achieving sustainability may be accomplished by continuously cycling through the steps in the Sustainability Roadmap. It is unlikely that an organization would achieve sustainability by completing the steps just one time. This type of operational and organizational transformation does not happen overnight; it typically requires full engagement from an entire company and years or decades to accomplish. It is possible for a company to achieve the concept of sustainability or move more closely towards it. The process starts with setting and reaching small goals, and then continuing to set and reach increasingly aggressive goals over time.

Challenges to Implementing the Sustainability Roadmap

In practice, there are a number of challenges that organizations must overcome in order to implement the Sustainability Roadmap. Typical challenges include lack of the following: a plan to achieve sustainability, priority for sustainability efforts, resources (human, material, or financial) to perform sustainability efforts, and incentives for people to participate in them. In addition, general organizational resistance to change may also be a challenge.

The root cause for many of these challenges is not having support or direction from senior leadership. Senior leadership *must* support and lead the company towards sustainability from the very beginning, starting with setting sustainability goals, and make designing strategies for implementing sustainability efforts a business priority. Representatives from all functions should be included at various points in the Sustainability Roadmap development, from providing input to sustainability goals to participating in solution implementation. Leadership support must be visible and ongoing, through signing the corporate sustainability policy, communicating sustainability goals and focus of the organization clearly to the employees, and including those goals in every aspect of daily operations. In addition, leadership must allocate time for people to participate in sustainability efforts and provide incentives for them to do so, with recognition and rewards. Sustainability goals may even be included as a part of employee performance goals and compensation.

Examples of other commonly used environmental management programs and strategies that are strongly linked to sustainability goals and objectives are presented in the following sections. Selection of the programs has been based on their significance and direct impact on meeting discussed environmental management and sustainability strategies.

Occupational Health and Safety Management Systems

Many organizations implement an Occupational Health and Safety Management System (OHSMS) as part of their risk management strategy to address changing legislation and to protect their workforce. An OHSMS promotes a safe and healthy working environment. The purpose of an OHSMS is to systematically eliminate the possibility of accident, illness, injury, or fatality in the workplace by ensuring that the hazards in the workplace are eliminated or controlled in a systematic manner, rather than waiting for a crisis to occur. Employers have legal responsibilities to provide a safe workplace and systems of work, to consult with employees, and to keep employees informed about health and safety matters. Small businesses can use an OHSMS to meet their need to prevent injuries, illness, and accidents.

The primary benefits of OHSMS are meeting the moral and legal responsibilities of employers, prevention of occupational injury and disease, reduced loss of working days due to injury and accidents, lowered incidence of employee compensation claims, minimized work stoppages due to safety disputes, and improved work methods and worker morale thus leading to improved productivity. This system also provides a framework for meeting legislative responsibilities, although implementation of an OHSMS does not exempt an employer from meeting the requirements of the *Work Health Act* and *Work Health (Occupational Health and Safety) Regulations*.

Some companies have chosen to integrate their OHSMS with their own broader management systems, since many elements of OHSMS are the same as those found in effective management principles/activities. The extent to which organizations meet the **Occupational Health and Safety management Standard (OHSAS)** 18001 requirements depends on the size, location, culture, activities, legal obligations, nature, content, policy, scope, hazards, and risks of OHSMS. If an organization has an OHSMS program, a gap analysis approach can be used to maximize its effectiveness by comparing the existing OHSMS with the OHSAS 18001 requirements.[18]

Environmental Life Cycle Assessment

Environmental Life Cycle, or Life Cycle Assessment (LCA), is a system for identifying potential environmental aspects and impacts of a product (goods or services) during its life cycle. A product's life cycle includes all stages of a product system, from raw material acquisition or natural resource production to the disposal of the product at the end of its life, including extracting and processing of raw materials, manufacturing, distribution, use, reuse, maintenance, recycling, and final disposal (i.e., cradle to grave).

The LCA was originally developed in the late 1960s and throughout the 1970s to address the desire of enterprises and policy makers to understand the relative environmental LCA impacts of alternative packaging options. Initially, it was concerned with energy consumption and the production of solid wastes. The scope of environmental impacts has since been developed and includes analysis of air pollution and product type impacts. The Society of Environmental Toxicology generated the initial LCA Code of Practice, published by the Society of Environmental Toxicology and Chemistry (SETAC) in 1993. As a part of the ISO's standards for environmental management, four ISO standards (ISO 14040–14043) were published in the years 1997–2000, and then were replaced with two standards, ISO 14040 (2006) and ISO 14044 (2006). These standards describe the required and recommended elements of environmental LCAs.[19]

The LCA approach is widely recognized as a useful framework, and attempts are under way to integrate life-cycle thinking into business decisions. The ISO standards identify four phases for conducting an LCA: Goal and Scope, Life Cycle Inventory (LCI), Life Cycle Impact Assessment (LCIA), and Life Cycle Interpretation, in which the findings of the previous two phases are combined with the defined goal and scope in order to reach conclusions or recommendations.[20]

Life Cycle Costing

Traditional Life Cycle Costing (LCC) is a method of calculating the total cost of a product (goods and services) generated throughout its life cycle from its acquisition to its disposal, including design, installation, operation, maintenance, and recycling/disposal, etc. LCC can be used for a wide range of different purposes. In general, the most common uses of LCC are selection studies for different products and design trade-offs, relating to both comparisons and optimization. The construction industry is the main user of affordability studies, and cases from the energy sector often focus on the source selection for different services. The public sector uses LCC mostly in sourcing decisions, while the private sector also uses LCC as a design support tool.[21]

Life Cycle Engineering

Life cycle engineering (LCE) depends on understanding performance, cost, and environmental implications and translates them into engineering requirements, goals, and specifications. Related decisions are iterative in nature. LCE evaluation will review product design and development outcomes, reevaluate initial decisions, and expand the coverage to ensure that the broadest set of improvement opportunities are considered in product development. For example, substantial environmental implications are considered and effects are not shifted from one life cycle stage to another.[22]

Environmental Product Declaration

Environmental Product Declaration (EPD) is based on an LCA and ISO standards for LCA. It includes information about the environmental impacts associated with a product or service, such as raw material acquisition; energy use and efficiency; content of materials and chemical substances; emissions to air, soil, and water; and waste generation.

EPD is a voluntary program that attempts to provide easily accessible, quality assured and comparable information regarding the environmental performance of products. Two documents control how the calculations and data collection behind an EPD should be done and what information the EPD must contain:

Description of the product and the company. The first part of the EPD is very straightforward with descriptions of the product and the manufacturer. The functional unit, which is the unit to which all calculations are referred, can be stated here or in the second part. The functional unit reflects the actual function of the product.

Environmental performance. This part is the core of an EPD. It is based on an LCA of the product, which means that all processes, including extraction of resources, refining of raw materials, transport, and final production, are included.

In most EPDs, important air and water emissions are expressed both as inventory data and as potential influences on different environmental impact categories, for example, global warming (GWP). In this case, all emissions contributing to global warming are included in the impact category GWP.

Resource consumption is divided into nonrenewable and renewable resources. All results of calculations are presented per functional unit, which, for example, for chemicals is 1000 kg of the product. EPDs could also include a presentation of environmental impact from a typical transport to customer. The EPD fulfills the need for open and quantitative environmental information for a variety of target groups and markets. It is also supported by the international consensus regarding environmental declarations (such as ISO 14025). In summary, the EPD meets demands for objectivity, comparability and credibility.[23]

Product Stewardship

Product stewardship could be primarily defined as "responsible and ethical management of the health, safety and environmental aspects of a product" throughout its total life cycle. Under a product stewardship program, products must be managed and used safely via a management system that ensures safe development, manufacturing, packaging, distribution, use, and ultimate disposal of the raw material and by-products involved. Models and frameworks that are designed to ensure better management of product development should involve different team members in every stage of project development, including planning for sustainability projects and programs. Such a team effort would make the project more visible to all stakeholders, and as such could facilitate identifying R&D direction, goals and objectives such as moving toward "Zero Emissions," and using waste as inputs for other industries or processes.[24]

An example of a product stewardship program is the safety appraisal service from Shell Chemicals that was developed to ensure maximum safety at customer handling and storage facilities. An expert team trained in specialist risk appraisal techniques at Shell's Chester (United Kingdom) operation undertakes the safety appraisals of customer product reception facilities and trains Shell personnel and customers across Europe on how to identify potential risks. The program consists of a two-hour audit and appraisal with a customer representative. During the audit all electrical equipment, discharge facilities, emissions, and unloading procedures are checked against set standards. Also identified are the proximity to residential areas and access roads, earthing bonds on storage tanks, flame arrestors on vent pipes, etc.

Practical Sustainability Model and the SEA Framework

The Practical Sustainability Model is a strategic model that evolves from sustainable business practices and strategic decision making in accord with the following management components:

- Stakeholder values (S factor)
- Externality (E factor)
- Asset (A factor)

These factors constitute a framework that provides a clear, pragmatic approach for each stage of project management, including design, implementation, monitoring, and impact assessment. Rooted in the core concepts of sustainability, this framework can also shape business policies and strategies according to the strategic, operational, regulatory, reputation-oriented, and financial challenges and opportunities.

Application of the SEA practical sustainability framework. This model can assist managers in integrating sustainability concepts and rules on the level of business planning and project management simply by identifying how those projects contribute or respond to the main drivers of business sustainability. The application of this model can also provide opportunities for businesses to turn their social, economical, and environmental expertise into a tangible competitive advantage.

Notably, this is an elastic model with the potential to be customized according to the culture and technical specifications of any

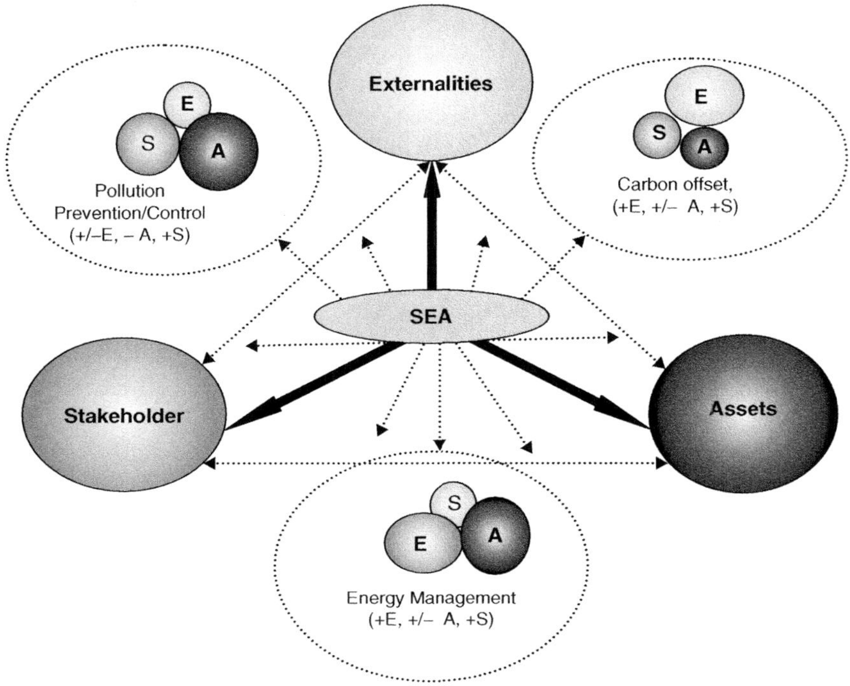

Figure 2.6 Practical sustainability model and SEA factors (S, stakeholder; E, externalities; A, asset).

industry. Using a qualitative or a quantitative approach, an industry can define how effective its sustainability strategy is and how it can be modified, for example, via a scoring system. Global application of the SEA framework could also include

- Assessing climate-related risks and opportunities
- Setting corporate goals for improving environmental and social performance
- Addressing increasing investor demand for companies to meet high environmental, social, and governance standards
- Addressing demand for products and services that are "green" and "sustainable"
- Participating in "fair trade"
- Meeting high expectations for labor market, human rights, community, and environmental benefits
- Communicating with stakeholders in regard to strategic decisions and responses
- Working with policy makers to explore how their actions could impact the industry

Table 2.2 Example Qualitative Assessment of Sustainability Projects

Example Project	*Stakeholder Score*	*Externalities Score*	*Financial (Asset) Score*	*Total Scores/ Relative Impacts*
Pollution Control Removes one pollutant but results in generation of another one, i.e., removal of SO_2 by scrubber results in generation of wastewater	+ Meets regulatory requirements	± Reduces negative impact on the environment	– Requires resources and use of company assets	+ A > S > E
Carbon Management Process modification, GHG reduction (control or pollution prevention), energy management	+ Meets certain stakeholders' expectations	+ Reduces negative externalities and impacts on global warming	± Depends on the project time horizon, intensity, and types: in the short term negative impact may be expected due to the use of resources; while in the long term positive impacts from participating in the carbon market, tax, regulatory compliance	+ E ≥ A > S
Energy Management Reducing energy use, changing equipment, changing sources of energy supply	+ Meets stakeholders' expectations	+ Reduces direct/ indirect GHG emissions	± Requires capital and technology limitations	+ E ≥ A > S

For example, if company X is exploring the possibility of participating in carbon disclosure programs, management must rigorously evaluate and assess all the benefits and costs associated with this strategic decision. Moreover, not only must the distinct value offered to the stakeholders be identified (S scores), but managers must also articulate the potential range of impact the project could have on the environmental externalities (E scores) and the company's assets (A scores). In conducting this trifold analysis, company X assesses the project's significance and impact, drawing upon the SEA scores for the project as shown in Figure 2.6 and Table 2.2.

Table 2.2 shows how the SEA qualitative assessment framework can be utilized. The impact assessment and the scoring system can be customized according to project type, sector, industry type, size, location, culture, resource availability, salient policy, regulatory requirements, and so forth.

Assessment. The assessment phase of the proposed strategic planning model was designed with consideration of the main factors of the model as well as their interactions. This requires the development of Balanced Scorecards (BSCs) for the three dimensions of business sustainability: financial performance (asset management), environmental performance (externality management), and social performance (stakeholder management). The SEA model can also be used to define customer satisfaction, effectiveness of internal business processes, innovation and learning (strategic use of human capital), and the profitability of the sustainability approaches undertaken.

Summary

Sustainability is a concept, a vision for business and society, a goal to be achieved, and a strategy to follow. It may also serve as an overarching goal or "umbrella" under which a company can guide and organize its environmental efforts. Environmental management provides the tools and techniques, such as pollution prevention and cleaner production, by which sustainability goals can be met.

This chapter presented multiple levels of strategies for the inclusion of sustainability core values in business decision making and strategy development practices. The term "strategy" is used at two different levels within this chapter: the corporate business strategy and operational-level strategy. The corporate strategy addresses incorporating sustainability into the overall business strategy for an entire organization as part of the strategic planning process. Operational-level strategy, however, is designed to address the tactical techniques and tools that are used to accomplish sustainability goals within individual projects or operations.

There are many approaches to strategic planning as well, but typically a three-step process is used to evaluate the *current situation* or *current state*; the *target situation*, which is the development of goals and objectives for an ideal state; and the *path*, which defines a possible route to meet the goals and objectives. The *current situation* analysis could include the analysis of the *markets* (customers), *competition*, *technology*, *supplier markets*, *labor markets*, the *economy*, and the *regulatory environment*. Sustainability strategies that are customer, culture, and product sensitive could differentiate an organization from its competitors. As such, inclusion of a sustainability strategy could create competitive advantage for the company by differentiating it from competitors via unique and valuable positions rooted in its system of activities.

As discussed in detail, a company may achieve "sustainability" by iterating through the *Sustainability Roadmap* many times and continuing to set, and reach, increasingly aggressive goals. The first and critical steps in the Sustainability Roadmap are setting sustainability goals and developing a corporate sustainability policy. Senior leadership should drive these activities, set direction, and visibly support them. This helps to mitigate a number of challenges that often occur, such as lack of resources or priority for sustainability efforts. Implementation of an EMS as a tool to implement the Sustainability Roadmap is highly recommended as it provides structure, formality, and detailed procedures on how to execute the steps. The most effective and common guidelines and strategies for the development and implementation of business strategies, programs, and models with core sustainability values at operational levels were also presented and discussed in this chapter. The word strategy can be used in a variety of different contexts. At an operational level, sustainability strategies should identify sustainability goals and objectives that are in line with corporate business values and list activities, tools, and techniques to achieve those goals. Environmental Management Systems, commonly used to identify environmentally related data and include environmentally related decisions in the development of sustainability projects, were presented to create a sense of what is and should be involved in the development and execution of sustainability-related activities at operational levels (e.g., Occupational Health and Safety Management Systems [OHSMS], Life Cycle Assessment [LCA] models and techniques, Environmental Product Declarations [EPDs], and product stewardship). Also discussed were scenario-based strategic development, eco-enterprise strategy systems, and conflict management strategy in order to broaden the scope of discussions.

Case Study

Sustainability Approach at CSX Corporation

Company Profile

Formed in 1980, CSX Corporation is the parent company of a number of subsidiaries that provide freight transportation services across America and around the world. CSX Transportation (CSXT) operates the largest rail network in the eastern United States, offering freight transportation over more than 23,000 route miles in 23 states, the District of Columbia, and two Canadian provinces. More than 41,000 people are employed by CSX Corporation and its subsidiaries. The automobile, metals, agricultural, chemical, forest, and waste industries as well as the government all use CSXT as part of their operations. CSXT serves a multitude of waste treatment and disposal facilities throughout the eastern United States, including landfills, incinerators, hazardous and nonhazardous treatment facilities, wastewater treatment plants, cement kilns, and deep well sites. Waste streams generated by the rail industry include air emissions (nitrogen oxides, volatile organic compounds, particulate matter, carbon monoxide, and carbon dioxide), steel, batteries, used oil, cross ties, paper and aluminum, and accidental releases.

EMS Design at CSXT

As a global transportation leader, CSX committed itself to protecting the environment and ensuring the safety and health of its employees and the public. In 1997, CSX became a partner in the Responsible Care Program. To support this commitment, the environmental professionals at CSX developed a comprehensive EMS. The EMS goal and objective were to provide guidance for all CSX employees and facilitate environmental compliance and continual improvement of environmental performance. The EMS included the following:

1. Developing of environmental and hazardous material policies
2. Defining provided practices and procedures
3. Planning waste reduction, management review, implementation and operation, and checking and corrective actions
4. Defining the goals and objectives
5. Defining structure to implement these goals on a continual basis
6. Designing regular evaluation program for the EMS in place
7. Pursuing annual compliance certification according to the environmental and operational criteria

Benefits

As a result of efforts to minimize waste and to recycle through their EMS, CSXT reclaims about 611,000 pounds of signal and other rechargeable batteries each year and reconditions approximately 75% of replaced locomotive engine batteries. The railroad recycles approximately 2.1 million gallons of oil each year from a variety of sources, including locomotive and track equipment crankcases. Approximately 2.12 million used cross ties are converted into a fiber fuel source or reused as landscaping timbers. Old locomotives, rail cars, rails, and other equipment are also recycled. At CSXT headquarters, more than 400 tons of office paper and aluminum are recycled each year.

High importance has been placed on environmental training and awareness through the EMS. CSX has developed an *Environmental Certification Program*, which is administered to employees in the Mechanical Operations and Engineering departments. Instruction provided to other railroad employees contains *environmental training specific to their job functions*. For the Hazardous Materials System Group, employees, customers, and the public are trained in *emergency response and community and customer outreach programs* focusing on *prevention and response* to incidents. These programs are frequently reviewed and updated to address regulations and procedures.

CSX has continued to have an excellent record for the safe handling of hazardous materials. In 2001, CSX transported approximately 445,000 carloads of hazardous materials, only 17 of which spilled any contents due to derailment. The company recognizes and promotes environmental excellence from its employees by administering an award program called the Green Spike Award. Nominees are selected for this award based on their personal environmental achievements. CSX has had two employees receive the Association of American Railroads (AAR) John H. Chafee Environmental Award for outstanding environmental achievement. An employee from CSX has been nominated for this award every year since its inception in 1996. The Environmental Protection Agency's (EPA's) Office of Air and Radiation chose CSX as the 2001 recipient of the Clean Air Excellence Award for its design, patent, and installation of the Auxiliary Power Unit (APU) in railroad locomotives. During idling, the APU reduces the following emissions:

- Nitrogen oxides by 91%
- Hydrocarbons by 94%
- Carbon monoxide by 96%
- Particulate matter by 84%

CSX continues to set goals for ongoing improvement through the EMS. Open and candid communication with employees, customers, and the public regarding the company's environmental program and any hazard that might arise from its operations is encouraged. The importance of conserving landfill space and raw materials through reducing, reusing, and recycling materials has been recognized through the EMS and continues to be a priority as evidenced by the awards given to the company and its employees.[25]

Notes

1. Deata Mebratu, "Sustainability and Sustainable Development: Historical and Conceptual Review," *Environmental Impact Assessment Review* 18 (1998): 403–520.
2. Daniel C. Esty and Andrew S. Winston, *Green to Gold: How Smart Companies Use Environmental Strategy to Innovate, Create Value, and Build Competitive Advantage* (New Haven and London: Yale University Press, 2006), 10.
3. Ibid., 104.
4. Ibid.
5. Michael A. Hitt, Duane R. Ireland, Robert E. Hoskisson, *Strategic Management Concepts: Competitiveness and Globalization* (Cincinnati: South-Western, 8th Edition, 2009), 36.
6. "Interface's values are our guiding principles", 2010, InterfaceFLOR, Mission Statement, http://www.interfaceglobal.com/Sustainability/Sustainability-in-Action/Energy.aspx.
7. Csaba Pusztai, "Sustainability Planning and Its Role in Creating Capacity for Learning: A Complex Adaptive System Perspective," Central European University, Budapest 1051, Hungary, ephpuc01@phd.ceu.hu.
8. Arthur C. Petersen and Bert J.M. de Vries, "Conceptulizing Sustainable Development: An Assessment Methodology Connecting Values, Knowledge, Worldviews, and Scenarios," *Ecological Economics* 68 (2009): 1012.
9. Paul D. Raskin, "Global Scenarios: Background Review for the Millennium Ecosystem Assessment," *Ecosystems* 8 (March 2005): 133–42.
10. Jean Garner Stead and Edward Stead, "Eco-Enterprise Strategy: Standing for Sustainability," *Journal of Business Ethics* 24 (April 2000): 313–29.
11. David I. Stern, "The Capital Theory Approach to Sustainability: A Critical Appraisal," *Journal of Economic Issues* 31 (March 1997): 145–73.
12. Thomas,Wiedmann, Manfred Lenzen, and John Barrett, "Companies on the Scale, Comparing and Benchmarking the Ecological Footprint of Businesses," *Journal of Industrial Ecology*, 13 (3) (2009): 361–83.
13. Laura Quinn and Jessica Baltes, "Leadership and the Triple Bottom Line: Bringing Sustainability and Corporate Social Responsibility to Life," Center for Creative Leadership (2007): page 6, 12.
14. UNEP, "Guidelines For Social Life Cycle Assessment of Products," 2009, United Nations Environment Programme,(accessed September 6, 2010), http:*//www.oeko.de/publications/reports_studies/dok/659.php*
15. Philip J. Stapleton, Margaret A. Glover, and S. Petite. Davis, *Environmental Management Systems: An Implementation Guide for Small and Medium-Sized Organizations* (Grasonville: Ann Arbor, Michigan NSF International, 2001), page 8.
16. Ibid., 16.

17. Andrew J. Hoffman, *Carbon Strategies: How Leading Companies Are Reducing Their Climate Change Footprint* (Michigan; University of Michigan Press, 2007), 11.
18. OHSAS 18001, Occupational Health and Safety Management standard, 2007, http://www.praxiom.com/ohsas-18001-intro.htm (accessed March 15, 2010).
19. UNEP, "Guidelines For Social Life Cycle Assessment of Products," 2009, United Nations Environment Programme (accessed September 6, 2010) 28, http://www.oeko.de/publications/reports_studies/dok/659.php
20. Ibid., 33–35.
21. Ibid., 33–35.
22. "Life Cycle Engineering Guidelines" 2001, Joyce Smith Cooper and Bruce Vigon, Battelle Columbus Laboratories, 505 King Avenue Columbus, Ohio 43201, EPA/600/R-01/101, http://www.epa.gov/nrmrl/pubs/600r01101/600R01101.pdf (accessed September 7, 2010).
23. Anita Gärling, Anne-Marie Imrell, and Karin Sanne, "Development of Interpretation Keys for Environmental Product Declarations," *Journal of Cleaner Production* 16 (March 2008): 4–10.
24. Thomas N. Gladwin, James J. Kennelly, and Tara-Shelomith Krause, "Shifting Paradigms for Sustainable Development: Implications for Management Theory and Research," *The Academy of Management Review* 20 (October 1995): 874–907.
25. USEPA Case Studies, CSX Corporation, May 30 2003, http://www.epa.gov/ems/resources/casestudies/csx.htm (accessed March 6, 2010).

CHAPTER 3

Laying the Foundation: Creating a Sustainable Culture and Shift in Business Paradigms

Roya Ayman and Erica L. Hartman

This chapter is about developing and managing a sustainability culture in organizations. It explains the different aspects of culture and the process by which it forms. It also discusses programs, methodologies, and tools proven to be effective in shifting organizational culture toward sustainability. Creating changes in organizational sustainability requires a multipronged approach; therefore, this chapter addresses issues related to policy changes, informational dissemination, and behavioral modification at individual and group levels. It also acknowledges continuous monitoring of performance through measurement. By following the principles and steps discussed in this chapter, an organization will be able to effectively create changes in its culture to create environmental sustainability.

Introduction

The Chief Executive Officer of British Petroleum (BP) committed the company to reducing its emissions of GHGs that contribute to global warming, especially carbon dioxide. He challenged each business unit to identify ways in which it could produce fewer GHGs and promised that, by 2010, BP's GHG emissions would be 10% less than the 1990 levels, even though the company expected its outputs to be roughly 50% greater in 2010 than they were in 1990. Although this was a drastic change for the organization, CEO John Browne believed that taking a leadership position on climate change would create a distinctive identity and culture. This culture change would impact the perceptions of government officials, scientists, stakeholders, and employees.

By announcing this initiative, BP leadership also believed that they would release the creativity of its employees and increase the employees' commitment to the company, to the extent that they perceived their own values as being aligned with those of the organization. After three years, they had identified various ways to cut emissions, improve efficiencies, and save money. Although the initial changes cost BP an estimated $20 million, it saved $650 million during the first few years.[1,2]

"Wal-Mart CEO Lee Scott committed to improving the company's energy use by 30%, aiming to use 100% renewable energy (e.g., wind and solar panels) and to double the fuel efficiency of its massive shipping fleet and in order to support these programs, the company will invest over 500 million dollars annually".[3] In addition, Wal-Mart pressured its suppliers to reduce their waste and fossil fuel use. These "requests" then turned into scorecards that suppliers were asked to complete about their packaging, energy use, and carbon footprints. Through this initiative, suppliers such as Kraft identified opportunities to reduce their impact and also implemented sustainability initiatives.[4]

Both BP and Wal-Mart realized that environmental concerns are of the highest priority for our world, the organizations, and their customers. They determined ways they could address these issues and implemented programs that had an impact on their organizational culture and their customers, suppliers, and competitors. This chapter, will discuss how these organizations, and others like them, were successful in creating cultures of sustainability.

Prior chapters in this book discussed the concept of sustainability and strategic tools used to achieve sustainability. This chapter, will focus on implementing sustainable practices and changes and creating a culture of sustainability. In other words, how an organization can best bolster its commitment to sustainable organizational practices. This chapter will begin by defining organizational culture, and will discuss how a culture is created within an organization. In addition, this chapter will discuss the concept of culture change, including change management techniques and how to manage resistance to change. Finally, this chapter will provide a case study of an organization that created a sustainable culture, and will offer practical solutions for other organizations wishing to create a sustainable culture.

Definition of Culture

Scholars have long debated the definition of culture. Almost all agree with Kluckhom's (1951)[5] definition that culture is comprised of acquired and transmitted shared values, beliefs, and behavioral patterns that distinguish one group of people from the other. Culture has aspects that are visible and aspects that are not observable.[6] Hofstede (2001)[7] and Schein (1985)[8] agree that, within a culture, values and feelings are not visible, but aspects of culture that remain observable are the manifestation of those values and feelings (such as policies and norms of conduct and habitual behavior and symbols).

The most noticeable and visibly accessible aspect of a culture is its symbols. However, scholars are not in agreement as to whether an organization's values or the observable aspects come first. When examining a culture or engaging in culture change efforts, it is clear that a multipronged approach (e.g., focus on values and symbols) will yield the best result. Therefore, when considering a culture of sustainability, the values of environmental protection and social responsibility need to morph into observable entities. Similarly, these observable entities clarify the organization's values or missions and further emphasize them for employees and society.

Figure 3.1 represents the Onion Model of the components of culture (inspired by Hofstede 2001), which is described from the deepest part of the Onion to the surface in relation to a culture of sustainability.

Values, Beliefs, and Feelings

Values determine people's goals for action and the affective aspect of goals. A strong and positive affect towards a goal has a higher probability to result in action than one with less positive affect. At a group level (e.g., organization or work group), when consensus exists on "the importance of each value item as a guiding principle in [the group's] life," this can be considered as a cultural value.[9] Values are passed to us through cultural processes that span both geography and age groups.[10] They are influenced by a variety of factors such as ideology, religion, gender, class, and economic and social rules, all of which help to form our perceptions of the world. Tilbury and Wortman[11] referred to United Nations Education and Scientific and Cultural Organization (UNESCO, 2002) and mentioned that beyond discussions of politics, knowledge, and technology, working towards sustainability is primarily a matter of culture. Further, they

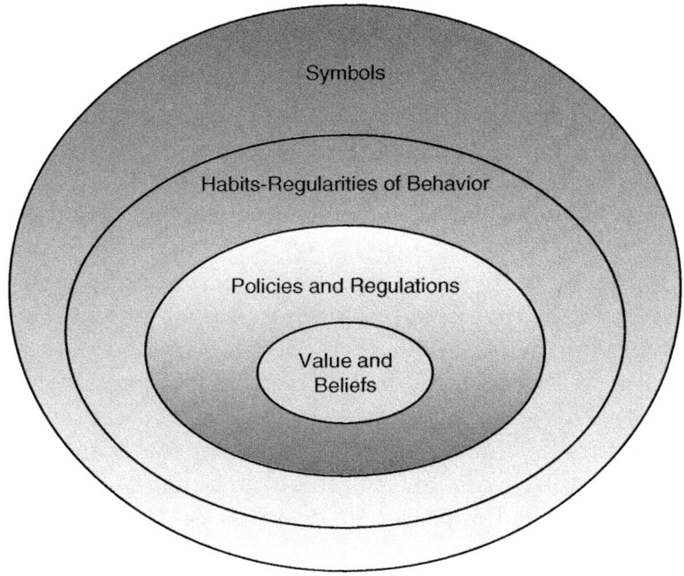

Figure 3.1 The Onion Model (inspired by Hofstede 2001).

clarified that culture and individual values are powerful forces that influence how people define problems and what they consider moral or ethical. Those who consider sustainability important would have a greater tendency to behave with respect towards the environment and engage in behaviors such as waste management, water conservation, carpooling, or telecommuting to work. They also think about the impact of their behavior on others around them and on future generations. Thus, their behaviors are guided by both their values of protecting the environment and of social justice.

Policies (Rules and Norms)

Policies set parameters for expected behaviors within a workgroup or organization. With these regulations or policies, employee behaviors are guided and the range of accepted behavior is clarified.[12] For example, if there are policies for how many hours or days employees need to be physically present in the organization, this is a demonstration of both the organization's response to the Clean Air Act and the flexibility to help employees manage work and family responsibilities (which is related to social justice and responsibility). Other examples of sustainability policies include paperless policies for the dissemination of documents or buildings that contain windows that open in comparison to buildings that monitor the air temperature internally, which can limit the energy needed to manage the air temperature.

During the implementation of the Clean Air Act in the early 1990s, many companies in the United States explored compressed work weeks and telecommuting options as a means of responding to this call. For example, Pattison[13] described a carpool mandate as a result of the Clean Air Act that required many urban areas to stop citizens from commuting by car. The effects of this decision were found not only to help reduce the carbon impact on the environment, but also reduced work-family conflict and had a positive impact on work performance.[14]

Habits and Behaviors

Habits and behaviors are observable actions of employees as individuals or in groups. An employee who makes an effort to conserve energy or resources could do so by keeping waste separated by categories (such as paper, plastic, and perishables), allowing for ease of recycling. At the group level, paper waste can be avoided by posting meeting agendas on a board or sending them by e-mail and conducting meetings that allow members to have their laptops or netbooks available during the session. Developing plans of action to either avoid excess use of material resources or to manage waste shows action-oriented responses to organizational sustainability.

Symbols

Symbols are very visible indicators of a culture, and they constitute the surface of a culture. For example, the current presence of hand-sanitizer dispensers in most public buildings (which began after the outbreak of the N1H1 virus) is a sign of concern for hygiene and health. Pictures and colors depicting nature (e.g., the color green) are used to convey environmental conscientiousness. In the last few years, professional conferences and companies have used the color green to show support for environmental sustainability.

In addition to the content of culture that is descriptive, some cultures are considered strong and others weak.[15] Strong cultures have clear norms and policies with which most people agree. These cultures have a long history of behavioral patterns that have formed over generations. Thus, expectations of behaviors are clear and reinforced by rewards and punishments (such as social sanctions). In weak cultures, the norms are not very clear and are not imposed with sanctions. The uniformity and consensus around policies and rules are not as high. In these cultures, individuals have more freedom of expression, and the anticipation of a given act is less possible. The implication of the differences between the two cultures are that in comparison to the weak cultures, in strong cultures behaviors of individuals and groups are predictable. On the other hand, these cultures are deeply rooted in tradition (e.g., habitual behavior and rules) and are less open to new learning and change.

Importance of Culture in Organizations

Studies in organizations have shown that organizational cultures, which represent the perception of the values and behavioral norms of the majority of the employees, have had an impact on organizational performance as determined by financial and market performance, customer satisfaction,[16,17,18] and safety behaviors. In all of these studies, the strong, positive perception of organizational policies and practices has had an impact on the bottom line. As now the various components of culture and its importance to organizations was defined, we will discuss what is considered a sustainable culture and follow that with how culture is formed and maintained.

How Is Culture Created?

Human beings gravitate to groups to be affirmed and to make sense of their surroundings. Groups allow for social comparison and provide clarity for individuals about their actions and standards that would otherwise be ambiguous. Thus, through their culture, groups guide individual behavior. Social conformity research in the twentieth century showed that individuals tend to rely on others for guidance, particularly when they are not sure of what to believe. Both Asch's paradigm[19] (1951) and Sharif's[20] (1935) classic studies showed that people in uncertain situations will conform to collective information. Asch showed how individuals gravitate to the majority opinion in his famous line-judging tests. In Sharif's studies, he demonstrated that once a group forms a perception, even if the perception of each of the members of the group is changed, the culture persists. In his studies, it took several generations of new members before the norms and beliefs of the group were questioned by its new members.

The group's culture can impact the individual in two ways: through informational social influence or through normative social influence. The former social impact provides clarity and convinces the individual of the acceptable values and behaviors. With the latter, the individual conforms because of the fear of rejection. While both are powerful processes, the first process is longer lasting and changes not only the person's public behavior, but also the person's private behaviors. When the social influence is based on an attraction to the group, it produces identification, whereas when the social influence is based on expert information, it may lead to internalization of that concept by the individuals in the group. Their impact varies on different individuals. For example, Werner, Sansone, and Brown[21] demonstrated that both informational and normative social influences are necessary when there is a need to change attitudes of men and women in relation to the use of toxic and nontoxic products. In their study, they showed that, for women, normative social influence mattered. For men, the informational influence was sufficient and others' opinions did not matter. Scholars would agree that both processes are needed to develop and maintain a culture.[22]

On the other hand, individuals who value their freedom of action and thought may perceive strong social pressure for conformity as a threat. At times, they may oppose influence and information and become deviant, which is referred to as "Reactance Theory"[23] (Santee and Maslach 1982). Some evidence shows that if the language of the messages for change and the method of social influence is inclusive, it would cause less reaction.

Once a group has formed a culture, which means it has a common set of values, mission, and norms, it provides mechanisms to maintain that culture. In other words, the conformity occurs partially because the person is fearful of being rejected. This fear is not unfounded. Schachter[24] (1951) showed that the group members control and protect the culture and ostracize deviant members. In his studies, he was also able to demonstrate that the group rewarded those who had initially disagreed with, but then accepted the group's values and norms. Therefore, organizations with strong culture can guide the beliefs and behaviors of their members and force compliance; however, this organizational culture can also have liabilities. While culture can initially serve as a guide for individuals' behaviors, it can also act as a barrier to change.

Unlike traditional organizations, learning organizations create an environment that allows for improvement and adjustment.[25] These organizations have cultures that promote change and flexibility in response to new information. The culture of these organizations is governed with values of openness to new ideas, inclusivity of all perspectives, concern for others, and self-examination for improvement. Thomas and Allen[26] state that what differentiates learning organizations from others is "their ability to continually expand their respective capacities to create their future or learn and transform themselves" (p. 125). In today's society, organizations are faced with many complexities such as a diverse workforce, changes in technology, and changes in the definition of success and effectiveness. It seems evident that there is a need for a systematic exploration of novel approaches and an openness to learn. These organizations would be more receptive to the change and adjustment needed for preserving resources and social responsibility.

Who Creates Culture?

Many attribute the creator and the instigator of a culture to the founder or CEO of a company.[27,28] However, a leader with a vision who is imposing it on an organization is not sufficient for a culture to form. As discussed in the formation and maintenance of cultures, it becomes evident that the influence process is very important. Scholars would argue that a charismatic and transformational leader has the capacity and the ability to take a value or a vision and gain the needed support from the organization to build the culture.[29]

A charismatic leader can be the role model for the value and the mission. A transformational leader can gain the trust of his or her people and can be the change agent to rally the employees and get buy-in.[30] The behavioral characteristics associated with this type of leader are known as the "4 I's"[31]:

Idealized influence: conveys a sense of joint mission, eases tension, shows sacrifice and commitment.

Inspirational motivation: creates a "can do" attitude among employees, sets examples, raises expectations, thinks of unforeseen opportunities, and brings hope.

Intellectual stimulation: encourages "thinking outside the box" and "behaving out of the comfort zone." Listens and considers any comment regardless of how foolish it may sound, and encourages revisiting problems with new perspectives.

Individual consideration: demonstrates awareness of the strengths and weaknesses of each employee, shows interest in others' well-being, promotes learning and development, and encourages two-way communication.

In essence, the leader can be the role model and hero who inspires others and exemplifies the behaviors that are needed to establish the culture. The leader can facilitate the three steps for developing a culture:

1. Clarify the values of the organization in regard to sustainability.
2. Establish beliefs and policies that provide parameters for behaviours—what is accepted in the organization.
3. Integrate organizational values with individual values (i.e., internalization).

In conclusion, an organization's culture has a major impact on employees and their effectiveness. In further exploring the factors that make a culture and how that culture is formed and maintained, the chapter provided tools for future leaders and managers. Leaders who adhere to transformational and charismatic values and behaviors can become the key agents of change in their organizations. Now we will elaborate on the mechanisms and steps of change management within an organization.

What Is Change Management?

When an organization sets out to change its organizational culture, it is bringing about planned change. According to Levy,[32] there are two goals of planned change: first, it seeks to improve the ability of the organization to adapt to changes in its environment; and second, it seeks to change employee behavior. Because an organization's success or failure is essentially determined by employee behaviors, planned change is focused on changing the behaviors of individuals and groups in the organization.

In planned change, an organization can either utilize first-order change or second-order changes. First order change is linear and continuous. Second order changes are multidimensional, multilevel, discontinuous, and result in radical changes in assumptions about the organization.[33] Given that the goal is to create changes in the organization, as well as in the individuals and groups associated within the organization, sustainable culture change is a multilevel concept. Each level must be addressed in change management efforts. In addition, many organizations that I have highlighted throughout this chapter have utilized multifaceted change management efforts in order to impact all areas of an organization and its organizational strategy.

How Are Meaningful and Sustainable Changes Created?

Although sustainable cultures are a relatively new concept, and no one has a clear sense of what a successful sustainable culture looks like,[34] we do know that there are several key actions that must be part of any successful culture change efforts.

Change Readiness Assessment

Before embarking on an organizational change, it is beneficial to assess the "change readiness" of the organization. There are various methods for assessing the readiness of an organization. For an example of this type of assessment, see Table 3.1. Many of these evaluations focus on assessing the success and impact of past change initiatives, the support by leadership and management, the communication within the organization, and employee satisfaction.

Organizations can prepare for readiness by engaging in what Lewin[35] discussed as part of his classic concept of the three-step model of the change process. The first step is to "unfreeze" the status quo of the organization. According to Lewin, the status quo is a state of equilibrium that needs to be altered in order to do this and to overcome individual resistance and group conformity. The readiness assessment is done to ensure that this alteration has happened. He further recommends using force field analysis that capitalizes on the driving forces (which direct behavior away from the status quo) and restraining forces (which hinder movement from the existing equilibrium) to position the organization towards change. Once the organization has shifted from equilibrium, the change can be introduced. Once the change has been introduced, the process of "refreezing" occurs, in which the organization takes on efforts to ensure the change is permanent. The following ideas, which are presented in Figure 3.2, enable the movement and refreezing process.

Table 3.1 Example Change Readiness Assessment

Employees' willingness to change determines how quickly and thoroughly a team or organization can move forward. A change readiness assessment will determine employees' willingness to accept new and different processes, customers, equipment, ideas, and more. The assessment measures the following dimensions:

Information Dissemination: How well have you communicated the purpose and the process of the change?

Stakeholder Involvement: Which groups need to be involved in the planning and change process? Which groups report positive levels of job involvement? How are employees going to be involved in the change process?

Attitudes Towards Change: How have previous change initiatives been managed in the organization? What are people's attitudes towards change in the organization?

Reaching the Goal: Are your change initiatives succeeding in the eyes of employees? Who will be communicating the success of the change initiatives?

Project Activities: What are the initial impressions of the new initiative? On follow-up administrations of the survey, what are later impressions?

Leadership and Management Support

In order for any change initiative to work, it is imperative that there be support and buy-in from both the leadership team and management. Organizational leaders set the vision, values, and goals; therefore, change initiatives must start at the top of the organization and the messages must be consistent, comprehensive, and inclusive.[36] In addition to setting the vision and values of the organization, the support of leadership also brings with it the credibility and importance of making the initiative a success.

Once the executive team has decided upon a green initiative, or to make sustainability changes in their culture, the leaders and managers tasked with making it happen (on top of all their other responsibilities) often find that they are not as supportive of the change efforts as their employees. This concept is called the "middle management squeeze."[37] If these managers and leaders are uncertain of their responsibilities and do not champion the changes, organizations will see a cascading effect of these attitudes to their employees. Therefore, before any change effort begins, it is critical to secure the support of leadership and managers.

There are several ways an organization can assess and obtain support from these individuals. First and foremost, the business case for creating a culture of sustainability must be developed and communicated to leadership. In order for leadership to be fully committed, they need to have a clear understanding of the issue and its importance. For more information on this concept, see chapter 4. One of the easiest ways to obtain commitment to the change initiative is to involve leadership and management in the change efforts. This will be discussed in greater detail in the next section.

Stakeholder Involvement

Buy-in and involvement are not limited to the executive leadership and management. A more positive, proactive approach is to actively engage a range of stakeholders to have them develop, *in conjunction with the leadership team*, a clear and shared vision. By engaging key

Figure 3.2 Lewin's Three-Step Change Model.

stakeholders in this process, commitment and ownership will be created, which will help them inspire and motivate themselves and others. Many times, these stakeholders also form the basis of a task force or committee that can be used to collect data regarding the issues, help to analyze the issues and problem-solve, and serve as champions of the project for the rest of the organization.

When identifying stakeholders and task force team members, it is important to carefully consider the "right" members. These teams should be comprised of employees from different departments and different levels from within the organization so that the issues can be examined from various different perspectives. The ideas that are generated from heterogeneous groups are representative of more groups in the organization and therefore tend to generate more buy-in across the organization. Some organizations may also wish to include board members and customers, depending on the identified changes being addressed.

Once these stakeholders and team members have been identified, it is important that they are provided with the appropriate level of decision making and influence. This task force needs to be empowered with the right resources to further investigate the issues at hand; to be given the latitude to develop innovative, creative solutions; and to have the ability to take ownership for change. In addition to the stakeholders and the task force members, organizations should also provide sustainability education and training for employees (to be addressed later in the chapter). This will enable everyone to participate in the changes, and research has shown that sustainability plans are most successful when they are based on the active involvement and contribution of everyone in the environment.[38]

Linkage to Organizational Strategy and Practices

In order to make sustainable culture changes and to make changes that are sustainable, the changes need to be linked to the broader organizational strategies. In other words, environmental thinking needs to be considered and integrated into every strategic decision.[39] In addition to looking at each decision with an "environmental lens," all organizational practices need to be realigned with a focus on sustainability.

Two of the most common areas that people consider when aligning their practices with their environmental strategy are *measurement* and *compensation*. Organizations reward what is important to them;

therefore, it is critical that environmental performance be incorporated into the compensation structure of the organization. Similarly, if it is also true that "what gets measured gets managed," then key performance indicators need to include environmental performance measures.

Many times, these two organizational practices go hand in hand. This may mean that, many times, the environmental performance measures are used for determining bonuses, merit increases, or even promotions. Another way in which the culture can be reinforced is to align reward and recognition programs around environmental performance. Companies like 3M, FedEx, and Timberland all have reward programs specifically focused on environmental performance.[40]

Another organizational practice that should be aligned to the environmental agenda is the organization's hiring practices. It is critical that employees who are brought into the company are aligned with the values of the organization and understand that sustainability is a core value. Assessing person-environment fit will help ensure that the person takes ownership of the environmental performance of the organization.

Communication

Tell them what you are going to do, tell them what you are currently doing, and tell them what you did. In other words, communicate, communicate, and communicate! Whatever changes are occurring, communication is the glue that holds different functions, groups, and individuals together.[41] As mentioned earlier in the chapter, social and informational influences are key drivers in the formation of culture. Utilizing a well-structured communication plan will facilitate the change management process.

One popular model of organizational communication is the CPR (Content–Process–Roles) model of organizational communication.[42,43] This model provides three key steps to organizational communication:

1. Exactly what is being communicated (content)?
2. How is it communicated (processes)?
3. Who does the communicating (roles)?

In this model, the most important aspect of communication is to understand what is being communicated (content). Without understanding this, it is impossible to understand what the preferred methods of transmission processes are and what group or individual (roles) should be responsible for transferring the information.

In addition to communicating information about the forthcoming changes, it is also important to communicate what actions and changes have been made and the results of those changes. Both internal and external stakeholders want to see progress and that the organization is "walking the talk." When organizations begin to see a link between changes in behaviors and attitudes and improvements in performance, change has begun to institutionalize itself.[44] Therefore, as stated earlier in the chapter, it is key to put performance measures in place around the change initiatives.

Education

Implementing changes in an organizational culture many times requires employees to learn new skill sets and acquire new knowledge in order to be successful. Therefore, learning organizations tend to have more rapid change adaption. Specifically, it has been found that organizations that have open communication and information, risk-taking and new idea generation, and resource availability to perform one's job have rapid change adaptation.[45] When creating sustainable cultures, it is critical to equip employees with the knowledge of sustainability so that they can participate in actions for change.[46] Esty and Winston[47] highlight three types of training programs that sustainable organizations have utilized to make successful culture changes:

1. Training on focused topics like regulatory compliance or eco-efficiency
2. Education to raise general knowledge of environmental issues and help employees adopt sustainability in their own lives
3. Executive-level, big-picture programs on sustainability

Resistance to Change

The concept of change is difficult for individuals and organizations to understand, accept, and implement. As a result, organizations run into resistance when implementing changes. In order to successfully create sustainability changes, organizations must expect resistance and plan their responses to create acceptance among their employees. Three main reasons for resistance include fear and anxiety (natural responses that can be used as learning opportunities), concern with performance measurement (which means different things to different stakeholders), and the dangers of innovations becoming isolated from the organization.[48]

Some of the ways to overcome resistance to change initiatives have already been highlighted in this chapter. These include forming a task force with members of the organization, which will increase their commitment to the change and allow them to serve as champions of the project to others who are in doubt. Communication is another driving force in overcoming resistance to change. This can occur during town hall meetings, through communications from the CEO and/or senior leadership, or through written publications. Another valuable tool that can help overcome resistance is the use of focus groups. Gathering a group of employees together to discuss the upcoming changes, their importance, what will occur, how it will impact them and the organization, and taking the time to listen to their concerns and answer questions they may have can be very helpful.

Some examples of questions that can be used in a focus group setting to help alleviate fears related to sustainability changes are adapted from Church, Waclawski, and Kraut)[49]:

- Describe your fears regarding these changes. What negative results could come from this and why?
- Describe what positive outcomes you expect to see from these changes.
- What can be done to make the changes more meaningful and beneficial?
- What are the main issues facing your organization that you would like to see addressed by the changes?

Table 3.2 Checklist for Change Management

1. **Change Readiness Assessment**: Make sure your organization is ready for the changes you are thinking of making. Don't set yourself up for failure if the organization is not in a place that is willing to embrace these new initiatives and ideas.
2. **Leadership and Management Commitment**: Ensure that both leadership and middle management is fully committed. Not only does leadership set the vision for the organization, they also have a large influence on the degree to which the employees accept the changes.
3. **Stakeholder and Task Force Involvement**: Involve people in the organization. They will be more committed to the changes and will take more ownership.
4. **Link to Strategic Objectives**: Ensure that there are measurement and reward systems in place that are linked to the environmental initiatives.
5. **Communication**: Communicate, communicate, communicate!
6. **Education and Training**: Provide people with the knowledge, skills, and abilities they need to actively contribute to the changes

- What things do you like about your organization that you would like to see remain the same?

By following the principles and steps discussed in this chapter, organizations will be able to effectively create changes in their culture to create environmental sustainability. See Table 3.2 for a list of the change management steps and techniques discussed in this chapter.

Summary

Culture is comprised of acquired and transmitted shared values, beliefs, and behavioral patterns that distinguish one group of people from another. Culture has aspects that are visible and others that are not observable.[50] The most noticeable and visibly accessible aspect of a culture is its symbols. However, scholars are not in agreement as to whether an organization's values or the observable aspects come first. When examining a culture or engaging in culture change efforts, it is clear that a multipronged approach (e.g., focus on values and symbols) will yield the best result. Therefore, when considering a culture of sustainability, the values of environmental protection and social responsibility need to morph into observable entities. Similarly, these observable entities clarify the organization's values or missions and further emphasize them for employees and society. Further, scholars clarified that culture and individual values are powerful forces that influence how people define problems and what they consider moral or ethical.

Those who consider sustainability important would have a greater tendency to behave with respect towards the environment and engage in behaviors such as waste management, water conservation, carpooling, or telecommuting to work. They also think about the impact of their behavior on others around them and on future generations. Thus their behaviors are guided by both their values of protecting the environment and social justice.

Studies in organizations have shown that organizational cultures that represent the perception of the majority of employees' values and behavioral norms have had an impact on organizational performance, as determined by financial and market performance, customer satisfaction,[51,52,53] and safety behaviors.[54] (Clarke 2006). In all of these studies, the strong, positive perception of organizational policies and practices has had an impact on the bottom line.

Case Study and Examples

Following are examples of change management efforts around the world in various organizations for review, reflection, and take away lessons for your organization.

Australia's Brisbane Institute of Technical and Further Education

Australia's Brisbane Institute of Technical and Further Education developed renewable energy courses and placed sustainability at the core of its engineering studies. The courses provide opportunities to learn about the social, environmental, and economic impacts of sustainability and the barriers to the increased usage of renewable energy. Best practices are demonstrated in the learning setting, and instructors use a multidisciplinary systems approach that presents learners with real problems in the community. The institute also works with industry and the community on course development, implementation, and review.[55]

Hewlett-Packard

Hewlett-Packard (HP) is a leading global supplier of technology solutions to consumers, businesses, and institutions and has a very strong commitment to global corporate citizenship. One of the key initiatives that HP is known for is its product stewardship program based on a life-cycle analysis of its products. Life-cycle analysis incorporates design for environment, energy efficiency, materials innovation, design for recyclability, packaging, and product reuse and recycling. HP involves stakeholders in the life-cycle analysis and works collaboratively with them to minimize environmental impacts. This is an example of systemic thinking at work.[56]

SC Johnson

SC Johnson is a household products company that has committed to sustainability by creating value for those most in need of support around the world. SC Johnson partnered with Cornell University, the University of North Carolina, the University of Michigan, the World Resources Institute, and the Johnson Foundation to develop a "Base of the Pyramid" (BOP) Protocol that informs its sustainability strategy. Financial support was also provided by DuPont, Hewlett-Packard, and Tetra Pak. This partnership aims to link the private sector and local communities to build economic, social, and environmental value for the poorest sections of the global society. The BOP Protocol defines three key phases to generate value for all stakeholders:

1. ***Opening up***: Facilitating two-way stakeholder dialogue to understand the local environment and to generate ideas for change
2. ***Building the ecosystem:*** Generating a network of partnerships among multinational corporations, local individuals, and organizations that support change for sustainability and win-win strategies
3. ***Creating the enterprise:*** Piloting a test, evaluating results, and then further launching change initiatives that generate value for all stakeholders

Following the BOP Protocol, SC Johnson and other multinational corporations identify and develop sustainable new products and businesses in partnership with BOP suppliers and consumers, resulting in lasting value that stems from a deep understanding of their needs, perspectives, and capabilities.[57]

Notes

1. Daniel C. Esty and Andrew S. Winston, *Green to Gold: How Smart Companies Use Environmental Strategy to Innovate, Create Value, and Build Competitive Advantage* (Hoboken, NJ: Yale University Press, 2009), 2.
2. Kimberly O'Niel Packard and Forest Reinhardt, "What Every Executive Needs to Know about Global Warming," *Harvard Business Review on Green Business Strategy* (July–August 2000): 29–30.
3. Daniel C. Esty and Andrew S. Winston, *Green to Gold: How Smart Companies Use Environmental Strategy to Innovate, Create Value, and Build Competitive Advantage* (Hoboken, NJ: Yale University Press, 2009), 7.
4. Ibid., xiii–xiv.
5 C. Kluckhohn, "The Study of Culture," in *The Policy Science,* eds. D. Lerner and D. H. Lasswell (Ed.) (Stanford, CA: Stanford University Press, 1951), 86-101.
6. Roya Ayman and Karen Korabik, "Leadership: Why Culture and Gender Matter," *American Psychologist* 65 (April 2010): 157–70.
7. Greet Hofstede, *Culture's Consequences* (Thousand Oaks, CA: Sage, 2001).
8. Edgar H. Schein, *Organizational Culture and Leadership* (San Francisco: Jossey-Bass Publishers, 1985).
9. S.H. Schwartz and K. Boehnke, "Evaluating the Structure of Human Values with Confirmatory Factor Analysis," *Journal of Research in Personality* 38 (2004): 230–55.
10. Darin Saul, "Expanding Environmental Education: Thinking Critically, Thinking Culturally," *Journal of Environmental Education* 31 (2000): 5–7.

11. Daniells Tilbury and David Wortman, "Education for Sustainability in Further and Higher Education: Reflections along the Journey," *Planning for Higher Education* 36 (July–September 2008): 5–16.
12. Edgar H. Schein, *Organizational Culture and Leadership* (San Francisco: Jossey-Bass Publishers, 1985).
13. S. Pattison, "Carpools; Pennsylvania; United States; All Other Transit and Ground Passenger Transportation," *Consumers' Research Magazine* (January1994): 38.
14. M. LoVerde, R. Ayman, and N. Delay , "The Effects of Psychological Needs on Telework's Impact on Performance." A paper presented at the Society of Industrial and Organizational Psychology. Orlando, FL, USA (April 2003).
15. R. Ayman and S.J. Adams (in press), "Contingencies, Context, and Situation in Leadership," in *The Nature of Leadership*, eds. D. Day and J. Antonakis.
16. Y. Berson, S. Oreg, and T. Dvir, "CEO Values, Organizational Culture, and Firm Outcomes," *Journal of Organizational Behavior* 29 (2008): 615–33.
17. B. Schneider, W.H. Macey, W.C. Lee, and S.A. Young, "Organizational Service Climate Drivers of the American Customer Satisfaction Index (ACSI) and Financial and Market Performance," *Journal of Service Research* 12 (2009): 3–14.
18. M. Schulte, C. Ostroff, S. Shmulyianm, and A. Kinicki, "Organizational Climate Configurations: Relationships to Collective Attitudes, Customer Satisfaction, and Financial Performance," *Journal of Applied Psychology* 94 (2009): 618–34.
19. S. Asch, "Effects of Group Pressure upon the Modification and Distortion of Judgment," in *Groups, Leadership, and Men* , eds. H. Guetzkow (Pittsburgh: Carnegie Press, 1951).
20. M. Sherif, M., "A Study of Some Social Factors in Perception," *Archives of Psychology* 27 (187) (1935): 1-60.
21. C. Werner, C. Sansone, and B. Brown, "Guided Group Discussion and Attitude Change: The Roles of Normative and Informational Influence," *Journal of Environmental Psychology* 28 (2007): 27–41.
22. M.E. Shaw, *Group Dynamics: The Psychology of Small Group Behavior,* (3rd ed). (New York: McGraw Hill Book company, 1981).
23. R. T. Santee and C. Maslach, "To Agree or Not to Agree: Personal Dissent Amid Social Pressure to Conform," *Journal of Personality and social Psychology* 42 (4) (1982), 690-700.
24. S. Schachter, "Deviation, Rejection, and Communication," *Journal of Abnormal and Social Psychology* 46 (1951): 190-207.
25. P. Senge, *The Fifth Discipline: The Art and Practice of a Learning Organization* (Sydney: Random House, 1995).
26 K. Thomas and S. Allen, "The Learning Organisation: A Meta-Analysis of Themes in literature." The Learning Organisation, 13 (2) (2006): 121-139.
27. Y. Berson, S. Oreg, and T. Dvir, "CEO Values, Organizational Culture, and Firm Outcomes," *Journal of Organizational Behavior* 29 (2008): 615–33.
28. S.C. Chang and M.S. Lee, "A Study on Relationships among Leadership, Organizational Culture, the Operation of Learning Organizations and Employee's Job Satisfaction," *The Learning Organization* 14 (2007): 155–85.
29. B.M. Bass and B.J. Avoilio, "Transformational Leadership: A Response to Critiques," in *Leadership Theory and Research: Perspectives and Directions*, eds. M.M. Chemers and R. Ayman (San Diego: Academic Press, 1993), 49–80.
30. N.A. Gillespie and L. Mann, "Transformational Leadership and Shared Values: The Building Blocks of Trust," *Journal of Managerial Psychology* 19 (2004): 588–607.

31. B.M. Bass and B.J. Avoilio, "Transformational Leadership: A Response to Critiques," in *Leadership Theory and Research: Perspectives and Directions,* eds. M.M. Chemers and R. Ayman (San Diego: Academic Press, 1993), 49–80.
32. A. Levy, "Second-Order Planned Change: Definition and Conceptualization," *Organizational Dynamics* 15 (1986): 4–20.
33. Ibid.
34. Robert Prescott-Allen, *Wellbeing of Nations* (New York: Island Press, 2001), 2.
35. K. Lewin, *Field Theory in Social Science* (New York: Harper & Row, 1951).
36. D. Buchana, L. Fitzgerald, D. Ketley, R. Gollop, J.L. Jones, S.S. Lamont, A. Neath, and E. Whitby, "No Going Back: A Review of the Literature on Sustaining Organizational Change," *International Journal of Management Review* 7 (2005): 189–205.
37. Daniel C. Esty and Andrew S. Winston, *Green to Gold: How Smart Companies Use Environmental Strategy to Innovate, Create Value, and Build Competitive Advantage* (Hoboken, NJ: Yale University Press, 2009), xvi, 242–43.
38. S. Calvo Roy, J. Benayas, and J. Gutierrez Perez, "Learning in Sustainable Environments: The Greening of Higher Education," in *Education and Sustainability: Responding to the Global Challenge,* eds. D. Tilbury, R. B. Stevenson, J. Fien, and D. Schreuder.(Gland: International Union for Conservation of Nature and Natural Resources Commission on Education and Communication, 1951), 91–98.
39. Ibid., 207.
40. Ibid., 224.
41. A.H. Church, J. Waclawski, A.I. Kraut, *Designing and Using Organizational Surveys: A Seven Step Process* (San Francisco: Jossey-Bass Publishers, 2001).
42. A.H. Church, "The Character of Organizational Communication: A Review and New Conceptualization," *Internal Journal of Organizational Analysis* 2 (1994): 18–53.
43. A.H. Church, "Giving Your Organizational Communication C-P-R," *Leadership and Organizational Development Journal* 17 (1996): 4–11.
44. J.P. Kotter, "Leading Change: Why Transformation Efforts Fail," *Harvard Business Review* 73 (1995): 59–67.
45. C. Kontoghiorghes, S.M. Awbrey, and P.L. Feurig, "Examining the Relationship between Learning Organization Characteristics and Change Adaptation, Innovation, and Organizational Performance," *Human Resource Quarterly* 16 (2005): 185–211.
46. D. Tilbury, "Environmental Education for Sustainability: A Force for Change in Higher Education," in *Higher Education and the Challenge of Sustainability: Problematics, Promise, and Practice,* eds. P.B. Corcoran and A.E.J. Wals (Dordrecht: Kluwer Academic Publishers, 2004), 97–112.
47. Daniel C. Esty and Andrew S. Winston, *Green to Gold: How Smart Companies Use Environmental Strategy to Innovate, Create Value, and Build Competitive Advantage* (Hoboken, NJ: Yale University Press, 2009), 230–32.
48. P.M. Senge and K.H. Kaeufer, "Creating Change," *Executive Focus* 17 (2000): 4–5.
49. Adapted from A.H., Church, J. Waclawski, and A.I. Kraut, *Designing and Using Organizational Surveys: A Seven Step Process* (San Francisco: Jossey-Bass Publishers, 2001).
50. Roya Ayman and Karen Korabik, "Leadership: Why Culture and Gender Matter," *American Psychologist* 65 (April 2010): 157–70.
51. Y. Berson, S. Oreg, and T. Dvir, "CEO Values, Organizational Culture, and Firm Outcomes," *Journal of Organizational Behavior* 29 (2008): 615–33.

52. B. Schneider, W.H. Macey, W.C. Lee, and S.A. Young, "Organizational Service Climate Drivers of the American Customer Satisfaction Index (ACSI) and Financial and Market Performance," *Journal of Service Research* 12 (2009): 3–14.
53. M. Schulte, C. Ostroff, S. Shmulyianm, and A. Kinicki, "Organizational Climate Configurations: Relationships to Collective Attitudes, Customer Satisfaction, and Financial Performance," *Journal of Applied Psychology* 94 (2009): 618–34.
54. S. Clarke, "The Relationship Between Safety Climate and Safety Performance: A Meta-Analytic Review," *Journal of Occupational Health psychology,* 11. (2006) (4): 315-327.
55. D. Tilbury and D. Wortman, *Education for Sustainability in Further and Higher Education: Reflections along the Journey* (Ann Arbor, MI: Society of College and University Planning, 2008).
56. Ibid., (www.hp.com/hpinfo/globalcitizenship/gcreport/pdf/dfe_life_cycle.pdf).
57. Adapted from www.scjohnson.com/PR05/cnv_4_npn.asp#; D. Tilbury & D. Wortman, *Education for Sustainability in Further and Higher Education: Reflections Along the Journey* (Ann Arbor: Society of College and University Planning, 2008).

CHAPTER 4

Business Case for Sustainability

Nasrin R. Khalili

Sustainability is becoming a top priority for leaders of governments, businesses, and society. Pursuing sustainability, however, entails careful assessment of the business models in practice, business culture, and value systems. Translating a sustainability concept into actionable steps requires setting priorities, defining principles, and forming strategies for the development of the guidelines and systems as a "business case" that can justify the need, identify the risks, and define the benefits of pursuing sustainability. Although it may vary in style and format, the development of a business case assists businesses in determining what sustainability means to them, what the perceived values are, and how they can create those values via a proper and systematic transformation of their business strategy, structure, and order. Development of an ingenious business case for sustainability will assist businesses with the design of realistic sustainability goals and objectives; identify systematic changes necessary to successfully address sustainability; and design codified methodologies to assess the impact of sustainability on business social, environmental, and financial performance (triple bottom line). This chapter discusses the need, and steps involved in the development of a business case for sustainability. Also presented is a framework for the analysis and assessment of sustainability business cases.

Introduction

In order to succeed in the new competitive market, corporations must address social values and honor the environment by mitigating environmental and social risks associated with their operations.

Such mitigation strategies have commonly focused on identifying environmental concerns within the realm of corporate strategy and responded to it by developing codified management, audit, and reporting schemes for a wide range of operations. The most effective response, however, requires integration of various environmental policies and programs into the operations strategies. Environmental management and risk mitigation programs such as Quality Management, Six Sigma, Environmental Management Systems (ISOs 14000–18000), Product Stewardship, and Life Cycle Assessment have been put in place to strengthen firms' distinctive competence in terms of their operations objectives (highest quality products at lowest costs).

Traditional business economic views suggest that any corporate effort to address environmental pollution and externalities involves costs. These costs would be transferred back to the firms with negative impacts on corporate financial performance. Alternatively, it has been documented that corporate strategies that factor in environmental issues could improve the firm's level of financial performance and overall competitiveness in the market. Generally, poor environmental performance reduces a firm's market valuation.[1]

During the last two decades, a growing body of research has focused on identifying best practices that can concurrently reduce or eliminate the negative impact of a firm's activities on the natural environment and contribute to the creation of a competitive advantage in the product markets. Different best practices, however, could affect different types of competitive advantage. Best practices could be either distinction between cost and differentiation advantages, which has previously been used to classify types of competitive advantages created by a firm's environmental strategy, or cost advantages that can result from adopting best practices focusing on a firm's production processes, namely transition toward sustainability.[2]

Corporations in North America, Europe, Japan, and in most newly industrializing nations are now embracing environmental protection as part of their international competitive strategies. For many firms, the shift to proactive environmental management is driven by pressures they face from the government, by regulatory and legal liabilities for environmental damage, from customers who desire sustainable products and corporate responsibility, from employees, and also from competitors. The strongest driver, however, has been the growing evidence that firms that adopt proactive environmental management strategies and subsequently pursue sustainability would become more efficient and competitive. Therefore, environmental sustainability, the need to protect the environment and conserve natural resources, is now a value embraced by the most competitive and successful multinational companies.[3]

Theories of cultural, economic, and environmental sustainability and the sustainability of political and social structures have been proposed in pursuit of the achievement of sustainability.[4] Sustainable development has been increasingly adopted as a goal of government policy and planning for environmentally sustainable development. From a business perspective, sustainability means achieving financial objectives without sacrificing social or environmental and economic values. Corporations that do not understand the implications of these issues could face increasing difficulty in the market as consumers and industries begin to impose sustainability requirements on manufacturers and suppliers of raw materials, goods, and services.

The goal of a business transition toward sustainability is to provide high quality of life now and for future generations while preserving resources. These goals, however, are achievable only within the constraints set by resources and the environment. In their crusade toward becoming sustainable, organizations must identify both the "greatest threats" and the "opportunities" they could encounter while pursuing sustainability.

A wide range of approaches, strategies, and programs have been initiated by policymakers in partnership with industry in an attempt to assist businesses and corporations in addressing and managing their sustainability goals and objectives. Examples include the development of *sustainable business codes*, *sustainable business ethical responsibility*, *green procurement*, and *Global Reporting Initiatives (GRIs)*, which is in line with the concept of *Corporate Social Responsibility*.[5,6]

This chapter suggests the development and use of a "business case" for sustainability movements as the first strategic tool. A business case for sustainability both attends to the existing business strategies and programs and provides opportunities to factor in parameters linked with the environmental and social responsibilities, research and development, technological innovation, financial instruments, new policies and regulations, and stakeholder values. As presented, scenario-based analysis techniques included in the sustainability business case framework allow for the inclusion of sustainability risk and opportunities in the decision-making stages of business strategic development.[7–9]

Developing a Business Case for Sustainability

The development, implementation, and measurement of sustainability strategies means improving profitability, competitiveness, and market share in response to consumer awareness and demand. At the theoretical level, the concept of sustainability makes sense, but translating the concept into actionable steps with financial viability and investments has been a significant obstacle for organizations. The development of a business case for sustainability demonstrates how sustainability-based strategies can assist organizations with meeting government, customer, and market expectations while assessing their impact on the natural environment.

The practical sustainability concept and the Stakeholder, Externality, and Asset (SEA) strategic model presented in chapter 2 were developed in support of the transition to sustainable business practices. This model can be used to assess and illustrate the relationship, interaction, and interdependency among the SEA factors for any sustainability project. We have also discussed the contributing factors, such as the need for cultural change, in chapter 3. The present chapter, however, continues to unfold the concept of business sustainability and the significance of fostering business case development for sustainability projects.

The design of an effective business case specifically for "sustainability" requires a full understanding of the concepts and logic behind the development of a successful generic business case. Accordingly, an analysis of the methodologies and models used to develop a business case are provided prior to discussing the framework for sustainability business cases (*how to include sustainability in the corporate strategic planning and business models or characterize and assess sustainability projects*).

The equity market, which has an important influence over corporate thinking and direction, views sustainability and sustainable development as factors that can both define and impact current and future business activities. Therefore, there is a need for an explicit analysis of the potential opportunities and threats posed by sustainability issues, particularly in the areas of strategic concern to businesses.

What Is a Business Case?

An effective business case is a multipurpose document that generates the support, participation, and leadership commitment required to transform an idea into reality. A business case is also the first step in capital planning and investment models. It presents financial justification for the allocation of corporate resources, such as funding, labor, and technology, and identifies effective tools for obtaining financing from public or private sources while setting direction from a range of strategic alternatives.

A business case is the key document that senior managers review when deciding whether to allocate funding and resources required for a project to move forward. Accordingly, it should detail the benefits of the project, how those will be achieved, what the costs will be, and how long it will take to see the results. Writing a business case provides an understanding of the specific outcomes, the key assumptions, the baselines against which the company can track the scope, the time lines for delivery of benefits, and the scope of stakeholder involvement.[10]

The business case for a project that changes the strategic direction of a company needs to be built on rigorous analysis of the broad business environment and key influences that are likely to affect a company's markets and operations.

To win the support of the Board of Directors and investors, business cases must be communicated in standard business terms. For example, for a new product, the business case should identify, among others, the size of the market opportunities and the expected impact on financial performance and shareholder values. Regardless of the methodologies used, the development of a business case and alternatives for a project should involve six global constituents: project goals, expectations, scope, knowledge, stakeholders, financial constraints, and resource constraints.

Example of a Business Case Template

When developing a business case, it is important to remember that this is a "business"-oriented task; therefore, it is essential to approach it from a "business" perspective.

A template provides guidance on the information that should be collected and entered for the business case. If a project's information is not provided at any level, or is not complete, the business case is unfinished and should not be forwarded to the approving authority, such as corporate officers, stakeholders, or financial, technical, and operation managers.

A business case should provide a brief but concise summary and justification for the project, including a clear description of how the project closes (*partially or completely*) any identified performance gap. It should also provide a brief statement of the mission requirement for the proposed project and indicate if the project is required by legislation, is mandated, or is exploratory or voluntary in nature.

In order to understand the purpose and the importance of the project, the beneficiaries, partners, and stakeholders should be identified; an explanation of how the proposed project would help achieve company mission requirements should be provided; and any anticipated mission performance gaps need to be listed and explained. Also required is a classification of the competing activities, programs, and requirements for collaborations or requisites for building alliances with other sectors or organizations. A business case must present and justify the costs and benefits of the project (*cost-cycle analysis*), identify barriers to success, and anticipate risks and constraints of the project. Finally, the alignment of the project goals with organizational goals and objectives should be presented. Table 4.1 illustrates the main components of a generic business case. This table is provided to serve as a guideline only, as most companies tend to design and customize templates for the development of business cases according to their requisites and specifications.

A Business Case for Sustainability

Sustainability issues are emerging as companies are forced by regulatory requirements or stakeholders' demands to internalize their externalities

Table 4.1 Example Business Case Template

Main Components
Executive Summary
Company Background
Project Description
Strategic Alignments
Project Context Analysis
List of Alternatives to the Project
Business and Operational Impact Analysis for the Project and Alternatives
Risk, Barrier, and Performing Constraint Analysis
Cost/Benefit Analysis for the Project and Its Alternatives
Qualitative and Quantitative Comparison Analysis of the Project and Alternatives
Results and Conclusion
Recommendations
Project Accounting, Project Responsibility, Reporting
Implementation Strategies
Review and Approval Process
Business Case Signoff
Appendix: Supporting Data, Assessment and Modeling Techniques

(*negative impact of their operations on the environment*). To address sustainability, companies must develop strategies, tools, and programs that are capable of internalizing their externalities in a cost-effective manner and also of addressing the three aspects of social, environmental, and economic sustainability (*the triple bottom line for sustainable business*). The development of managerial concepts and tools such as a business case for sustainability is a logical response to reduce the negative externalities and generate positive externalities for the company.

Achieving sustainability is more than just taking responsibility for effective resource management. Sustainability has become a fundamental business planning element to sustain returns and enhance competitiveness. At a minimum, sustainability is the ability to develop and execute growth and development strategies in a resource-constrained economy.

Since a business case for sustainability is characterized by creating economic success through a certain environmental or social activity, it would require a firm understanding of the links between both monetary and nonmonetary social and environmental activities and business or economic success. Figure 4.1 presents the three requirements of any business case for sustainability and the initial steps involved with the design of an effective business case.

Drivers of a business case for sustainability are similar to those identified for conventional business cases and thus should include elements of cost (reduction/increase), sales and profit margin, risk (reduction or increase), reputation and brand value, influence on stakeholders including employees, and innovation, market entry, and development according to the company strategy and business outlook.

An overall approach for developing a sustainability business case consists of several main activities, including articulating current program elements, identifying market and strategy alternatives, identifying program improvement areas, and developing a program implementation roadmap for data collection.[11]

Information presented in the business case for sustainability is used during the strategic planning process to determine how an organization or a company will incorporate the concept of sustainability into its overall business strategy. For example, some companies may aspire to be out in front of their competitors by offering green products or services, while others may simply want to stay in compliance, manage costs, and maintain their reputation. Once the company's goals and objectives for pursuing sustainability are known, the sustainability concepts should be incorporated directly into the company's business strategy. This is one of the most critical steps toward

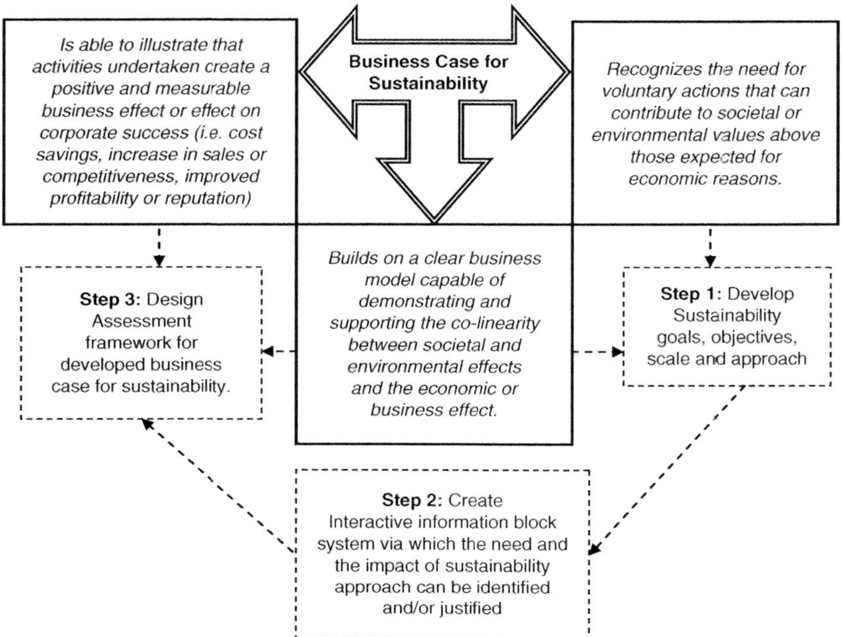

Figure 4.1 Business case for sustainability: three requirements and initial steps.

meeting sustainability goals. This inclusion would result in the successful design of a sustainability strategy, its successful implementation, and assurance of meeting presumed goals.

While there may be some specific sustainability goals that exist separately from other business goals, the best approach is to make them the foundation of operations, business planning, and decision making. Over time, sustainable thinking should fully permeate the company culture and become inherent to the way business is conducted, from the design of new products/services and production processes to building a new facility to ordering paper and office supplies. When setting sustainability goals, a company must decide what it wants to accomplish and how aggressive it wants to be when trying to achieve the goals.

Approaching sustainability is a dynamic process. It happens over time via careful planning. Accordingly, the best practice is to start with small, accomplishable goals and increase their scope and magnitude over time. Smaller, incremental goals are typically stated in percentage reductions, for example, in emissions, material use, and waste generation (externalities). If goals are set too aggressively to start, they may not be reached, resulting in low morale and a loss of momentum for sustainability efforts. A sustainability goal could be a "zero waste" processes or becoming "carbon neutral," which typically requires reducing emissions and offsetting the rest through purchasing Green Power, Renewable Energy Credits (RECs), and carbon offsets. For example, Dow Chemical sustainability goals are directed toward reducing its energy intensity by 25% from 2005 to 2015, and the long-term direction for all IKEA Group buildings is for them to be supplied with renewable energy generated through energy sources other than fossil fuel and to improve IKEA Group's overall energy efficiency by 25% by 2015, compared with 2005. DuPont has pledged to further reduce its GHG emissions by at least 15% from a base year of 2004, and by 2015 it will further reduce air carcinogen emissions by at least 50% from a base year of 2004. This will bring total reductions since 1990 to 96%.

Building a Team: Integrating Internal Resources

Business case development is a collaborative effort and is commonly a business-driven idea led by the business or program area that is making the proposal. Depending on the project, industry, business culture, and sector, the business case development for sustainability could involve, among others,

- Information technology representative(s)
- Change management representative(s)
- Business process engineering units
- Financial and policy analyst representative(s)
- Any or all stakeholders who will be impacted by the business case proposal, to ensure approval and ongoing support
- A benefits sponsor[12]

Business Case Value System via Interactive Information Block System

A business case for sustainability must be created actively through an intelligent sustainability management approach that calls for identifying different decision situations and information requirements before developing an integrative approach that can systematically and successfully create and manage a sustainability case. The main question is how can profit-maximizing societal and environmental activities be identified and managed, and how can the management of a business case be linked to sustainability accounting and performance measurements?[13] Companies now have room to maneuver in terms of a valid business case for sustainability as long as external regulations are still being determined.[14] In developing a business case for sustainability companies should consider the following:

- The business case for sustainability must be built on incremental improvements aimed at resolving environmental and social issues at no or little extra cost. As such it must show how economic and environmental performance could be achieved via internal cost reductions, product differentiation, setting private standards, or lobbying for tighter regulation, as well as redefining markets by focusing on cost reduction and increase in consumer perception of value (i.e., willingness to pay for green products). Overall, it must focus on how to manage environmental business risks.[15]
- No matter how important environmental and social considerations are, the financial implications of any strategy are in fact the main and crucial element of decision making. This is particularly the case for quoted companies that must maintain the support of shareholders, especially institutional investors.[16]
- Equity analysts employed by institutions work predominantly with financial data. To win their understanding and support for a sustainability strategy, it is essential to be able to convey its potential benefits using standard business terms.
- The business case for sustainability should clearly demonstrate the impact of the proposed project or strategy on revenues, cost levels, investment needs, the cost of and return on capital, or the economic value added.
- Prior to building a business case, managers need to identify opportunities a project provides to create and conserve values.

The project thrust and promise for value creation and conservation of sustainability goals and objectives can be tested using a stepwise "Information Block System" similar to the one presented in Figure 4.2. Each block lists the core project information including sustainability-related data. For example, Information Block A focuses on the company and provides information on the current status of the company, business values, business models, company vision and mission statement, planned subject or projects, activities to be generated, and any information on the existing environmental and sustainability programs and initiatives. Information Block B, on the other

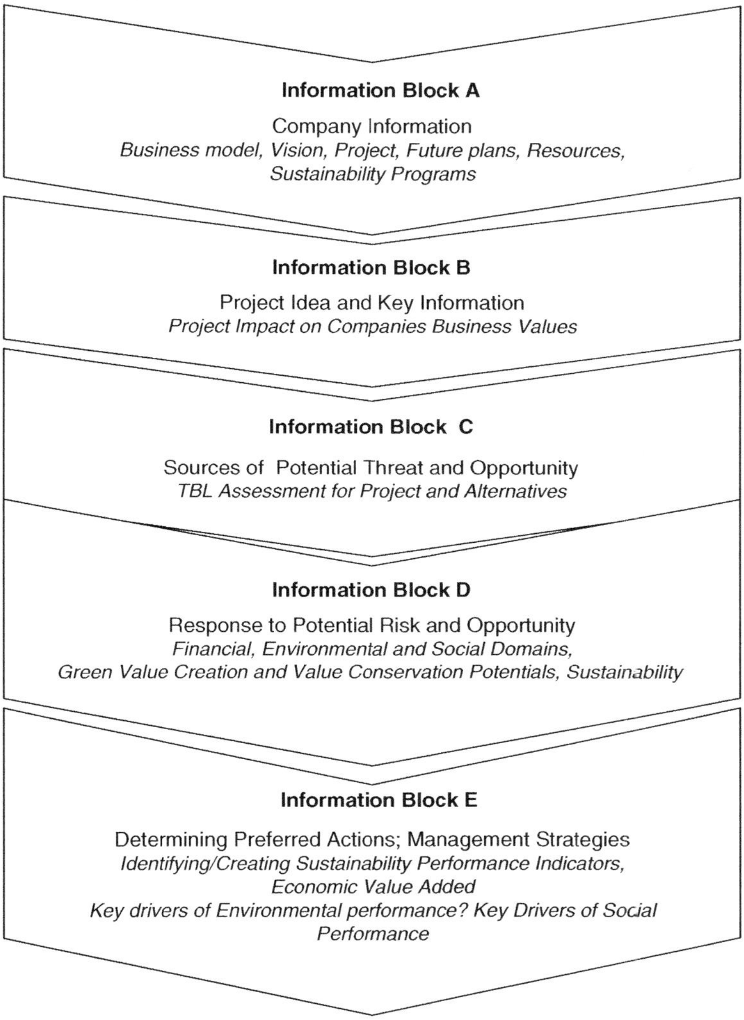

Figure 4.2 Information Block System for development of business case for sustainability.

hand, is concerned with the project itself. As such, it would identify information on the project, its significance, assumptions made, project scope and boundary, and its link to the company's business objectives (recall that we are talking about a sustainability project that is primarily concerned with environmental and social factors and values). Information Block E should identify which combination(s) of actions within the project could offer quantifiable business, environmental, and social benefits, or links with the key drivers of financial performance.

Interactive Information Block Systems by which project analysis can be started are essential to the development of a well-informed and successful business case for sustainability projects. The key concepts and tools presented for developing a business case for sustainability can be used both by companies and in the equity markets, and thereby provide a common basis for identifying and assessing the benefits of a project.

All voluntary societal and environmental activities associated with a proposed sustainability project must be analyzed in terms of financial, social, and environmental drivers. Reporting on implementation progress and monitoring overall sustainability performance may require the development and use of company-specific sustainability indicators.[17]

Assessment Framework for Sustainability Business Case Development

A qualitative ranking system is proposed to assess the relative impact of each principal component of sustainability business cases. The goal of the assessment is twofold: (a) to maximize the efficiency and effectiveness of the business case development, and (b) to benchmark a company's sustainability performance against its competitors. The value drivers and principal components involved in the development of a business case for sustainability include the following:

Level of Strategic Planning for Sustainability

This component identifies the level of corporate commitment to sustainability (environmental policies/programs, corporate value systems, sustainability team/human resource developments, strategic partnership with external stakeholders, brand reputation).

Commitment to Developing Business Cases for Sustainability

This component identifies the existence of a framework or a roadmap for data collection, financing, and economic, social, and environmental impact analysis of the activities and commitment to meeting the TBL accounting.

Developing Sustainability Goals and Objectives

This component identifies the level of commitment and the rate of success in setting goals, objectives, and sustainability direction. The sustainability vision and mission statements and cultural shifts to embed sustainability core values in everyday operation are identified and scored.

Developing a Pilot Project for Sustainability

This component examines potentials for the modification of the existing processes, design of sustainability projects, and activities. This could include scores for the efficiency of current operations, future plans, potentials for growth in a resource-constrained economy, sustainable product development, the existing environmental programs, and inclusion of the new environmental policies/regulations in decision making.

Developing Strategic and Guidelines for Full Implementation of Sustainability

This component characterizes the existing policies, procedures, and frameworks for a long-term commitment to sustainability. This assessment could include firm-, plant-, or process-level sustainability programs within a single or all business units and the involvement of stakeholder values in policy development.

Developing Strategies for Monitoring, Assessment, and Verification of Sustainability Programs

This component focuses on the temporal economic, environmental, and social impact analysis; the use of national or internal social, environmental, financial, and economic indicators; and stakeholder/shareholder views and assessment in managerial decision making.

Figure 4.3 illustrates the application of a spider mapping technique in a qualitative assessment of sustainability business cases according to each principal component. For demonstration purposes only, I have selected scoring scales between 0 and 5, 5 and 10, 10 and 15, and 15 and 20. The assessment outcome, however, could vary depending on the methods used for the measurements (expert judgment), time frames, and assumptions.

Although many businesses have tended to focus on the business case for sustainability, utilization of the proposed scoring system for business cases could vary across companies or countries as its use and application depends on the mindset of managers, corporate culture, knowledge gap, regulatory barriers, new business opportunities, top management leadership, and nurturing corporate culture.

The main thrust of this approach is on defining how firms can further their economic sustainability by paying attention to social and environmental issues by developing strategies that can result in increasing their ecological and social efficiency.

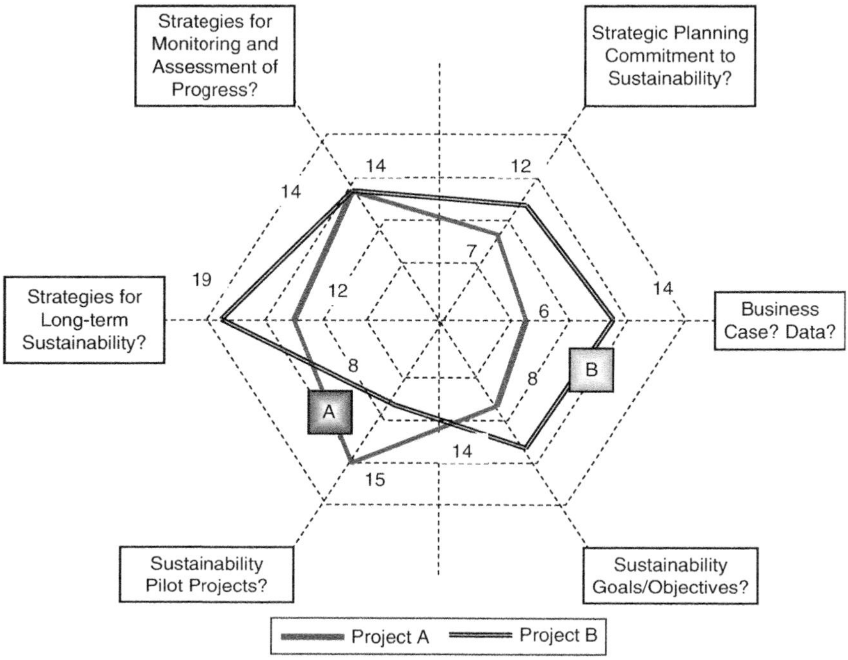

Figure 4.3 Spider mapping assessment of the sustainability business cases (project A, project B).

As shown, a project could be selected for implementation, be modified, or be eliminated altogether according to either the highest scores, the lowest scores, or total score assigned to the principal components of the developed sustainability business case. For example, project B with a total score of 80 (out of 120) could be accepted by one company and be rejected by the others depending on the project goals and objectives, resource availability, anticipated impacts, policies and regulations, market pressure, and overall level of organizational commitment to meeting sustainability goals and objectives.

The assessment must be specific, measurable, actionable, repeatable, relevant, and time bound. Performance in each area could be assessed and managed further via methods such as effectiveness or efficiency measures. The strategy alternatives and program improvement areas identified in a sustainability business case are the foundation for developing a comprehensive plan to build internal competencies, communicate activities, and expand market opportunities. The performance of organizations post–business case development can also be measured using quantitative tools. Selecting the right measures and establishing appropriate targets can communicate expected levels of performance and value added to customers and stakeholders.

Built on understanding the rapidly changing technological, political, and regulatory environment and related market opportunities, the business case for sustainability must address all existing multilayer and multifaceted business activities, value investments, and risks embedded in market participation. The business case for sustainability should also demonstrate how to align organizations' financial and technological capabilities, human resources, and R&D for investing in monitoring, reporting, and compliance with sustainability core values across the entire enterprise. The impact of sustainability strategies on organizations' economic and financial viability and competitive advantage in the marketplace must be evaluated and communicated to both internal and external stakeholders.

Summary

A review of recent benchmark studies and competitive analysis suggests that sustainability can and will offer firms and organizations a strategic competitive advantage. The inclusion of sustainability in business planning, however, should start with developing a well-structured program including a business case for sustainability that can recognize the need for change in the organizational culture, the scarcity of resources, the possible expected changes in the existing fundamental economics pricings, and what is acceptable to society.

Reconciling economic and environmental performance in business models via business cases entails knowledge of internal costs, product differentiation, and existing private standards and external regulations, as well as understanding the risks and market behavior. Building the business case for sustainability could validate how firms can remain competitive when addressing sustainability concerns. Three types of outcomes can be expected for sustainability efforts:

1. A win-win-win situation referring to the best practices.
2. Establishment of empirical evidence based on observed correlations between the exercised sustainability efforts and the measured impacts. This outcome varies depending on the measures, time frames, and assumptions.
3. Assuming that there is or could be a positive correlation between sustainability efforts and performance, the third outcome focuses

on the development of tool sets to manage corporate sustainability actions and recommend an appropriate organizational setting.

The business case must also describe "how" and "who" will be affected by the outcome of a project. The "how" and "who" typically evolve around individual or organizational behavioral changes, also known as "change management." Change management involves the "people" and "process changes" that would be required. The need for the "change in corporate culture" was discussed in detail in chapter 3.

Business case development is a collaborative effort and is commonly a business-driven idea led by the business or program area that is making the proposal, depending on the company and the proposed project, information technology representative(s), change management representative(s), business process engineering units, financial and policy analyst representative(s), and any or all interested stakeholders. At a minimum, a business case should include an executive summary, introduction and background, problem definition and desired business goal(s) and objectives, alternatives, assumptions, benefit estimates, and benefit metrics, cost estimates, risk assessment, financial analysis, recommendation, implementation, approach/timeline, and the need and justifications for a pilot project before full implementation.

Case Study

A Business Case for Managing GHG Emissions at the Stuart School of Business[18]

Proposed Project/Initiative

This Business Case for Sustainability (BCS) evaluates greenhouse gas (GHG) emissions and energy cost reduction opportunities at 565 West Adams and presents a low-risk, low-cost strategy for completing an Energy Audit.

Description of Proposed Project/Initiative

- The Energy Audit will evaluate building operations, historical energy consumption, and GHG emissions.
- A Final Report consisting of an energy reduction project portfolio will summarize energy reduction projects, project costs, energy and GHG savings, and payback.

Opportunity Statement

- The Stuart School of Business will develop a GHG emissions and building operational cost reduction strategy at 565 West Adams via an Energy Reduction Program, which is based upon executable turn-key energy reduction projects.

Opportunities for Emission Reduction

- Lighting
  - Switch to energy-efficient lighting and install motion sensors.
  - Turn off the lights when offices and meeting rooms are empty.
  - Purchase compact fluorescent lamps (CFLs) for the offices.
- Building and Facilities
  - Replace old air conditioning equipment with energy-efficient systems and save 25% to 35% of electricity use in the building.
  - Upgrade old boiler to a more energy-efficient system.
  - Office temperature set points: night and weekend setbacks, summer and winter setbacks.
  - Building management software systems (i.e., Siemens).
- Equipment
  - Ensure equipment is off when not in use.
  - If equipment has an energy-efficient mode, use it!
  - Use timers for equipment such as photocopiers and printers.
  - Employ "Switch Me Off" stickers, as reminders.
  - Turn off computers when away from office.
  - Purchase Energy Star–rated equipment (rated by the EPA).
- Computers
  - Shrink the Data Center footprint.
  - Shut down office computers and other equipment.
  - Cut back on the number of printers and print less.
- Use Green Energy (NOT UNDER CONSIDERATION)
  - Consider purchasing green power (solar, wind, biomass, etc.).
- Offsets (NOT UNDER CONSIDERATION)
  - If emission reduction targets have not been met, you may choose to purchase carbon offsets.

According to the EPA, energy costs for a typical office building in the United States are $1.50/square foot. Energy-efficient equipment can reduce those costs by 30%.

Key Performance Indicators (for Energy Audit)

- Building energy consumption (GJ) – historical data required.
- Building surface area (m^2) – historical data required.
- Building energy costs ($) – historical data required.
- GHG emissions (tons CO_2) – historical data required.
- Energy efficiency intensity (GJ/m^2) – historical data required.

Alternatives

- *Alternative #1 – Hire a consulting firm to complete the following tasks:*
  - Conduct building energy audit for 565 West Adams (Stuart and Kent building footprint).
  - Generate energy audit report (includes energy reduction project list, energy and emission savings, and project payback).
  - Develop an energy reduction project portfolio and execution strategy.
- *Alternative #2 – Add one contractor to provide the following services, with the option of hiring as a permanent employee after one year, if necessary:*
  - Conduct building energy audit for 565 West Adams (Stuart and Kent building footprint).
  - Generate energy audit report (includes energy reduction project list, energy and GHG emission savings, and project payback).
  - Develop an energy reduction project portfolio and execution strategy.
- *Alternative #3 – Use existing staff (faculty and graduate students) to complete the following tasks (status quo option):*
  - Conduct building energy audit for 565 West Adams (Stuart and Kent building footprint).
  - Generate energy audit report (includes energy reduction project list, energy and emission savings, and project payback).
  - Develop an energy reduction project portfolio and execution strategy.

Assumptions

- Energy savings estimates are based on industry norms, which result from energy reduction project calculations, as defined in the Energy Audit summary.

- It is assumed that any costs associated with the Energy Audit will be offset by energy cost savings and will be verified by utility meters and invoices.
- Energy and GHG reductions will not be recognized until projects have been executed.

Costs and Benefits

Alternative #1 – Hire a consulting firm

- Consultants generally guarantee a 10% to 20% reduction in energy consumption.
- Deliverable is a project portfolio, with project costs/savings/payback time frame.
- Savings will be recognized within 12 months of completing an energy reduction project (additional funding is required for projects).
- GHG emission and energy cost reduction of ~10% to 20%.
- Cost $5 thousand to $20 thousand.

Alternative #2 – Add one contractor

- Not as effective as consultant; assume 5% to 10% reduction in energy consumption.
- GHG emission and energy cost reduction of ~5% to 10%.
- Savings will be recognized within 12 months of completing an energy reduction project (additional funding is required for projects).
- <$5 thousand cost.
- Time required to hire and bring contractor up to speed.
- Uncertainty about contractor's expertise.
- Costly (time and money) to replace if not performing.

Alternative #3 – Existing staff, in-house management or the status quo

- No additional labor costs.
- Minor energy and GHG savings.
- Lesser energy cost savings and emission reduction (~2.5% to 5%).
- Longer project execution timeframe (>12 months).

Recommendation and Rationale

- *Alternative #1 – Hire consulting firm*
- *Rationale:* This option was selected for the following reasons:
  - Generates the highest potential savings of GHG emissions.
  - Maximizes energy cost avoidance for Stuart/Kent.

- Yields the largest reduction in energy consumption (10%–20%).
- Short-term impact (<12 months).
- Consulting firm provides Stuart/Kent with a portfolio of specific projects along with energy reduction calculations (per project), anticipated cost and GHG savings, and payback.

Summary and Conclusions

This opportunity is important because it allows Stuart/Kent to reduce building operational costs and GHG emissions by adhering to a low-risk, high-return strategy that has been proven to be successful for years in the industry. The Energy Audit provides an energy reduction project portfolio that can be managed according to current budgetary conditions.

Notes

1. Charles J. Corbett and Robert D. Klassen, "Extending the Horizons: Environmental Excellence as Key to Improving Operations," *Manufacturing & Service Operations Management* 8 (2006): 5–22.
2. Petra Christmann, "Effects of 'Best Practice' of Environmental Management on Cost Advantage: The Role of Complementary Assets," *Academy of Management Journal* 43 (2000): 663–80.
3. Michael A. Berry and Dennis A. Rondinelli, "Proactive Corporate Environmental Management: A New Industrial Revolution," *The Academy of Management Executives* 12 (1993): 38–50.
4. James Meadowcroft, "Planning, Democracy and the Challenge of Sustainable Development," *International Political Science Review* 18 (1997): 167–89.
5. Ulrich Steger, Aileen Ionescu-Somers, and Oliver Salzmann, "The Economic Foundation of Corporate Sustainability," *Journal of Corporate governance* 7 (2007): 162–77.
6. Thomas Wiedmann, Manfred Lenzen, and John Barrett, "Companies on the Scale, Comparing and Benchmarking the Ecological Footprint of Businesses," *Journal of Industrial Ecology* 13 (2009): 361–83.
7. Jerrell D. Coggburn, "Achieving Managerial Values through Green Procurement," *Public Performance and Management Review* 28 (2004): 236–58.
8. Joseph R. DesJardins and Ernest Diedrich, "Learning What It Really Costs: Teaching Business Ethics with Life-Cycle Case Studies," *Journal of Business Ethics* 48 (2003): 33–42.
9. Muel Kaptein, "Business Codes of Multinational Firms: What Do They Say?" *Journal of Business Ethics* 50 (2004): 13–31.
10. John Mclaughlin, "Winning Project Approval: Writing a Convincing Business Case for Project Funding," *Journal of Facilities Management*, 2 (2004): 330–37.
11. Randy Wilson and Ken Hooper, "Building a Business Case for Sustainability," KPMG's Global Energy Institute, February 2008, http://www.docstoc.com/docs/18796483/building-a-business-case-for-sustainability/ (accessed April 18, 2010).

12. "Guidelines for Developing a Business Case and Business Case Template, State of Oregon," Oregon Department of Human Services, http://dhsresources.hr.state.or.us/WORD_DOCS/DE0096.doc (Accessed September 7, 2010). http://www.oregon.gov/DAS/EISPD/docs/Bus_Case_Template_V1.1.doc (accessed April 15, 2010).
13. Stefan Schaltegger, "Managing the Business Case for Sustainability," *Proceedings of the EMAN-EU 2008 Conference on Sustainability and Corporate Responsibility Accounting—Measuring and Managing Business Benefits*, Budapest, Hungry, October 5–7, 2008.
14. Ulrich Steger, Aileen Ionescu-Somers, and Oliver Salzmann, "The Economic Foundation of Corporate Sustainability," *Journal of Corporate governance* 7 (2007): 162–77.
15. Oliver Salzmann, Aileen Lonescu-Somers, and Ulrich Steger, "The Sustainable Business Case—Establishing a Sound Research Base for the Development of a Case-Building Tool," *IMD Business School Research Working Papers* (June 2002).
16. Vicky Kemp, "To Whose Profit? Building a Business Case for Sustainability," *United Kingdom: World Wild Fund Press (2001)*, http://www.wwf.org.uk/filelibrary/pdf/towhoseprofit.pdf (accessed April 18, 2010).
17. Ulrich Steger, Aileen Ionescu-Somers, and Oliver Salzmann, "The Economic Foundation of Corporate Sustainability," *Journal of Corporate Governance* 7 (2007): 162–77.
18. Brett A. Whittleton, Nasrin R. Khalili "Development of a Business Case for Managing Carbon Emission at Office Buildings" Stuart School of Business, working paper (May 2010).

CHAPTER 5

Sustainable Supply Chain Management

NAVID SABBAGHI AND OMID SABBAGHI

Regulators, customers, courts, shareholders, directors, partners, and (indirectly) competitors place demands on products or firms to reduce their ecological footprint. These demands are known now, but in the future they may be uncertain. In order for firms to survive and compete, they must supply operational innovations both within their firm and further upstream (e.g., their suppliers and their suppliers' suppliers) in order to meet future sustainability demands. These demands and the supply chain's response in terms of innovations create sustainability risks that endanger the firm's survival. The need for firms to manage sustainability risk has driven the evolution of supply chains from operating in forward-only modes to operating in symbiotic modes. This chapter presents an overview of sustainable supply chain management and its focus on managing product and process waste, by-products, and energy consumption in order to manage sustainability risks. Building upon this background of sustainable supply chains, the chapter describes sustainability risks that firms in a supply chain face and surveys methods for inducing sustainable practices among supply chain partners, particularly upstream partners.

Introduction

A *supply chain* can be defined as the physical processes (potentially owned or controlled by multiple firms) as well as the material, information, and payment flows that are involved in transforming supplies of raw materials into finished goods in order to satisfy customer demand. Figure 5.1 depicts a classic product-centric view of a supply chain. The main stages or *echelons*, from left to right, are as follows:

- Upstream raw materials are extracted, treated, and then sent to facilities that create product parts.
- Parts are then sent to factories that manufacture subassemblies, which in turn are sent to plants that assemble the final product.
- The final product is then sent to distributors and retailers downstream, from which customers purchase the finished good.

The hollow-arrow lines depict the materials that flow out from each of the processes. Information and payments also flow among the firms managing these processes and play an essential role in the field of *supply chain management*, which studies supply chain systems with the goal of optimizing the overall financial and operational performance of the supply chain. Although our discussion in this chapter focuses on supply chains that provide products, a similar treatment follows for supply chains that provide services

In these systems, there are various sources of uncertainty (e.g., customer demand, future order quantities, future prices, and availability of materials) resulting from the limited information flowing among the firms managing these processes. And, as a result, there are a number of risks that the firms must manage. For example, firms face *inventory risk* when there is a possibility that the amount of goods they prepare exceeds demand. Alternatively, firms face *supply risk* when there is a possibility that there will be insufficient supply to meet demand. Managing the risks associated with the sources of uncertainty becomes essential when optimizing any process, let alone the entire supply chain.

Closed-Loop Supply Chain

Future demands on sustainability create *sustainability risks* that we describe further in the following section. These forms of risk motivate the evolution of the supply chain from a classic output-oriented system, as depicted in Figure 5.1, to a system that is in greater symbiosis with its environment as described below.

A more sustainable view of a product-centric supply chain includes the material flows resulting from customers or processes disposing of any fraction of the product (wastes), depicted by the solid-arrow

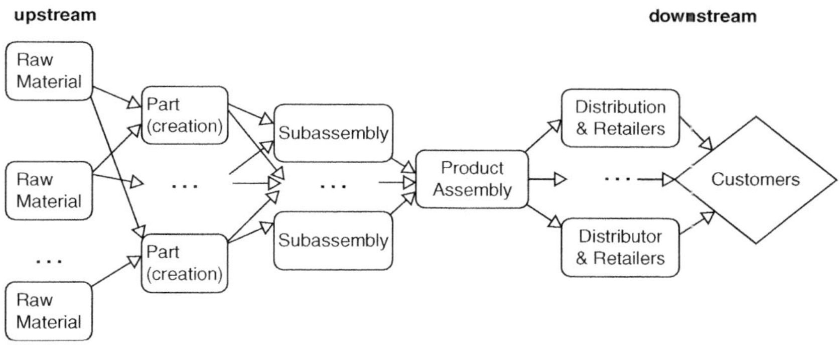

Figure 5.1 A classical output-oriented product supply chain. Processes are depicted by rounded rectangles and material flows are depicted by the hollow-arrow lines.

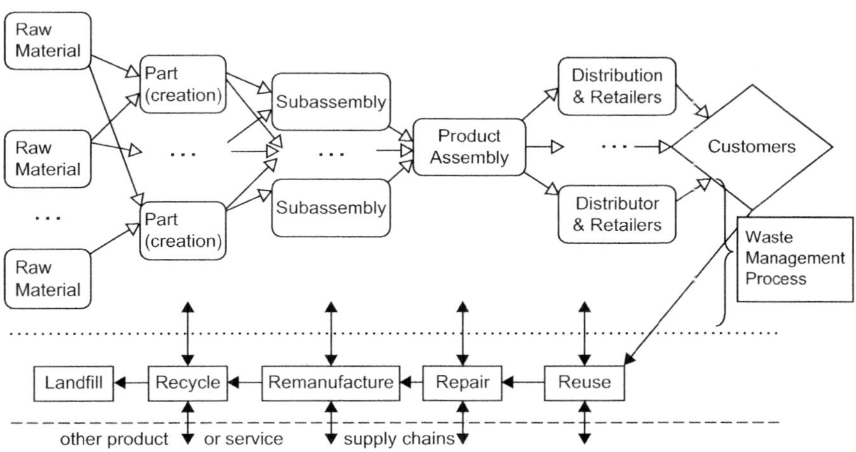

Figure 5.2 A closed-loop product supply chain. Material flows back from the customer or various stages of the supply chain and is reintegrated into the original supply chain or other supply chains.

lines in Figure 5.2, as well as additional processes for treating and transforming those disposed elements (wastes and environmental externalities) into elements useful for the main supply chain or other supply chains, if technologically feasible and economically viable. Otherwise, those elements will ultimately end up in a landfill. This more sustainable supply chain configuration is often referred to as a *closed-loop supply chain*.

The closed-loop supply chain depicted in Figure 5.2 accounts for the material waste flows resulting from the customers and the quality control policy within each process; however, it does not account for the by-product flows and ecological footprint that each process creates. Figure 5.3 provides an even more sustainable view of the system towards which supply chains are evolving:

- By-products and energy are traded among firms participating in the supply chain or other supply chains and are reintegrated into supply chain processes when feasible and profitable.
- Furthermore, the ecological footprint (e.g., natural resource usage, greenhouse gas emissions) is accounted for.

We term this evolved supply chain configuration a *green supply chain*. As mentioned, the need for firms to manage sustainability risk has driven this evolution of supply chains operating in forward-only modes as represented in Figure 5.1 to supply chains operating in symbiotic modes as depicted in Figure 5.3. Building upon this background of sustainable supply chains, the next section elaborates on sustainability risk and introduces the topics for the rest of the chapter. In particular, we present a survey of methods for inducing sustainable practices among supply chain partners, particularly upstream partners.

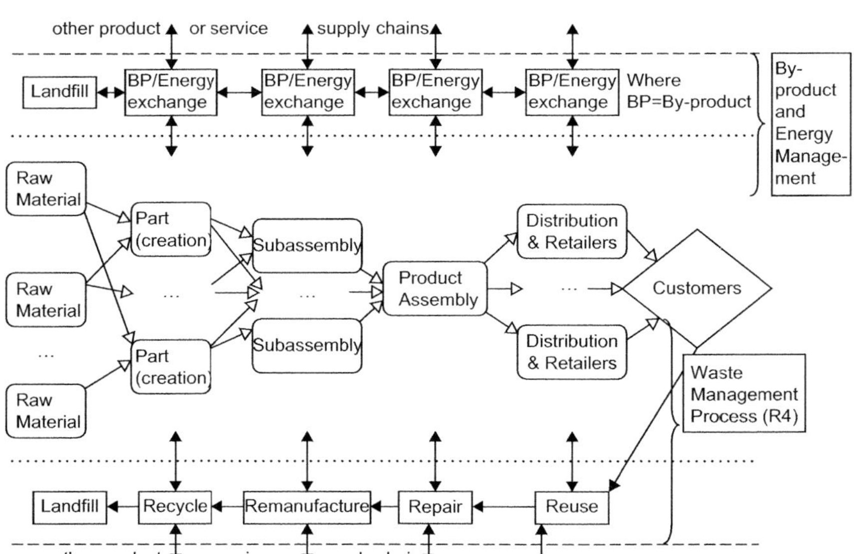

Figure 5.3 A green (product) supply chain. Processes account for ecological footprint and by-products and energy flow between stages of the supply chain before being reintegrated into the supply chain or traded with other supply chains.

Managing Sustainability Risk by Matching Supply and Demand

Firms are often forced to deal with customer demand uncertainty, and sometimes supply uncertainty, in the markets within which they operate. And if firms fail to properly match supply with demand, they face costs that otherwise could have been avoided (e.g., excess inventory that will be salvaged at a cost or the opportunity cost of unmet demand). In practice, how does a firm better achieve this matching objective? There are a number of quantitative models within the field of supply chain management that address this question.

Many of these models require the firm to look beyond its boundaries and work with other firms to better match supply with demand. For example, the firm may negotiate alternative contracts with its suppliers, enabling it to order an inventory level that achieves a better match.[1]

The supply chain management tools are not limited to handling only customer demand and product supply uncertainties. They can be generalized to deal with a variety of demands and supplies. In particular, regulators, customers, courts, shareholders, directors, partners, and (indirectly) competitors may place demands on products or firms to reduce their ecological footprint. These demands may be known now, but in the future they may be uncertain. In order for firms to survive and compete, they must supply operational innovations both within their firm and further upstream (e.g., their suppliers and their suppliers' suppliers) in order to meet future sustainability demands. Therefore, a firm faces *innovation supply risk* if there is a possibility that an upstream firm undersupplies operational innovations to deal with future sustainability demands (e.g., on the ecological footprint).

The possible existence of such a firm would cause all the firms following that firm, further downstream, to face this form of sustainability risk. Alternatively, a firm faces an *innovation inventory risk* if there is a possibility that an upstream firm overinvests in operational innovations relative to market incentives and available funds, thus endangering the solvency of the company and the source of supply for firms further downstream, thereby resulting in extra costs for the firms further downstream. A quantitative approach to better match the supply of innovations with sustainability demands in a supply chain could demonstrate how firms can balance these two types of sustainability risks. We emphasize that both of these sustainability risks result from the operational decisions of processes or firms upstream, potentially not under the direct control of the firm facing the sustainability risk.

Any firm that aims to green the operations within their own firm usually faces organizational challenges unless executives are involved in promoting the change. Greening operations outside the firm, further upstream in the supply chain, however, is even more difficult due to the lack of direct control. As a result, the question that this chapter focuses on is "how can a firm induce its suppliers to take on sustainability initiatives?" In particular, what are the mechanisms used in industry today? And what mechanisms are or can be used for greening suppliers further upstream (e.g., the suppliers' suppliers)?

Why do we focus on suppliers, the suppliers' suppliers, and so on? Because more than 40% of a company's ecological footprint resides upstream in its supply chain as mentioned in Brickman and Ungerman[2] (2008). As a result, working with suppliers is critical to greening any supply chain. However, promoting operational change outside of an organization, further upstream in the supply chain, is not an easy task. And for that reason incentives are critical to promoting external operational change. Therefore, in this chapter, we survey mechanisms that induce upstream partners to undertake "greening" initiatives.

Why should firms look beyond their organizational boundaries, within their supply chains, and ensure that sustainability initiatives are occurring there? Isn't it enough to just take care of sustainability initiatives within their own firm and let other firms sustain for themselves? It's not enough because although firms compete with other firms in the same industry, they also rely on firms in their supply chain to deliver products and services to their customers. Competition creates a strong incentive to better manage costs and revenues relative to other firms in the industry. However, the dependency among firms in the supply chain creates risks that firms must also manage in order to compete effectively over time. IBM is a prime example of a firm that must manage the sustainability risks of its end-to-end supply chain in order to survive and compete. IBM manages a $40 billion supply chain, depending on more than 28,000 suppliers in more than 90 countries. If the upstream suppliers fail to keep up with regulations, fail to obtain natural resources, or become targets of public relations campaigns focusing on the lack of corporate social responsibility, IBM will face additional costs in delivering its goods and services, which in turn will hurt its competitive positioning.[3] Managing sustainability risk throughout the supply chain, and in particular from suppliers upstream where a firm may exert more control, is absolutely critical for a firm's long-term survival and success.

How to Green the Supply Chain: A Greening Managerial Mindset versus Merely Greening Products

We distinguish between two categories of mechanisms that induce sustainability initiatives upstream based on whether they induce a long-term and strategic shift in managerial thought or simply induce a change in a product. We define a firm that has a *greening managerial mindset* as one whose management undertakes preemptive actions that green its products and processes in anticipation of demands from external entities. We contrast this managerial mindset with a mindset that is insensitive to greening initiatives and merely undertakes them to react to demands from external entities.

Wal-Mart exemplifies a greening managerial mindset in that the firm, at the CEO level, claims to preemptively engage in green measures for long-term economic benefits as described in LaMonica.[4] Kanellos[5] provides examples of firms exhibiting a greening managerial mindset.

A firm may require that its suppliers supply a greener product without asking the supplier's management to adopt a green mindset beyond the part being supplied. Figure 5.4 illustrates this distinction. For example, the Restriction of Hazardous Substances (RoHS) directive took effect in July 2006 in the European Union and restricts six hazardous materials from being used in the manufacture of a number of electrical components. RoHS aims to reduce damage to the environment and people in third-world countries where these components usually pile up at the end of their life cycle. As a result of this regulatory directive, a manufacturer must green the products affected by this directive regardless of whether or not, as part of its mindset, the firm's management tends to seize greening opportunities.

Rather than solely relaying regulatory requirements to their suppliers in order to green a product, a number of firms are proactively adopting policies to green the managerial mindsets of their suppliers and suppliers further upstream. For example, IBM's vice president for global supply and chief procurement officer strongly encouraged its suppliers to transition towards a greening managerial mindset when he said, "If a supplier cannot be compliant with requirements on the environment and sustainability, we'll

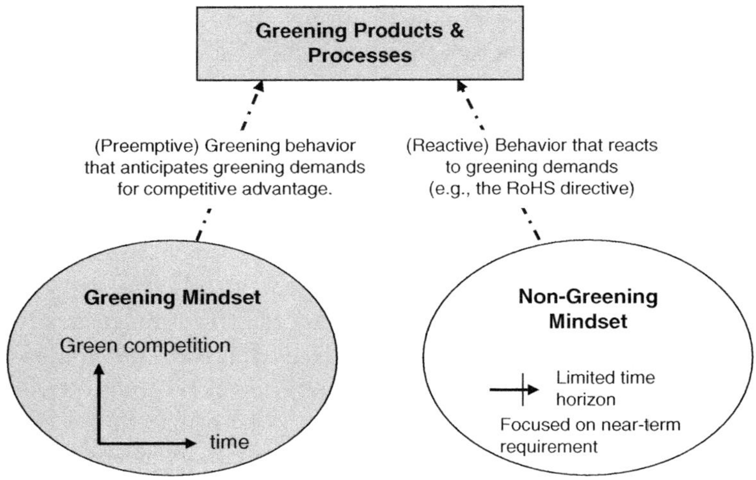

Figure 5.4 A supplier with a greening managerial mindset takes on greening initiatives even when not asked/required in order to attain a competitive advantage.

stop doing business with them."[6] Furthermore, IBM has requested that their suppliers ask their suppliers to take large steps in monitoring sustainability indicators if the products and services are a critical part of the IBM supply chain. IBM clearly sees the benefits in transforming a supplier's mindset to a green one over simply greening the supplier's product. IBM and its suppliers also see the costs, especially in the short term. However, by proactively managing sustainability risk, IBM expects its upstream supply chain to be better off.

A firm aiming to green its upstream supply chain must distinguish mechanisms that solely green a supplier's products from mechanisms that green products with the potential of also transforming the supplier's managerial mindset to a greening mindset. Otherwise, the firm may implement costly mechanisms over time that ultimately green a number of components rather than mechanisms that induce a supplier's management to shift towards green behavior, thereby becoming a strategic long-term supply chain partner.

In practice, when using mechanisms to induce supply chain partners to take on sustainability initiatives, it is important to compare the mechanisms and decide based on the benefits, costs, and impact on the managerial mindset. In the remainder of this chapter, our focus is on providing examples of different mechanisms used in practice and some qualitative suggestions as to the benefits, costs, and impact on the managerial mindset.

Table 5.1 provides a roadmap categorizing the mechanisms that we emphasize in the following text for inducing sustainable supply chains.

Collaborating on Specifications and Logistics

Often firms simply induce their suppliers to partake in greening initiatives by having their procurement or design groups work closely with the suppliers to require or prohibit certain materials. IBM is a prime example of a firm that must ensure the sustainability of its end-to-end supply chain given its dependence on so many suppliers and the negative impact a supplier can have on the supply chain if it suddenly incurs distress.

Requiring Certain Materials

In 2009, the state of New York, through an executive order from the governor, required all its state agencies, public authorities, and public benefit corporations to buy products from their supply chains that are Energy Star compliant, contain recycled content, avoid

Table 5.1 Mechanisms for Inducing Sustainable Supply Chains

Categories	*Specific Mechanisms*
Collaborating on specifications and logistics	Requiring materials (e.g., recycled content) Prohibiting dependence on materials
	Redesigning supply chain logistics
Promoting product and production stewardship	Creating product take-back initiatives Requiring waste treatment
	Adopting eco-labels or disclosures
	Creating stewardship competition among suppliers
Aligning incentives via contractual relationship	Changing from a product to a service contract Shifting to gain-sharing contracts
	Rewarding suppliers with more capacity
Using environmental criteria in supplier selection/promotion	EMS and EHS reviews
	Supplier recognition and differentiation
	Executive and employee compensation scheme
	Ecological footprint campaigns
Promoting industrial symbiosis	Anchor tenant when setting up industrial park Procuring renewable energy together

toxic chemicals, and promote reuse.[7] As a result of this executive order, the state was required to set up monitoring and auditing processes in order to verify that the procurement policies were carried out. Did this executive order transform the mindsets of some suppliers to a greening managerial mindset, or did the suppliers simply conduct business as usual for their other customers? We do not have any direct evidence, but it is possible that initially smaller firms transformed to a business model that involves a greening mindset. However, once the number of competing firms with such a mindset increases to a certain threshold, we feel it would be less likely for a firm to transition towards a greening managerial mindset, unless the amount of demand also increases. We'd expect to find a similar relationship describing the number of green startups as a function of time.

Ford exemplifies another firm that works with its suppliers to specify sustainable parts for use in its products. Lombardi[8] states that Ford uses engine covers made from post-consumer recycled plastics and prevents an estimated 25 million pounds of plastic from going into landfills. In addition, their seat fabrics are produced using recycled yarn, and their storage bins are produced from wheat straw–reinforced plastic. The firm's goals include avoiding petroleum products and moving towards compostable products. Ford's evolution towards sustainable practices requires close collaboration with suppliers to specify parts and materials and a supply chain R&D budget to produce these innovations, if they do not already exist.

Prohibiting Dependence on Certain Materials

Sometimes the prohibition of certain materials results purely from legal rules or directives. For example, the ban on dichlorodifluoromethane (CFC-12) and the regulations on other chlorofluorocarbons (due to the Montreal Protocol) limit their use by suppliers. The RoHS directive we've described is another example in which the law prevails in greening suppliers. However, preventing dependence is not always purely due to government regulation (e.g., Ford's goal of preventing dependence on petroleum-based products induces its suppliers to take on sustainability initiatives).

We should mention that Ford's sustainability decisions are not completely voluntary and are taking future vehicle end-of-life regulations into account. We describe these regulations further in the product stewardship section below.

Redesigning Supply Chain Logistics

IBM works closely with its suppliers so that it can monitor their environmental indicators. For example, IBM succeeded in convincing one of its suppliers, COSCO in China, where sustainability initiatives are not as high a priority as in the United States and Europe, to redesign its upstream logistics supply chain to reduce the carbon footprint by 15%.[9] COSCO had an opportunity to increase operational efficiencies and reduce emissions because it had acquired other logistic service providers, which helped it gain market position but resulted in redundant facilities and routes in its network.[10] As a result, solving an appropriate network flow problem and implementing the recommendation resulted in significant savings and reduction in emissions. In this case an additional external organization, the United Nations Global Compact, also motivated COSCO's decision to move forward on its sustainability initiatives as it would be a way to improve upon its corporate social responsibility.

Promoting Product and Production Stewardship

There are a variety of regulations that require firms to be responsible for their products and production processes post consumption and production, respectively. In the European Union there is an end-of-life directive for vehicles with the goal of making vehicle disassembly and recycling environmentally safer. There are well-defined goals for reuse, recycling, and recovery of vehicle parts in the directive. Konz[11] and Kanari et al.[12] elaborate further on the end-of-life directive, providing technical details. Promoting product and production stewardship is another mechanism for inducing upstream suppliers to take on sustainability initiatives.

The end-of-life directive motivated firms to consider potentially tighter regulations and become stewards; however, there are also examples of firms that motivated their suppliers to voluntarily become stewards through incentives: PepsiCo is a prime example.

Creating Product Take-Back Initiatives

PepsiCo's recycling program incents consumers of its beverages to return the aluminum can or plastic bottle at the end of its product life cycle. In particular, it has partnered with one of its suppliers, the recycler Waste

Management, to place recycling kiosks across the United States that accept the containers and in return give consumers coupons that are tailored to the kiosk location.[13] In addition, using a key fob, consumers also accrue rewards points with each returned container. The main reason proposed for PepsiCo's product take-back initiative is that its main competitor Coca-Cola claims to be the beverage industry's leader in recycled content. If this is indeed true, that would be a competitive cost disadvantage for PepsiCo over time as Coca-Cola grows its use of recycled materials and as the cost of scarce raw materials continues to rise. However, if PepsiCo is able to convince consumers to bring back their containers, it will be able to reuse the containers after they are recycled and better compete with Coca-Cola. In addition to advertising the reward benefits to consumers, PepsiCo appeals to consumer goodwill to bring back their containers by promising to donate to wounded veterans for every container brought back.[14] PepsiCo clearly has become a product steward and brought its supplier on board so that it can compete more effectively with Coca-Cola. Stewardship is not limited to products alone, however. Production processes also require stewardship, as Gap demonstrates.

Requiring Waste Treatment

The fashion retailer Gap is taking on the role of a steward for the production processes that occur upstream. In December 2008, as a participant in the Business for Social Responsibility (BSR) Sustainable Water working group, Gap introduced a new denim laundry policy requiring every supplier to meet specific wastewater quality guidelines.[15] It undertook this initiative because it realized that its consumers were becoming increasingly concerned about the sustainability impact of the clothes they wore. Asking its suppliers to become stewards for its production processes has a large enough impact on demand, relative to costs, because of the importance consumers place on brand in the apparel industry.

Adopting Eco-Labels or Disclosures

Firms can also notify their suppliers that they will be adopting eco-labels or disclosures that describe the ecological footprint of their products or the parts in their products. This creates an opportunity for the firm to offer a differentiated set of products to the market and incentivizes suppliers to join the "green club" if there is not too much competition and cost relative to the rewards.

Wal-Mart uses this mechanism with its seafood suppliers.[16] In particular, Wal-Mart motivates its seafood suppliers to obtain the Marine Stewardship Council's independent blue eco-label, which certifies sustainable fishing practices, then distinctly advertises products with those eco-labels and touts the advantages in the store.[17] This mechanism is very important for Wal-Mart because it is one of the largest sellers of seafood and it must control seafood costs from skyrocketing, which would eradicate Wal-Mart's profit margins and market.

Eco-labels and disclosures have the effect of motivating suppliers to volunteer to take on sustainability initiatives and customers to notice, in turn creating pressure on more suppliers to volunteer.

Creating Stewardship Competition among Suppliers

Wal-Mart has also helped its suppliers to compare themselves with other suppliers in assessing their stewardship, thereby implicitly setting up a competition to encourage suppliers to take on sustainability initiatives. On November 1, 2006, Wal-Mart introduced a packaging scoring system that allows suppliers to compare themselves with other suppliers on the following sustainability metrics, which are combined into an overall packaging score: GHG/CO_2 per ton of production, material value, product/package ratio, cube utilization, transportation, recycled content, recovery value, renewable energy, and innovation.[18]

Wal-Mart followed up this scoring mechanism with another scoring mechanism, the sustainability index, which induces competition among suppliers that promote sustainability initiatives. The sustainability index is being rolled out in three phases. The first phase will provide a means for Wal-Mart's more than 100,000 global suppliers to provide sustainability assessments in the area of energy and climate, material efficiency, natural resources, and people and community. The second phase will focus on developing a database of information on products' life cycles. The final phase will provide customers with information that enables them to purchase consumer products that are more sustainable.[19]

Aligning Incentives via a Contractual Relationship

Sometimes in supply chains a change of contract type can result in better financial performance for the entire supply chain. For example, in some settings a wholesale price contract may not result in maximal profit for the entire supply chain, whereas a revenue-sharing contract can induce the decision makers within the supply chain to make decisions that maximize the entire supply chain's profit.[20]

Changing from a Product to a Service Contract

In the past, firms that dealt with chemical suppliers engaged in a product-oriented contract in which they would buy the chemicals from the suppliers and be solely responsible for the usage of the chemicals and disposal of the waste and by-products. However, this type of contract releases the chemical supplier from any responsibility for waste and damage to the environment.

Furthermore, the incentives in the contract are usually misaligned so that the supplier wants to sell more chemical supplies, yet the buyer wants to purchase less. However, Reiskin[21] points out that the contractual relationship between buyers and their chemical suppliers in the automobile and electronics sectors has shifted from a product contract to a service contract in which the chemical supplier becomes responsible for maintaining chemical inventory for the buyer, using the chemicals in the buyer's facilities, collecting and disposing of waste, and recycling. The chemical supplier works for a service fee and, as a result, the chemicals and chemical life cycle become an operational cost for the supplier. As a result, the incentives start to align the goals of the chemical service supplier and buyer.

Shifting to Gain-Sharing Contracts

When the contracts have a gain-sharing provision, in which profit gains from better chemical efficiency and use reduction are shared, the incentives align their goals ever further so that suppliers take on more sustainability initiatives as suggested by Reiskin et al. (1999). Mont et al.[22] studied the economic and environmental advantages of a shift to these contracts and found that the gains are not always guaranteed. They elaborated with a list of important factors.

Rewarding by Giving More Capacity to Environmentally Sound Suppliers

Suppliers can be further incentivized to take on sustainability initiatives by rewarding them with more business. Wal-Mart's sustainability index may ultimately achieve this goal by its customers demanding more products from sustainabilility-minded suppliers rather than other suppliers.

Using Environmental Criteria in Supplier Selection

The use of environmental criteria in supplier selection and promotion will naturally motivate suppliers to take on greening initiatives. However, it is not always clear whether suppliers will simply green their products or if their mindset will transform to a greening managerial mindset.

Environmental Management Systems and Environmental, Health, and Safety Reviews

A simple way to make suppliers more aware of and responsible for their environmental impact is to require them to install Environmental Management Systems (EMS) to track their environmental resource usage. The vice president for IBM's global supply and chief procurement officer touted an initiative that requires their suppliers to install environmental management systems to track environmental resource usage with the ultimate aim of making the suppliers more accountable for their environmental externalities. The systems will gather data on energy use, GHGs, waste, and recycling, among other sustainability indicators as described by Woody.[23] The advantage of Environmental Management Systems is that they provide a consistent approach to environmental monitoring, regulatory compliance, and pollution prevention across suppliers.

Pfizer has gone one step further and, since 1998, has been conducting periodic environmental, health, and safety reviews at the site of its suppliers in order to minimize the different types of sustainability risks.[24] Wal-Mart is another company that is screening more than 10,000 of its suppliers in China to find energy efficiency opportunities and assess environmental impacts.[25]

Supplier Recognition and Differentiation

Rewarding suppliers when they take on environmental initiatives via awards that garner publicity can induce suppliers to take on a greening managerial mindset, because the "green" publicity may increase the supplier's future business dealings with other firms who hear about the supplier's environmental excellence. For example, on April 6, 2010, Konica Minolta received the 2009 Evergreen Award from the U.S. General Services Administration. The news made rounds on various environmental websites.

It would also be interesting to measure the effect of this "green" publicity. If the results of such a study are positive, there may be green marketing incentives for firms to achieve environmental excellence, suggesting that rewarding suppliers for environmental excellence is an effective mechanism for inducing a green managerial mindset among suppliers.

SRI/Surgical Express provides reusable surgical products to hospitals and surgery centers, which lowers disposal costs for its clients. For at least a third of U.S. hospitals, environmental purchasing plans are a priority. This has led the firm to differentiate itself and brand itself as the firm that provides "Environmental Solutions, Delivered Daily."[26] The incentive to stand out among suppliers and monopolize access to environmentally minded purchasers might cause suppliers to adopt a green managerial mindset; however, this may critically depend on the number of other firms also differentiating themselves and the amount of demand for environmentally conscious products.

Executive and Employee Compensation Schemes

In selecting suppliers, firms could seek out supply partners that already have a greening managerial mindset. How do you find them? Look for the firms whose executive and employee compensation packages incentivize sustainability initiatives. Lubber[27] finds that Intel, National Grid, and Xcel Energy are firms that fit this category. At Intel, since 2008, every employee's yearly bonus is based on the firm's performance on sustainability initiatives (e.g., product energy efficiency and completion of clean energy projects).

At the British utility company National Grid, the compensation of the CEO and other executives is tied to the firm's achievement of its greenhouse gas reduction goals. Xcel Energy ties executive compensation to emission reduction goals, but also publishes the details of these compensation packages in proxy statements rather than sustainability reports alone in order to signal to the market that sustainability is a core part of its business. As another example, Nissan added carbon dioxide emissions to its list of internal management performance indicators, which previously included only quality, cost, and time.[28]

Interestingly, Berrone et al.[29] found that firms that focus on pollution prevention rather than end-of-pipe pollution control pay their executives more. These findings suggest that when firms seek suppliers with a green managerial mindset, they should consider suppliers whose executives have more compensation at stake and whose compensation depends on sustainability indicators.

Ecological Footprint Campaigns

Another common mechanism that can induce a greening managerial mindset upstream is for firms to create ecological footprint campaigns and rally their suppliers around the cause (see also chapter 12). For example, in February 2010 Wal-Mart made it a general campaign goal to ask suppliers to cut 20 million metric tons of greenhouse gas emissions (GHGs) by 2015.[30] These ecological footprint campaigns are not tied to any particular product, and thus have the potential to change a supplier's mindset rather than products alone.

IBM has taken this mechanism one step further and asked that its suppliers and the subcontractors for those suppliers set public environmental goals and publicly report on their progress over time.[31] These campaigns are signals to the consumer and financial markets, and the firms running these campaigns will need the commitment of their upstream supply chain in order to succeed.

Summary

In this chapter we surveyed mechanisms that firms use to green products or induce a greening managerial mindset further upstream in the supply chain. We also qualitatively described research directions in the exciting area of green supply chain management. Our hope is that the qualitative descriptions of the mechanisms in this chapter will motivate the interested reader to pursue further quantitative analysis of these mechanisms.

Although we described a number of mechanisms that are in place in developed countries, there are opportunities to explore mechanisms that would be more appropriate in developing countries. IBM executives have acknowledged that one of their biggest challenges will be greening suppliers in emerging markets such as China, Brazil, and India where it spends a third of its supply chain budget, but where sustainability is not a priority for firms in those countries. With global supply chains, transparency becomes even more important. So although we surveyed some mechanisms for greening upstream suppliers, these mechanisms may have different levels of effectiveness around the world.

Mini-Case (CD)

Choose one of Wal-Mart's suppliers that discloses information on its ecological footprint. Is the supplier simply greening products or is there evidence that it has a greening managerial mindset? Describe the specific mechanism that Wal-Mart uses on that supplier in order to either green its products or induce a greening managerial mindset. What are the costs and benefits of this particular mechanism? Is there a mechanism that you feel would work better on that supplier? If so, describe the mechanism as well as its costs and benefits, comparing it with the current mechanism in use.

Notes

1. N. Sabbaghi, "Coordination and Competition in Resource-Constrained Channels." Doctoral thesis, Massachusetts Institute of Technology (July 2008), and N. Sabbaghi, Y. Sheffi, and J.N. Tsitsiklis, "Coordination Capability of Linear Wholesale Price Contracts," Technical report LIDS-P-2749, Laboratory for Information and Decision Systems, MIT (February 2007).
2. "Climate Change and Supply Chain Management," 2008, McKinsey Quarterly, http://www.mckinseyquarterly.com/Climate_change_and_supply-chain_management_2175 (accessed April 15, 2010).
3. S. T. Woody, "I.B.M. Suppliers Must Track Environmental Data," *New York Times*, April 14, 2010, http://green.blogs.nytimes.com/2010/04/14/ibm-will-require-suppliers-to-track-environmental-data/ (accessed April 17, 2010).
4. Wal-Mart Chairman: Go Green for Money, Not Image," April 12, 2010, CNET, http://news.cnet.com/8301-11128_3-20002313-54.html (accessed April 15, 2010).
5. 10 Green Giants That Could Change the World," April 22, 2010, CBS News, http://www.cbsnews.com/8301-504466_162-20003149-504466.html (accessed April 23, 2010).
6. Ibid.
7. M. Keating, "New York Issues Specifications for Purchasing Green Products," GovPro Media, March 10, 2010, http://govpro.com/green/content/new_york_green_specifications_7447/ (accessed April 19, 2010).
8. "Our Cars Are 85 Percent Recycable, Ford Says," April 22, 2010, CNET, http://news.cnet.com/8301-17938_105-20003169-1.html, (accessed on April 24, 2010).
9. S. T. Woody, "I.B.M. Suppliers Must Track Environmental Data," *New York Times*, April 14, 2010, http://green.blogs.nytimes.com/2010/04/14/ibm-will-require-suppliers-to-track-environmental-data/ (accessed April 17, 2010).
10. "Cosco Leverages Supply Chain Insights to Keep Its Distribution Center Network in Balance," *IBM*, October 14, 2009, ftp://ftp.software.ibm.com/software/solutions/pdfs/ODC03147-USEN-00_COSCO_final_SP_Oct14-09.pdf (accessed April 7, 2010).
11. R.J. Konz, "The End-of-life Vehicle (ELV) Directive: The Road to Responsible Disposal," *Minnesota Journal of International Law*, 18(2) (2009): 431-457
12. N. Kanari, J.-L. Pineau, S. Shallari, "End-of-life Vehicle Recycling in the European Union," *JOM*, 55(2003): 15-19.
13. J. McWilliams, "PepsiCo's New Recycling Program Billed as a Win, Win, Win," *Atlanta Journal-Constitution*, April 21, 2010, http://www.ajc.com/business/pepsicos-new-recycling-program-481104.html?printArticle=y (accessed April 23, 2010).
14. E. Fredrix, "New Kiosks Make Recycling Good for the Pocket Book," *Washington Post,* April 21, 2010, http://www.washingtonpost.com/wp-dyn/content/article/2010/04/21/AR2010042104462.html (accessed April 23, 2010).

15. A. Barenblat, "What's in a Label? Gap's New Clear Water Wash Messaging," August 17, 2009, http://blog.bsr.org/2009/08/whats-in-label-gaps-new-clean-water.html (accessed April 5, 2010).
16. "Wal-Mart Stores, Inc., Introduces New Label to Distinguish Sustainable Seafood," *Wal-Mart Press*, August 31, 2006, http://walmartstores.com/pressroom/news/5910.aspx (accessed April 3, 2010).
17. M. Gunther, "Saving Seafood," *Fortune*, July 31, 2006, http://money.cnn.com/2006/07/25/news/companies/pluggedin_gunther_fish.fortune/index.htm (accessed April 2, 2010).
18. "Wal-Mart Unveils 'Packaging Scorecard' to Suppliers," *Wal-Mart Press*, November 1, 2006, http://walmartstores.com/pressroom/news/6039.aspx (accessed April 4, 2010).
19. "Wal-Mart Announces Sustainable Product Index," *Wal-Mart Press*, July 16, 2009 http://walmartstores.com/pressroom/news/9277.aspx (accessed April 4, 2010).
20. N. Sabbaghi, "Coordination and Competition in Resource-Constrained Channels." Doctoral thesis, Massachusetts Institute of Technology (July 2008).
21. Reiskin, White, Johnson, and Votta, "Servicizing the Chemical Supply Chain," *Journal of Industrial Ecology*, 3 (1999): 19-31.
22. Mont, Singhal, and Fadeeva, "Chemical Management Services in Sweden and Europe," *Journal of Industrial Ecology*, 10(2006): 279-292.
23. "I.B.M. Suppliers Must Track Environmental Data," April 14, 2010, *New York Times*, http://green.blogs.nytimes.com/2010/04/14/ibm-will-require-suppliers-to-track-environmental-data/ (accessed April 17, 2010).
24. GEMI, 2004, http://www.gemi.org/supplychain/G1B.htm (accessed April 2, 2010).
25. S. Mufson, "In China, Wal-Mart Presses Suppliers on Labor, Environmental Standards," *Washington Post*, February 28, 2010, http://www.washingtonpost.com/wp-dyn/content/article/2010/02/26/AR2010022606757.html?hpid=topnews (accessed March 10, 2010).
26. M. Manning, "Growing Green at SRI," *Tampa Bay Business Journal*, April 23, 2010. http://tampabay.bizjournals.com/tampabay/stories/2010/04/26/story1.html?b=1272254400%5E3232781 (accessed April 27, 2010).
27. "Compensation and Sustainability," April 21, 2010, *Harvard Business Review*, http://blogs.hbr.org/cs/2010/04/compensation_and_sustainabilit.html (accessed on April 23, 2010).
28. "Nissan Announces Nissan Green Program 2010," Nissan press release, December 11, 2006, http://www.nissan-global.com/EN/NEWS/2006/_STORY/061211–01-e.html (accessed April 19, 2010).
29. P. Berrone, L.R. Gomez-Mejia, "Environmental performance and executive compensation: An integrated agency-institutional perspective," *Academy of Management Journal* 52(1) (2009):103-126.
30. S. Rosenbloom, "Wal-Mart Unveils Plan to Make Supply Chain Greener," *New York Times*, February 25, 2010, http://www.nytimes.com/2010/02/26/business/energy-environment/26walmart.html?scp=4&sq=walmart&st=cse (accessed March 24, 2010).
31. S. T. Woody, "I.B.M. Suppliers Must Track Environmental Data," *New York Times*, April 14, 2010, http://green.blogs.nytimes.com/2010/04/14/ibm-will-require-suppliers-to-track-environmental-data/ (accessed April 17, 2010).

CHAPTER 6

Green Marketing: A Future Revolution

SIVA K. BALASUBRAMANIAN AND GAURAV JAIN

This chapter highlights the significance of marketing products and services to customers from the sustainability perspective using green technology. It argues for proper awareness in the practice of environmental marketing. Figure 6.1 captures the essence of this approach by linking three abstract concepts: green marketing, environmental justice, and industrial ecology.[1] We explore the conceptual relationship between marketing and green marketing, and affirm that understanding sustainable/biodegradable/natural packaging hugely impacts sustainability practice. The past few decades have contributed substantially to increased consumer awareness of sustainable products and services.

Introduction

Definition

What is *marketing*? **Marketing** is the process of promoting, advertising, selling, planning, pricing, and distributing products, ideas, or services.

What is *green marketing*? **Green marketing** refers to a firm's orientation to provide environmental benefits when promoting its products or services. Note that such products or services may be inherently environmentally friendly or may be merely packaged in an environmentally friendly way or both.

There is a lack of consensus on the definition of "green marketing." Apart from showcasing the environmental orientation while promoting, selling, or advertising products, some believe that a truthful

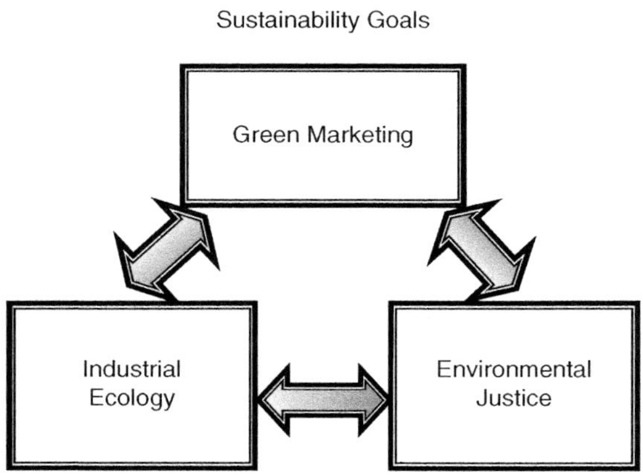

Figure 6.1 Green marketing balances business considerations with key principles of industrial ecology and environmental justice.

and altruistic signal toward enhancing human and planetary welfare that goes beyond profit goals (e.g., "recyclable" products that truly reduce waste) is a key aspect of green marketing. A contrarian school of thought is that a green orientation is an integral part of remaining profitable in the long term. In other words, savvy consumers will have the ability to independently and objectively discern if a firm is truly environmentally friendly, regardless of the "environmentally oriented" signal it chooses to convey in its messages.

Green marketing (or synonyms such as *environmental marketing*, *ecological marketing*, and *sustainable marketing*)[2] represents a widely used term that is often applied to consumer goods, industrial goods, and some services. It captures a variety of activities, including product modifications and changes to production, packaging, distribution, and marketing communication processes.

Significance of Green Marketing

Green marketing became prominent in the late 1980s and early 1990s. In the United States, the American Marketing Association (AMA) organized an early workshop on Ecological Marketing in 1975. In 1987, the World Commission on Environment and Development defined sustainable development as conforming to the needs of the present without adversely affecting the ability of future generations to meet their own needs. Publications on *green marketing* by Ken Peattie[3] in the United Kingdom and Jacquelyn Ottman[4] in the United States proposed that, from an organizational standpoint, environmental considerations should be integrated into all aspects of marketing. In other words, the environmentally friendly theme should pervade the new product development process through marketing communications and all points in between.[5]

Environmental considerations should ideally inform, and be responsive to, all customer needs.[6] Although the related modification of business or production processes may involve startup costs, they also generate significant long-term savings that justify these costs. As a result, new and improved products and services have emerged with the singular focus on *environmental impact*, thereby creating new markets that have the potential to increase both *profitability* and *competitive advantage*.

Although sustainable packaging is now a common concern (i.e., most major brands use sustainable materials for packaging), finding sustainable solutions to meet the increasingly demanding "green expectations" of both firms and their end consumers remains a daunting challenge for packaging professionals.[7] Potential outcomes include reducing toxicity, pollution, and waste; improving energy efficiency and resource use; using renewable feedstock instead of petrochemical inputs; and developing products that are readily metabolized in biological and ecological systems.[8] Analysis of the value of environmental certification and eco-labels remains a promising area of research inquiry, from the customer perspective.[9]

Green marketing is a broad concept that can be applied to a wide range of goods and services. There is a growing sense of urgency among product manufacturers, especially consumer packaged goods (CPG) firms, to develop sustainable business practices. These firms are attempting to optimize consumption such that the needs of the current generation are fulfilled without compromising the needs of the future generation. Optimizing packaging materials, reducing shipping weight, and increasing packaging cubic densities can produce significant overall savings. That is, although material savings in direct packaging costs may appear minimal at first glance, it may generate a multiplier effect on other costs such as transportation, handling, and storage. In this regard, technology has

1. Facilitated a green orientation in every aspect of a firm's operations
2. Increased the use of eco-labeling for products
3. Enhanced customer involvement in waste minimization/elimination efforts such as e-bills and the use of recycled products
4. Catalyzed the adoption of a life-cycle usage approach to decision making[10]

5. Encouraged a shift away from a physical world toward a web-based or digital world

Creation of Regulations

There is evidence that strategic framing of mediated messages about sustainable consumption could enhance understanding and perceptions about sustainable consumption among the general public.[11] However, Jacquelyn Ottman (founder of J. Ottman Consulting and author of *Green Marketing: Opportunity for Innovation*) argues that consumers generally fail to understand the sustainable consumption concept, so a lot of confusion persists in this area. Many firms take advantage of this confusion to make false or exaggerated *green* claims. Critics refer to this practice as *green washing*. For instance, the environmental organization CorpWatch issues an annual list of the top ten green-washing firms, including BP Amoco for advertising its "Plug in the Sun" program, in which the firm installed solar panels in two hundred gas stations while continuing to aggressively lobby to drill for oil in the Arctic National Wildlife Refuge. To discourage such misleading or confusing information the Federal Trade Commission (FTC) established guidelines for environmental marketing claims in products or services tied to recyclable, biodegradable, or environmental issues.

The FTC and the U.S. Environmental Protection Agency define environmentally preferable products or services as those with reduced detrimental effect on human health. The label "environmentally preferable" considers how raw materials are acquired, produced, manufactured, packaged, distributed, reused, operated, and maintained, or how products are disposed off.[12] Sample guidelines for consumers include the following:

- Determining whether environmental claims apply to the product, the packaging, or both. For example, if a label says "recycled," check how much of the product or package is recycled.
- If a product is labeled "recycled" because it contains used, rebuilt, reconditioned, or remanufactured parts, the label must clearly define it. Consider a used auto parts store that sells used components salvaged from damaged cars and labels them *recycled* (without any additional qualification or description). In this instance, the store may believe that there is no need to define or qualify the recycled label. But is it appropriate?

- Labels on *recycled* products must clarify the origin of the recycled materials. If an envelope manufacturer recycles the paper clippings that are generated when paper is cut to generate envelopes, this needs to be communicated.
- A firm's product that claims to use less material than former or competing products should clarify what has been reduced, by how much, and compared to what. For example, a claim stating "15% less waste than our previous package" is unclear because it does not state details about the previous package.

The preceding guidelines seek to ensure that consumers have access to information to properly evaluate environmental claims. Similarly, the American Wind Energy Association has established guidelines for manufacturers about product content and related claims[13] that include the following:

- Disclosing information on power from renewable resources (wind, solar, geothermal, etc)
- Avoiding the distinction between "existing" and "new" renewable resources
- Disclosing product contents fully so that any information needed for verification is available to all consumers
- Avoiding excessive prices
- Avoiding the collection of premiums (for environmentally friendly products) in advance
- Avoiding donation programs (designed to stimulate environmentally responsible behaviors)
- Supporting a common disclosure system for price, fuel mix, and emissions information
- Supporting policies that advance sustainable energy goals

Sustainability and Marketing Strategy

Effective green marketing practices may powerfully reinforce a firm's environmental capabilities. According to Hosfeld and Associates,[14] these practices entail several steps including efforts to establish awareness among consumers for green products, exploring the potential for successful eco-branding, refining value propositions for products/services based on social/environmental factors, avoiding green washing, accounting for externalities, and creative deployment of strategic planning and market segmentation to achieve a superior market position. For example, many firms have adopted the concept of waterless printing on recycled materials that is significantly less damaging to the environment (when compared with conventional lithography) by conserving resources and reducing pollution, while also improving productivity by reducing setup time and simplifying operations. Similarly, many firms such as Comcast and Bank of America urge customers to use electronic statements rather than paper-based statements; others encourage the use of e-tickets for live webcasts to reduce paper use, or publish electronic versions of journals, brochures, or other targeted publications to eliminate printing and distribution costs in a manner that is environmentally friendly.

The 2009 BBMG Conscious Consumer Report shows that approximately 80% of Americans believe it is a positive difference to purchase products from eco-friendly firms. To promote green marketing products, the following steps appear important at the firm level:

- Choose a realistic price for a product/service.
- Offer personalized benefits.
- Minimize the effects of climate change.
- Set the right green objectives following government regulations and FTC guidelines.
- Demonstrate social responsibility as the approach to realize corporate and profit objectives.
- Provide precise information.
- Make information readily available and easy to use for customers.
- Identify products with green characteristics and highlight how they differ from competitors'.
- Orient product development activities around the sustainability concept.

Using the website www.green.ebay.com and other advertisements, eBay encourages the purchase of used products as an environmentally sound approach to facilitate conservation and recycling. In fact, eBay classifies featured items as *green* (e.g., a $34 cobalt blue vase made of recycled glass from a seller in Virginia) or *resource saving* (e.g., a $14.95 stainless steel water bottle from a seller in California). eBay depends on Cooler's (www.climatecooler.com) ability to compute the carbon footprint to determine how much carbon shoppers save by buying something used instead of new. For example, a leather handbag arguably saves as much energy as a flight from London to Paris.[15] Other similar websites include www.carbonfootprints.com and www.nature.org.

Global Survey on Green Marketing

Green marketing is becoming critically important to reaching and persuading consumers. Given significant recent scientific evidence about global climate changes and their potentially devastating consequences, consumers generally realize that Green marketing is vital to preserve our environment and its resources. Survey evidence from several countries[16] shows individuals believe that the environment is on a wrong track. Nevertheless, the majority of Indian and Chinese respondents (approximately 65%) asserted that the environment is on the right track, highlighting the perceptual adjustment about acceptable environmental risks when they are traded off against the benefits of rapid economic growth in those countries.

Generally, consumers make a conscious effort to buy green products (81% in Brazil), and they intend to spend more on green products. India, China, and Brazil scored the highest on this item, but this could be because the green marketing trend is just emerging in these countries, unlike in other markets where consumers can already access green products.

Consumers in all countries documented obstacles to buying green products, but the reasons vary by country. Price appears to be the main hurdle in developed countries, but consumers in India and Brazil find it difficult to locate green products. On the other hand, Chinese consumers are concerned about unclear labeling of products. Buying from firms that are environmentally responsible appears to be very important (to more than 93% of the respondents) in emergent economies.

In Brazil, consumers report heavy reliance on advertising to learn about green products. Western countries appear to be less receptive to this approach, possibly because of distrust of the media. In general, governments seem to be skeptical of green initiatives (or at least they appear to be slow in executing green initiatives). In contrast, consumers appear very open to green products. The future will no doubt present more opportunities for brands to capitalize on this green trend among consumers.

Rich Feeding on the Poor: Is It a Misuse of Green Marketing?

Effective marketing strategies have helped many consumer brands to successfully grow into global brands. Similarly, green marketing has emerged as a significant tool to promote awareness about sustainability. Green marketing has helped to encourage awareness and consumption of more eco-friendly products. In turn, this has stimulated the development and promotion of products that are ecologically sensitive and safe. However, we face imbalances in consumption: developed (richer) nations are characterized by excessive consumption while less-developed (poorer) nations reflect less consumption.

According to a recent World Wildlife Foundation study,[17] the ecological footprint of the United States in 2005 was 9.4 global hectares per person, while the world average was 2.7 global hectares per person. Comparable figures for high-income and low-income countries were 6.4 and 1.0, respectively. Although the incidence of poverty has decreased consistently over recent decades, the World Bank estimated that 1.4 billion people still lived on less than US $1.25 a day in 2005. To narrow the rich-poor gap mentioned earlier, it is useful to note the diminishing order of importance of the following 4 P's: *people, planet, product,* and *profit.*

Green Marketing: Trend or Just a Whim?

According to a recent study, 71% of participating firms indicated that they are involved in or are pursuing green technology or sustainability. This claim appears persistent and may reflect a significantly high level of corporate commitment to the green marketing approach. Twenty-eight percent of marketers think that green marketing is a more effective way to promote the products than other marketing methods. Firms are also realizing that green marketing helps to promote the concept of Corporate Social Responsibility.

In general, firms with lower marketing budgets are investing disproportionately more in green marketing endeavors. Firms with a budget of about $250,000 appear to spend just over 26% on green marketing efforts, while those with a budget exceeding $50 million spend 6% on green marketing. Research shows that the most common approach to promoting green marketing is via the Internet (74.2% of respondents), followed by print (49.8%), direct marketing (40%), outdoor advertising (7%), radio and TV (7%), and mobile communications (6%).

Research evidence shows that smaller firms believe green marketing is more effective when compared with larger firms.[18]

Hurdles to Green Marketing

Although the green marketing approach has become immensely popular, significant problems remain in the manner in which this approach is implemented. Firms adopting this business philosophy have a significant responsibility not to mislead customers or other firms. As noted earlier, they also have to comply with the related labeling rules established by the FTC.

Firms that modify their products/offerings in order to better appeal to their customers (from an environmentally friendly perspective) must also recognize that consumers' perceptions are not always correct. In such instances, firms also have the added responsibility to educate consumers about environmentally responsible consumption.

From a social responsibility perspective, firms have to balance the environmental implications of any decisions they make for the future. For instance, an aerosol firm that switched from CFCs (chlorofluorocarbons) to HFCs (hydrofluorocarbons) has to reconcile the fact that HFCs represent a greenhouse gas. Similarly, firms that use DME (dimethyl ether) as an aerosol propellant have to recognize its harmful consequences for the ozone layer in the earth's atmosphere. These examples underscore the significant complexity of any problem with perceived consumer benefits that also extract a heavy price in the form of detrimental environmental consequences.

Although governmental regulations attempt to provide guidelines for firms seeking to offer environmentally friendly products, one must recognize that establishing rules that address all environmental implications is practically impossible. For example, Mobil Corporation introduced "biodegradable" plastic garbage bags. It was found that these bags were technically biodegradable, but the usual conditions under which they were disposed of did not allow the biodegradation process to occur. Mobil was sued by several U.S. states for their misleading advertising claims.[19]

Summary

Overall, *green marketing* has emerged as very useful concept to promote or advance sustainability goals. Firms are attracted to the green marketing approach because consumers demand it. Consumers have also become more receptive to this philosophy over time. Nevertheless, firms need to recognize the numerous hurdles and challenges involved in developing a successful green marketing strategy. They also need to carefully balance consumer demands, environmental implications, government guidelines, and competitive advantages embedded in the green marketing approach. Similarly, from a demand perspective, it is essential to educate consumers to verify the authenticity of environmentally friendly claims on products.

A Case Study: Green Marketing Campaign 2010

Hanes Launches Green Ad Campaign "For Future Generations"

Hanes is a brand of apparel products owned by Hanesbrands. In 2010, Hanes launched a green marketing approach with a TV campaign called "For Future Generations."

Consumers can also access a related website to learn more about the brand's environmental responsibility effort, watch the "For Future Generations" advertisement, and find information and ideas about making more responsible environmental decisions.

"Hanes products are in nearly nine out of 10 U.S. households, and research shows that consumers want to buy products from companies they believe are environmentally responsible," says Sidney Falken, senior vice president for the Hanes brand. "We want to share what we've been doing in the area of environmental responsibility because it's important to us that our customers feel even better about purchasing Hanes products, knowing that the brand they've known and trusted for generations is taking steps to help ensure a greener future for generations to come."

The company's commitment to environmental stewardship is broad based. In addition to this green marketing campaign, over the past few years, Hanes also

- Manufactures EcoSmart Fleece apparel that is made in part from recycled plastic bottles. Hanes plans to reuse the equivalent of 25 million plastic bottles for its fleece products in 2010.
- Offers EcoSmart Socks that are made with 55% recycled cotton fiber.
- Uses renewable energy in the production of the fabric for 67% of Hanes men's and boys' undershirts.
- Lowered the amount of energy used to make products by 11%, cut carbon dioxide emissions by 12%, and increased its use of renewable energy to 25% of its overall energy needs (all compared to a 2007 baseline.)
- Was recognized by the U.S. Environmental Protection Agency as an Energy Star® 2010 Partner of the Year. The award showcases the company's energy savings and reduced carbon dioxide emissions.

- Became a member of the U.S. Green Building Council, with three U.S. facilities certified by the Council's Leadership in Energy and Environmental Design standards, including one of the largest certified warehouses in the world: the company's 1.3-million-square-foot distribution center in Perris, California.[20]

Notes

1. Philemon Oyewole, "Social Costs of Environmental Justice Associated with the Practice of Green Marketing," *Journal of Business Ethics* 29 (2001): 239–51.
2. "Understanding Green Marketing," *BNET Editorial*, 2007, http://www.bnet.com/2410–13237_23–168370.html (accessed March 8, 2010).
3. K. Peattie, *Green Marketing. The M + E Handbook Series* (London: Longman, 1992), 10-11, 101-105.
4. J.A Ottman, *Green Marketing-Opportunity for Innovation* (Business Books: Illinois NTC, 1993), pp. 16-24
5. World Commission on Environment and Development's (the Brundtland Commission) Report, Oxford University Press, 1987. http://www.worldbank.org/depweb/english/sd.html (accessed March 12, 2010).
6. Johanna Moisander, Annu Markkula, and Kirsi Eraranta, "Construction of Consumer Choice in the Market: Challenges for Environmental Policy," *International Journal of Consumer Studies* 34 (2010): 73–79.
7. Carolyn Allen, "Recently in Sustainable Packaging Design Category," *Solutions for Green Marketing*, 2009, http://www.solutionsforgreenmarketing.com/management/marketing-communications/packaging-design/ (accessed April 8, 2010).
8. Alastair Iles, "Shifting to Green Chemistry: The Need for Innovations in Sustainability Marketing," *Business Strategy and the Environment* 17 (2006): 524–35.
9. Antonio Chamorro, Sergio Rubio, and Francisco J. Mirando, "Characteristics of Research on Green Marketing," *Business Strategy and the Environment* 18 (2009): 223–29.
10. Michael Jay Polonsky and Alma T. Mintu-Wimsatt, *Environmental Marketing: Strategies, Practice, Theory, and Research* (New York: The Haworth Press, 1995), pp. 183-185, 225-236.
11. Komathi Kolandai-Matchett, "Mediated Communication of 'Sustainable Consumption' in the Alternative Media: A Case Study Exploring a Message Framing Strategy," *International Journal of Consumer Studies* 33 (2009): 113–25
12. Jacquelyn Ottoman and Edmond Shoaled Miller, *Green Marketing Opportunities for Innovation* (New York: McGraw-Hill, 1999).
13. American Wind Energy Association (AWEA), "Principles of Green Marketing," 2009, http://www.awea.org/policy/greenprins.html (accessed March 10, 2010).
14. Hosfeld and Associates, "Sustainability and the Path to Transformed Marketing," 2009, http://www.hosfeld.com/upload/3_pdf_20090819195945_1/Transformation%20of%20Marketing%20Chart.pdf (accessed March 18, 2010).
15. Claire Cain Miller, "eBay Highlights Conservation as a Benefit of Buying Used," *New York Times*, March 7, 2010, http://www.nytimes.com/2010/03/08/technology/08ebay.html (accessed May 2, 2010).

16. Cohn & Wolfe, Landor Associates, and Penn, Schoen & Berland Associates, "Green Brands, Global Insights," 2009, http://www.landor.com/index.cfm?do=thinking.article&storyid=749&bhcp=1 (accessed May 2, 2010).
17. World Wildlife Foundation, "Living Planet Report," 2008, http://assets.wwf.org.uk/downloads/lpr_2008.pdf (accessed March 2, 2010).
18. "Green Marketing: What Works, What Doesn't: A Market Study of Practitioners," *Environmental Leader and Media Buyer Planner Report*, 2009, http://www.aimme.es/archivosbd/observatorio_oportunidades/GreenMarketingReport_ExecutiveSummaryEL.pdf (accessed April 8, 2010).
19. Michal J. Polonsky, "An Introduction to Green Marketing," *Electronic Green Journal* 1 (1994): 1–11.
20. Tim Albinson, "Hanes Launches New Green Ad Campaign 'For Future Generations,'" 2010, http://2sustain.com/2010/04/hanes-launches-new-green-ad-campaign-%E2%80%9Cfor-future-generations%E2%80%9D.html (accessed March 3, 2010).

CHAPTER 7

Sustainability Measurement, Assessment, and Reporting

NASRIN R. KHALILI

Sustainability is a characteristic of dynamic systems that maintain themselves over time rather than a fixed endpoint that can be defined in a short time. Equally, environmental sustainability refers to the long-term maintenance of valued environmental resources in an evolving human context. Different models, formulas, indicators, and principles have been developed and proposed in the literature to guide strategic planning for sustainability measurement, assessment and reporting. The emphasis has mostly been on accounting approaches that focus on the maintenance of capital stocks, the measurement of natural resource depletion, or the determination of whether or not the current rates of resource use can be sustained into the distant future. The emphasis on sustainability assessment, however, should be broader and more policy oriented. This chapter presents contemporary approaches to monitoring, measuring, and reporting sustainability efforts. The application and use of environmental indicators in measuring success toward meeting sustainability goals and objectives are presented, and methods are described for organizations to follow to either develop or adopt benchmarking frameworks as a points of reference for assessing the trends, and to measure their progress toward sustainability. Also discussed are the types, characteristics, and application of the sustainability indicators; benchmarking techniques; and reporting guidelines.

Introduction

Sustainability is emerging as a critical concept and business objective for most corporations. An increasing number of CEOs are outlining their sustainability objectives and their corporate commitment to sustainable development. In October 2006, DuPont's chairman and CEO, Charles O. Holliday, Jr., unveiled the DuPont 2015 Sustainability Goals in a town hall meeting and global webcast while discussing the company's approach to sustainability. Further evidence of the importance of sustainability is also contained in the ever-growing number of public annual sustainability reports.

The industry sectors contain a mixture of international corporations, national companies, entrepreneurial smaller and medium-size enterprises (SMEs), and/or informal local businesses. Each part of a sector may have a different impact and dependence on the ecosystem services. As such the sectors should focus on the development of sustainability strategies and approaches that are specific to their operation. The following are examples of the key factors and actions that are essential for leading movements toward sustainable operations:

- Realization by the leaders of major companies that their long-term business interests, survival, and profitability depend on understanding and addressing a wide range of the expectations of their key stakeholders and audiences
- Understanding the range of drivers for sustainability, which could include ethical cases for action
- Setting policies and business objectives that include differentiation within the sector and seeking relative competitive advantage
- Designing consultation processes, typically over a number of years, to identify stakeholder expectations and establish how to address them
- Developing strong and mutually supportive partnerships with external organizations as key components of the implementation of agreed-upon action plans
- Voluntarily committing to processes and actions that deliver better environmental and social outcomes, with external verification
- Developing a strategy for engagement with public policy development and, by example, influencing the development of legislation that affects all parts of the sector, thus raising performance across the industry
- Committing to transparent reporting and accountability for performance[1]

Since an organization's long-term viability is dependent on sustaining "profitability" over all three dimensions (financial, environmental, and social), these dimensions should be measured, reported, and assessed on a periodic basis in a manner that is conceptually similar to the current financial reporting model (see chapter 9). Further, stakeholder groups, such as socially responsible investors, nongovernmental organizations, green consumers, and governmental regulators and agencies, are increasingly calling for information related to the social and environmental dimensions to be communicated systematically.[2] The business world, however, is still seeking any sort of comprehensive set, or index, of indicators for sustainability performance that are context based and full triple bottom line (TBL) in scope (meeting financial, social, and environmental objectives simultaneously).

For the past ten years, various successful attempts have been made to pilot, test, and evaluate the quotients approach to sustainability metrics in ways that are consistent with the Global Reporting Initiative's (GRI's) call for a "sustainability context" in sustainability measurement and reporting and to bring "context" to sustainability metrics by factoring in actual environmental, social, and economic conditions when designing and applying such metrics.

Sustainability auditing and reporting are used to evaluate the sustainability performance of a company, organization, or other entity using various performance indicators. Popular strategic tools for auditing procedures available at the global level, such as ISO 14000, ISO 14031, Natural Step, and TBL accounting, and input-output analysis were presented and discussed in chapter 2. Both of these techniques can be used for any level of organization with a financial budget, and as such are capable of relating the environmental impacts of organizations to the expenditures by calculating the resource intensity of the produced goods and services.

The following sections provide example frameworks, strategies, models, and quantitative and qualitative tools and techniques that can be used in principle and have been used in practice to measure, report, and manage sustainability efforts and programs at various levels. These include the application of decision analytical frameworks in assessing sustainability efforts; the development of sustainability indicators, indices, and scorecards used for sustainability benchmarking; and a review of the GRI sustainability reporting guidelines.

Decision Analytical Frameworks for Sustainability Management

The diverse characteristics of the decision-making situations associated with *ecosystem*, *biodiversity*, and ultimately *sustainability* management imply the need for a range of decision analytical frameworks (DAFs) and tools.

A DAF is defined as a coherent set of concepts and procedures aimed at synthesizing available information from relevant segments of an ecosystem management problem in order to help policy makers assess the consequences of various decision options. In general, DAFs can be used to organize the relevant information in a suitable framework, apply a decision criterion based on some paradigms or theories, and identify the best options under the assumptions characterizing the analytical framework and the application at hand. Several factors determine what type of DAF can be applied and what sort of framework can provide useful information for decision making. According to these factors, DAFs can be classified as *normative*, such as decision analysis and cost-benefit analysis, which deal more directly with valuation and commensuration; *descriptive*, which consider outcomes that may result from certain actions such as game theory; or *deliberative*, which deal with the discovery of information from people and by people, such as simulation gaming.

A number of DAFs, such as behavioral decision theory or portfolio theory, have elements that may be described as either normative or descriptive. There are also DAFs in traditional and transitional societies that can be typified as ethical and cultural. The context of the decisions made according to sustainability objectives incorporates *social, economic, and environmental* dimensions. Such decisions are heavily influenced by the prevailing social norms and aspirations, and by the existing rules and institutions. Most of the decisions affecting ecosystems are made by individuals (as owners, operators, or users) or by firms focusing on efficiency and attempting to maximize expected profits.

The DAF focusing on sustainability could include such systems as strategic decision analysis, cost-benefit analysis, cost-effectiveness analysis, portfolio theory development and analysis, game theory, public finance theory, behavioral decision theory, policy exercises, focus groups, simulation gaming, and ethical and cultural perspective rules. Selection of each method depends on its compatibility/usability. For example, cost-benefit and cost-effectiveness analyses are essential decision principles for optimization, efficiency, and equity management and can be used as direct interventions for projects at all levels (global, national, regional, local, and firms).[3]

Sustainability measurement is a term that denotes the measurements used as the quantitative basis for the informed management of *sustainability.* The metrics used for the measurement of sustainability (*i.e., sustainability of environmental, social, and economic domains both individually and in various combinations*) include the development of sustainability *indicators, scorecards, benchmarks, and accounting and reporting* systems. From an environmental perspective, sustainability measurement and management can be regarded as a quantitative aspect of resource management that compares the demand on *ecosystem services* with the available supply as described below.

Sustainability Indicators

The term "indicator" traces back to the Latin verb *indicare,* meaning to disclose or point out, to announce or make publicly known, or to estimate or put a price on. Indicators communicate information about progress toward social goals such as sustainable development. Indicators can be used for many purposes at many levels: community; sectoral; national; or international. National or international decision-making indicators focus on top-level policy attention or provide a framework for collecting and reporting information within nations and for reporting national data to international bodies such as the United Nations Commission on Sustainable Development.[4]

Progress toward sustainability design and the management and development of sustainability indicators requires directing policy attention to all three interacting economic, social, and environmental factors of sustainability. The question is whether existing economic and social indicators such as GDP, the consumer price index, or the unemployment index are useful measures of progress toward sustainable development. So far, no consensus has been formally formed on indicators of sustainable development. Despite the challenges involved, many highly aggregated economic and social indicators have been widely adopted and are frequently reported as a means for addressing efforts toward sustainability.

The interactions among environmental, social and economic factors are important and must be noted and linked to specific economic sectors or social concerns when possible. Indicators are developed to address such interactions, but they are only tools and must be used with wisdom and restraint, particularly when they are aimed at building support for a needed change. Although counting species or listing endangered species can in some sense measure biodiversity, it has been a challenge to measure social equity in environmental exposures.[5]

The first step toward developing environmental sustainability indicators is the design of a framework according to the main defining factors.

Indicator Frameworks Development: OECD Pressure-State-Response Model

Indicator frameworks provide the means to structure sets of indicators in a manner that facilitates their interpretation and understanding of their interrelationship. The OECD Pressure-State-Response model is a framework that is widely used to develop and set *national*-level indicators. At the project level, however, indicator frameworks are developed from the project cycle itself. Indicators are further classified as the *input, output, outcome,* and *impact.* The input indicators monitor the project-specific resources; the output indicators measure goods and services provided by a project; the outcome indicators measure the immediate or short-term results of project implementation; and the impact indicators monitor the longer-term or more pervasive results of a project.

According to the OECD model, human activities (*agriculture, industry, transport, energy, and waste*) create *pressure* and pollution burden on the *state* of the environment (*air, water, land, living resources,* etc.); different agents (*such as administration, households, enterprises, or international*) generate *responses* to address pressures on the states of the environment. More specifically, the elements of *pressure, state* and *response* can be described as follows:

- The *pressure* is the state of the project and activity. The pressure variables describe the underlying cause of the environmental problems. Pressure may be an existing problem such as soil erosion or air pollution resulting from a new project or investment.
- The *state* variable usually describes some physical, measurable characteristic of the environment that results from the *pressure.*
  - Ambient pollution levels of air or water are common *state* variables used in analyzing pollution (for example, particulate concentrations in micrograms per square meter of air or BOD loads to measure water pollution).
  - For natural or renewable resources other measures are used: the extent of forest cover, the area under protected status, the size of an animal population, and grazing density are all *state* variables.

- The *response* variables are **policy related investments** that are introduced to solve the problem.
  - Bank projects that have important environmental components can be thought of as *responses* to environmental problems. As such, they can affect the *state* either directly (for example, by installing pollution control equipment or by creating protected areas) or indirectly by acting on the *pressures* at work (for example, by providing alternative income sources for farmers who would otherwise clear forests).
  - A similar distinction can be made in the case of projects that have an adverse impact on the environment (for example, port construction might have a direct effect by displacing natural areas and an indirect effect by stimulating additional traffic and hence increased pollution).
  - In some cases, projects also seek to improve the *responses* to environmental problems (for example, by increasing the institutional capacity to monitor environmental problems and enforce environmental laws).

Developing scientifically defensible indicators to establish *environmental baselines* and *trends* is a universal need at a variety of levels. Federal governments in the United States and Canada (Environment Canada and U.S. EPA 2003), Europe (www.eionet.eu.int), and Australia[6] have developed programs for routine reporting on ecological indicators. Environmental indicators reflect all the elements of the causal chain that links human activities to their ultimate environmental impacts and the societal responses to these impacts. Ecological indicators are then a subset of environmental indicators that apply to ecological processes.[7] (Environmental indices are commonly developed utilizing a wide range of environmental indicators at different levels.

Environmental Sustainability Index

The Environmental Sustainability Index (ESI) provides a gauge of a society's natural resource endowments and environmental history, pollution stocks and flows, and resource extraction rates as well as institutional mechanisms and abilities to change future pollution and resource use trajectories.

Sustainability in this broader sense is the dynamic condition of society that depends on more than the protection and management of environmental resources and stresses as measured with the ESI. For a complete measure of sustainability, the ESI needs to be coupled with equivalent economic and social sustainability indices to provide an integrated set of measures of the efforts of countries to move towards full sustainability. With such measures, it will be easier to explore and understand the interactions between the economic, social, and environmental dimensions of the human system.

The Yale Center for Environmental Law and Policy published the 2005 Environmental Sustainability Index (ESI) report, which provides a composite profile of national environmental stewardship based on a compilation of 21 indicators that derive from 76 underlying data sets. The ESI offers a tool for shifting pollution control and natural resource management onto firmer analytic underpinnings. In this regard, the heart of the ESI is not the rankings but rather the underlying indicators and variables. By facilitating comparative analysis across national jurisdictions, these metrics provide a mechanism for making environmental management more quantitative, empirically grounded, and systematic.

The ESI was categorized into five components for analytic purposes, which in turn encompasses between three and six "indicators" of environmental sustainability. The 2005 ESI report considers the 21 indicators (i.e., *air quality, biodiversity, land, water quality, water quantity, reducing air pollution, reducing ecosystem stress, reducing population pressure)* and 76 variables (examples include *Environmental Hazard Exposure Index, Energy Efficiency, and Innovation Index*) to be the fundamental building blocks of environmental sustainability. Aggregation of the 21 indicators created the ESI.[8]

The ESI score quantifies the likelihood that a country will be able to preserve valuable environmental resources effectively over a period of several decades. In fact, the ESI could evaluate a country's potential to avoid major environmental deterioration, increase responsiveness to environmental pollution, and commit to sustainable development. For example, it was shown that the top-ranked country, Finland, has high scores across all five of the ESI's components. Because it is doing relatively well across such a broad range of environmental sustainability dynamics, Finland is expected to be more likely to provide its citizens with high levels of environmental quality and services into the foreseeable future. The bottom-ranked country, North Korea, scores low in many dimensions, but not all. Its weak performance in a large number of indicators generates the low overall score, which supports the conclusion that North Korea's medium-term environmental prospects are not good.

Because the different dimensions of environmental sustainability do not always correlate with one another, the ESI score taken by itself does not identify the relative contribution of the different indicators to the overall assessment of a country's medium-term prospects, nor the particular types of challenges that are most likely to pose acute problems. Although North Korea has the lowest ESI score, for example, its Environmental Stress score is closer to the world median. The United States, by contrast, has a far higher ESI score (45th) than North Korea, but has a worse Environmental Stress score. Therefore, although one would conclude that the United States is more likely to be able to effectively preserve its valuable environmental resources than North Korea, it is probably more likely to encounter problems that stem from high levels of pollution or high rates of conversion of natural land. In some areas the United States has extremely poor scores (greenhouse gas emissions are a notable example). However, these are balanced by above-average scores in many others areas, especially the preservation of wilderness and investment in capacity.[9]

The ESI as a basic conceptual and analytical framework has been introduced to the discourse on environmental policy making in the Philippines. As a member of the Committee on Appropriations and Vice-Chair of the Committee on Ecology, Neric Acosta, Congressman, Philippine House of Representatives Chair Committee, stated, "I learned of the ESI and argued for its inclusion as a framework for discussion in budget hearings for the Department of Environment and Natural Resources (DENR) and its enforcement arm, the Environmental Management Bureau (EMB). Noting the consistently dismal ranking (the lowest among the countries in Southeast Asia) of the Philippines, I insisted again on the government using the ESI as a policy tool in budget hearings in subsequent years. In advancing the Philippines Clean Air Act, I proposed that the ESI and its measurement criteria be utilized as a benchmark for the assessment and evaluation of environmental policies and sustainability in our country."[10]

Other Sustainability Indices

A sustainability index is an aggregate sustainability indicator that combines multiple sources of data. The Consultative Group on Sustainable Development Indices includes as examples such indices as the Air Quality Index, Environmental Performance Index, Emergy (*Embodied*) Sustainability Index, Human Development Index, Happy Planet Index, Gini Coefficient, Democracy Index, Child Development Index, Legatum Prosperity Index, Index of Sustainable Economic

Welfare, Perception Index, and Gender-Related Development Index. Most of these indices have been used in strategic planning processes at national, regional, and firm/corporate levels.

Ecological Indicators and Eco-Efficiency

Ecological indicators are mainly used to assess the condition of the environment, as early-warning signals of ecological problems, and as barometers for trends in ecological resources. These indicators are also used either to assess the condition of the environment (e.g., as an early-warning system) or to diagnose the cause of environmental change. For example, the widespread decline of the peregrine falcon in the 1950s is an excellent example of both such uses. The catastrophic decline of the species served as an early-warning signal of problems in the environment, and research on the cause of the decline led to the diagnosis of widespread contamination by chlorinated hydrocarbons such as DDT. The widespread decline of amphibians has also been viewed as an early-warning signal of problems in the environment, yet further research has failed to identify a specific cause for the decline. Amphibian declines are likely due to a variety of factors, including habitat change, global climate change, chemical contamination, disease and pathogens, invasive species, and commercial exploitation. The information gathered by ecological indicators can also be used to forecast future changes in the environment, to identify actions for remediation, or, if monitored over time, to identify changes or trends in indicators.[11]

Eco-efficiency has been widely accepted as a concept that can help businesses understand how achieving both environmental and business goals can be compatible. Eco-efficiency is also a significant subset of sustainable development, defined by the Brundtland Commission as "development which meets the needs of the present without jeopardizing the needs of future generations."

Eco-efficiency is significant because it offers an opportunity to engage business in the agenda of sustainable development on terms that support business goals. Its measures provide a practical tool for designing and implementing resource use programs for industry on sectoral, national, and international levels.

The WBCSD has also identified the following seven elements of eco-efficiency:

1. Reducing the material requirements for goods and services
2. Reducing the energy intensity of goods and services

3. Reducing toxic dispersion
4. Enhancing material recyclability
5. Maximizing the sustainable use of renewable resources
6. Extending product durability
7. Increasing the service intensity of goods and services

The WBCSD has attempted to solve some of the deficiencies of the classic eco-efficiency concept by proposing consideration of the environmental burden of a project and has developed a broader concept of eco-efficiency, in which "eco" combines a range of economic and ecological values. The WBCSD's working group, Eco-Efficiency Metrics and Reporting, recommends the use of the following ratio as a general equation to measure and report eco-efficiency:

Eco-efficiency = value provided/environmental burden.

The WBCSD eco-efficiency includes a range of performance criteria for innovative companies that are reducing the material and energy intensity of goods and services, reducing toxic dispersion, and enhancing recycling of material or increasing the use of renewable resources.[12]

Value of Eco-Efficiency Indicators to Businesses

The value of eco-efficiency indicators in helping businesses improve their financial and environmental performance is well documented. The values specific to the facility, corporate management, and employees are briefly described here.

Value to Facility Managers

Eco-efficiency indicators, when used for internal monitoring and reporting within facilities, have proven useful for justifying capital investments, identifying and prioritizing opportunities for improvement, tracking and ensuring continuous improvement, setting goals for improvement, and providing information for input into corporate strategic decisions.

Value to Corporate Managers

Companies have used eco-efficiency indicators as effective management tools. They have also found them useful for reporting to external stakeholders, setting goals for improvement, replying to external questions, and promoting resource stewardship and conservation. Companies also see the value of the indicators as a tool for benchmarking with similar facilities within a company or with other similar organizations. However, comparisons of indicators between businesses and business sectors should be made with caution. Businesses in the same sectors may be operating under different economic, political, environmental, and natural resource constraints. The manufacturing processes in different business sectors are inherently different, resulting in different achievable eco-efficiencies.

Value to Employees, Customers, Financiers, Regulators

The energy and water intensity indicators can be used to report performance to a variety of internal and external audiences (e.g., employees, shareholders, regulators, the public, and financial institutions). Because these two indicators are generally amenable to standardized calculating and reporting across most business sectors, their use could enable external stakeholders to compare similar organizations within business sectors, provided the denominators (units of production or service delivery) are comparable and details of the companies' product mix, operating conditions, and operating constraints are known.

How to Use Eco-Efficiency Indicators

Questions to consider when deciding on the uses and audience for the indicators are as follows:

- Will they be included in the company's corporate environmental report?
- Will they be reported internally to the company's board of directors?
- Will they be compared with the indicator results of similar companies within the same industry?
- Will facility managers use them as a tool in making their processes more efficient?
- What other uses will they have?

The intended use of the indicators will also help to determine the following:

- Appropriate project boundary

- *Corporate* (the entire company); *business unit* (a business unit within the corporation, which could include several different facilities or products); *product line* (a particular product line within the corporation, which could be produced at a single facility or at several facilities); *facility or facilities* (one or more facilities [sites] operated by the corporation); or *unit processes* (one or more unit operations within a facility).
- Reporting period
  - The decisions each company must make on the use, purpose, and scope of the indicators before it begins to calculate its indicators; advice on how to use the indicators for performance tracking and reporting; and caution about comparisons. Successful monitoring of eco-efficiency depends on the availability and quality of the data used.
- Denominator
  - The total production of the company in appropriate units (e.g., tons, dollars, widgets) for the project.[13]

Reporting of eco-efficiency could become as standard and routine as reporting currently accepted indicators of financial performance. Many leading companies have already developed key eco-efficiency indicators for their businesses and are routinely tracking and reporting *energy, waste,* and *water intensity* indicators. The problem is that because these indicators have been developed internally within businesses or business sectors, the results are not readily comparable. The standardization of definitions and decision rules for calculating and reporting eco-efficiency indicators could help companies to set measurable eco-efficiency targets and facilitate comparisons between companies and business sectors, essentially resulting in widely accepted, quantifiable, verifiable, and transparent indicators that could be broadly used.

Consumption and Production Indicators

Production and consumption activities require different indicators of resource use. The *consumption* and *production* indicators are designed to reflect developments in consumer demand. The final use of resources, such as land, fossil fuels, and biodiversity, and other environmental impacts can be obtained by combining these indicators with data on the environmental efficiency of production such as energy consumption and emissions from production processes, materials reuse, and losses from the production chain. *Production indicators* reflect production activities within a country and are more suitable for monitoring the environmental efficiency of specific production activities.

For example, the OECD has developed a number of indicators for monitoring changes in the sustainability of consumption. This list of indicators, along with the World Wildlife Fund (WWF) methodology, was used to develop indicators that can provide a good impression of the use of resources by the Dutch population. In this case, direct indicators associated with production and consumption were identified to be the fossil fuel, wood, food, and metals used. Indirect indicators associated with consumption and production were, however, listed as household, building, and demolition wastes. The contribution of each indicator to environmental impacts from consumption was then estimated according to the land use, damage to biodiversity, GHG emissions, and ecotoxicological impacts such as acidification of lakes, use of pesticides, etc. The highest contribution to environmental impact in this case was found to be 80% and was associated with the greenhouse gas effects from the use of fossil fuel. Wood and total food indicators contributed 56% and 36% of the land use, respectively.[14]

Energy-Waste-Water Intensity Indicators

Energy and water use and waste generation intensities (or *pollution intensity*) are the three core indicators developed by the National Round Table on the Environment and the Economy (NRTEE) to help companies evaluate their performance over time with respect to the WBCSD's first two elements of eco-efficiency: reducing material requirements through improved waste and water management, and reducing energy intensity.[15]

The pollution intensity indicators defined here are all direct and indirect fuels and water used or waste generated during the production processes or services per unit of production or service delivery. Calculations and accompanying reports should clearly demonstrate and justify the selection of the data and methods used to estimate the indicators. For example, in calculating the core waste intensity, the industry must determine the boundary for data collection, the total material entering the production boundary, and materials that are recycled and end up in the product or co-products. The core waste intensity indicator can be calculated using either a mass balance or waste output approach. For companies whose manufacturing processes are based largely on chemical reactions (e.g., *chemical and plastics manufacturers*) or have few input materials, the mass balance approach is relatively straightforward. For companies with a relatively large number of input materials (e.g., *food and automobile makers*), the waste output approach may be more practical.

The definitions and decision rules for the core water intensity indicator and instructions for its calculation must also be selected and justified. Water use is an increasing concern for companies, from both availability and quality perspectives. As a result, water intensity has been identified as an important subset of material intensity for companies. As for energy and waste, the core water intensity indicator represents the amount of water taken into the project boundary (*from wells, water bodies, or municipal supply, but excluding water taken in with raw materials, snow, or rain*) per unit of product or services. An example of how a food plant calculated its three core pollution intensity indicators is as follows[16]:

Core Energy Intensity

The project boundary identified was only one facility with a production capacity of 3,400 tons over a two-month period. Data collected from the facility indicated two sources for energy use: electricity (1,700,000 kWh = 6,120,000 MJ from electricity [3.6 MJ/kWh]) and natural gas (220,000 m^3 = 8,311,600 MJ [37.78 MJ/m^3]). Using the data provided the Core Energy Intensity was estimated to be 4,245 MJ/t of production.

Core Waste Intensity

Data collected from the facility indicated that 150,000 kg of waste is landfilled. The recycled waste was composed of 25,000 kg cans, 48,000 kg cardboard, 250 kg plastics, and 33,500 kg wood material. The Core Waste Intensity was then estimated to be 75 kg/t of production with a Waste Utilization Factor of 41.5% (estimated from total waste used/total waste generated: 106,750/256,750).

Water Use Intensity

The only source of water is the municipal water supply. With total water use of 900,000 ft^3 (or 25,485 m^3), water intensity was estimated as 7.5 m^3/t of production.

Providing example indicators would assist organizations with measuring and assessing their environmental performance and associated financial and social implications. The critical question, however, is to determine whether they are positioning their competitive advantage in the area of sustainability.

Sustainability Performance Evaluation and Benchmarking

Sustainability Balanced Scorecard Approach

The concept of the Balanced Scorecard (BSC) was developed in the early 1990s as a new approach to performance measurement. The concept of the BSC is based on the assumption that the efficient use of investment capital is no longer the sole determinant for competitive advantages, and that increasingly soft factors such as intellectual capital, knowledge creation, and excellent customer orientation are becoming more important. The BSC's four perspectives are the *financial*, *customer*, *internal*, and *learning and growth* perspectives. The purpose of a BSC is to build a hierarchical system of strategic objectives in the four perspectives that is derived from the business strategy and aligned towards the financial perspective.

Formulating a Sustainability BSC (SBSC), by definition, requires the integration of environmental and social management into business management objectives. It must be specific to the business units, and as such should target the specific characteristics and requirements of the strategy and the environmental and social aspects of the business units. Another important consideration is that the environmental and social aspects of each business unit must be integrated according to their strategic relevance.[17]

Scorecards are developed from a set of indicators or performance measures such as those presented in this chapter. Accordingly, they can be used to compare and benchmark a company's sustainability performance against its peers. Any single indicator taken for a benchmark is almost meaningless for assessing sustainability. Instead, sustainability benchmarking frameworks must use a systematic approach for comparing, reporting, and rating sustainability.[18]

Multicriteria Framework Approach to Sustainability Benchmarking

Sustainability management and planning is mainly a social decision process about the desired future. When dealing with sustainability indicators, an essential step is to identify the definition of sustainability standards, as well as the gap that needs to be filled in order to meet those standards. Munda proposed the application of a multicriteria framework approach for the benchmarking of sustainability indicators and suggested the following main steps for sustainability benchmarking:

- Clearly specify the policy purposes of the assessment exercise.
- Choose the spatial scale of analysis.
- Choose a set of relevant dimensions/indicators according to which the comparison has to be made.
- Calculate the scores of the various indicators for the firm or project assessed.
- Choose the direction of each indicator (minimization or maximization).
- Define some *reference points* that are considered desirable to be achieved on any single indicator.
- Compare the performance of the indicators with the reference points chosen according to some distance functions.

The main advantages of using this approach are that policy purposes can be immediately evaluated, process becomes transparent, and compensability among the different dimensions of indicators can be avoided since the indicators are not aggregated. The choice of indicators, their policy prioritization, and the choice of reference points are all technical and sociopolitical issues built against a history of scientific research and political controversy. These should be considered when selecting indicators and participatory approaches to the evaluation process.[19]

Example Industry Benchmarking Frameworks

A number of financial-oriented organizations have published a variety of sustainability indices and screening criteria that mostly measure companies' corporate responsibility and environmental performance. These published indices are analyzed closely by the companies who make up the roster of companies being analyzed. The following sections present example sustainability screening criteria used by leading companies and discuss the American Institute of Chemical Engineers (AIChE) Sustainability Index development methods and their application to the U.S. Chemical Industry.

Dow Jones Sustainability Index

The screening criteria for this index are codes of conduct, compliance, corruption and bribery, corporate governance, customer relationship management, investor relationships, risk and crisis management, environmental policy management, environmental performance (eco-efficiency), environmental reporting, corporate citizenship/philanthropy, stakeholder engagement, labor practice indicators, human capital development, social reporting, talent attraction and retention, and industry-specific criteria.

Calvert Social Index

The screening criteria for this index are governance and ethics, environmental workplace, product safety and impact, international operation and human rights, indigenous peoples rights, and community relations.

AIChE Sustainability Index

Aligned with other sustainability indices the AIChE Sustainability Index (SI) accounts for key factors that are fundamental to the chemical process industries. This index focuses primarily on the company's *operations*, *engineering*, and *research*.

To create a unique marketable index, the Work Group at AIChE identified a set of potential factors for consideration in the AIChE SI. Example industry components factored in include energy, environmental, and safety performance from a value chain perspective (i.e., including process, product, and supply performance), integration of sustainability thinking into research and development and business management processes, and the robustness of the industry and individual companies in preparing for emerging challenges such as climate change and the European REACH regulation. Data needed for the development of the AIChE SI are company- and sector-specific information.

Company-specific information can be obtained from annual sustainability/ Environmental, Health and Safety (EHS) reports, annual reports to the Securities and Exchange Commission (SEC), the U.S. Chemical Safety and Hazard Investigation Board (CSB), incident reports, patent databases, trade journal and general media reports, Socially Responsible Investment Analysis, and other sustainability indices. Sector-specific information can be extracted from U.S. EPA

Emission and Hazardous Waste reports; the U.S. EPA Greenhouse Gas Emissions Inventory; Canadian Broadcasting Center (CBC) incident reports; U.S. Bureau of Labor Statistic safety reports; U.S. Census Bureau Annual Survey of Manufacturer, Trade Journal, and General Media reports; Socially Responsible Investment Analysis; and any other sustainability indices.[20]

The AIChE index is composed of seven main elements. Each element is determined by a series of five to six metrics and indicators as follows:

1 – Strategic Commitment to Sustainability (*stated commitment, presence and extent of sustainability goals*)

2 – Safety Performance (*process safety, employee safety*)

3 – Environmental Performance (*resource use, waste and emissions [including greenhouse gases], compliance history*)

4 – Social Responsibility (*community investment, stakeholder partnership and engagement*)

5 – Product Stewardship (*product safety and environmental assurance process, systems in place to comply with regulations, i.e., REACH*)

6 – Innovation (*R&D in place to address societal needs [e.g., millennium development goals, integration of sustainability concepts and tools in R&D, new products related to sustainability*)

7 – Value Chain Management (*environmental management systems, supplier standards, and management process*)

Most of these elements are scored based on "quantitative metrics" (e.g., GHG emissions per sales in U.S. dollars and percentage of facilities with third-party environmental management system clarification). Others, however, are scored based on "qualitative" criteria (e.g., *reported use of sustainability decision support tools in research and development*).[21]

An example application of the AIChE SI in benchmarking performance of U.S. chemical companies in the global economy follows. To start, each identified metric and indicator area was weighted based on its relevance to the industry sector being analyzed. For each data series (*strategic commitment, safety performance, social responsibility, value-chain management, innovation, product stewardship, and environmental operations*), the individual companies included in the assessment were ranked according to their performance. The series obtained was then scaled to the index ranging from 0–7 (*within the seven major categories identified above*). Also, the individual data series in each category was weighted relative to its importance and influence within the major category. Once each major category was completed, it was displayed on the "spider" chart and compared to the overall SI. The result of this assessment indicated that the U.S. chemical manufacturing industry needs to increase its strategic commitments to sustainability, focus on innovation, and obligation to social responsibility in order to be compatible in the global market.

Each analysis applied according to the above references offers a tool for different companies and industries. For example, in the food industry sustainability patterns of employment will look very different from those in the financial market. However, comparisons within certain industries will look similar. The key areas for benchmarking are sustainability focus, industry specific, related to information quality, and comparability. It is also important to consider the elements of best practices, selected criteria, alignment of governance structure and focus, specifics and scenarios, key issues expressed, and defined usage of quantitative and qualitative data and data handling and presentation.

Reporting sustainability performance is another very important part of strategic planning for corporate sustainability. Accordingly, following is a review of triple bottom line accounting because of its appeal to common sense in modern business practice, and a review of the Global Reporting Initiative (GRI), which has pioneered the development of the world's most widely used sustainability reporting framework.

Sustainability Reporting Framework

Triple Bottom Line Reporting

The organization affects, and is affected by, both the social and natural systems, which have different goals, objectives, and performance criteria. The changes in one system, however, need to be monitored, assessed, and reported as they can significantly impact the other systems. Accordingly, when it comes to setting guidelines for corporate reporting on sustainability performance, careful observers such as the GRI explicitly devise sets of indicators that separately conceptualize and measure each system and their factors .[22]

Measuring social and environmental metrics is necessary for meaningful triple bottom line (TBL) assessments. TBL, as defined in the literature, is a term that was originally used by John Elkington to describe corporations moving from reporting only on their financial "bottom line" to assessing and reporting the three key elements of environmental, social, and financial bottom lines.

Relevant indicators derived from environmental rating systems provide performance scores for each area. The proper approach to reporting, however, should consider important social metrics representing the third element of the TBL tripod. Three TBL systems are identified in the relevant literature: *design*, *problem solving*, and *accountancy*. Each of these systems essentially conveys similar meanings but with different applications. For instance, because of its measurement capacity TBL accounting can be used as a reporting rule, in which design and planning functions will help to shape the valuation approaches. Example applications are defined to clarify the following:

Design: Architects derive their understanding of TBL from cost, aesthetics, and performance, which implies taking equal account of ecology, equity, and economy.

Problem Solving/Decision Making: Administrators and managers are beginning to use an interwoven triad of ecology, society, and economy as a conceptual approach to decision making.

Accountancy: Accounting professionals understand that TBL reporting is the disclosure of information about an entity's economic, social, and environmental performance.

TBL is being taken very seriously because of its appeal to common sense in modern business practice and its influence on the market, which is significant and must not be dismissed.[23]

The GRI has pioneered the development of the world's most widely used sustainability reporting framework and is committed to its continuous improvement and application worldwide. This framework sets out the principles and indicators (reporting guideline [RG]) that organizations can use to measure and report their economic, environmental, and social performance, correctly and homogeneously.

Reporting Guideline

Sustainability reporting is the practice of measuring, disclosing, and being accountable to internal and external stakeholders for organizational performance towards the goal of sustainable development. "Sustainability reporting" is a broad term that is considered synonymous with others used to describe reporting on economic, environmental, and social impacts. As a general rule, a sustainability report should provide a balanced and reasonable representation of the sustainability performance of a reporting organization including both positive and negative contributions.

In its G3 standard, GRI defines the "sustainability context" in measurement and reporting. By reporting performance information, organizations show how they contribute to the improvement or deterioration of economic, environmental, and social conditions at the local, regional, or global level. The report should also express organizations' performance in relation to broader environmental and social sustainability. The Key Performance Indicators (KPIs) must be identified and evaluated prior to being disclosed in the report.

GRI reports can be used for *benchmarking* and assessing sustainability performance with respect to laws, norms, codes, performance standards, and voluntary initiatives; for *demonstrating* how the organization influences and is influenced by expectations about sustainable development; and for *comparing* performance within an organization and between different organizations over time.

The Sustainability Reporting Guidelines (the Guidelines) consist of principles for defining report content and ensuring the quality of reported information. They also include standard disclosures made up of performance indicators and other disclosure items, as well as guidance on specific technical topics in reporting. The indicator protocols exist for each of the performance indicators contained in the Guidelines. These protocols provide definitions, compilation guidance, and other information to assist report preparers and to ensure consistency in the interpretation of the performance indicators. Also provided are the sector supplements to complement the Guidelines with interpretations and guidance on how to apply the Guidelines in a given sector, and they include sector-specific performance indicators.

The GRI also includes technical protocols that are created to provide guidance on issues in reporting, such as setting the report boundary. They are designed to be used in conjunction with the Guidelines and sector supplements, covering issues that face most organizations during the reporting process.

Standard disclosures that should be included in sustainability reports are as follows:

Strategy and Profile: Disclosures that set the overall context for understanding organizational performance such as its strategy, profile, and governance

Management Approach: Disclosures that cover how an organization addresses a given set of topics in order to provide the context for understanding performance in a specific area

Performance Indicators: Indicators that elicit comparable information on the economic, environmental, and social performance of the organization[24]

The GRI provides a set of tools to help organizations manage, measure, and communicate their overall sustainability performance: social, environmental, and economic. Together, they draw on a wide range of stakeholders and interests to increase the legitimacy of decision making and improve performance. GRI reporting focuses on categories such as direct economic impacts and environmental, social, human rights, society, and product responsibility. Also considered in the GRI are the aspects of these categories, for example, customers, suppliers, products and services, compliance, transport, employment, labor management, health and safety, training and education, diversity and opportunity, safety management, child labor, community, political contribution, customer health and safety, and advertising.

At a minimum a company's reporting on its sustainability effort should express environmental and social effects linked with its business objectives and strategy. For benchmark assessments to become relevant for companies and rating organizations, the benchmark must be built so that nonfinancial risks are in fact material and transparent to the business.

Summary

In order to manage and measure progress with respect to corporate sustainability rules and regulations, companies need dedicated indicators that are relevant, complete, measurable, universal, and most of all make sense to them. Increasing coherence between dedicated internal and external measurement and screening methods would significantly improve the availability and quality of the reporting and disclosure of information on a company's sustainability performance. Standardized methods of measurement, reporting, and rating would most importantly benefit corporate reporting standards with the purpose of developing a benchmark framework. The relationship between the key sustainability issues and transparency and materiality defined both on financial and stakeholder input is clearly vital benchmarking for the performance of companies.

Identifying sustainability issues and understanding how they link with investment value drivers can enhance a company's comparability, which is a clear advantage to the company. In a practical sense, organizations must perform a critical self-analysis from their own business perspective, and understand and account for the peer group of companies and the value of stakeholder involvements. The self-assessment and analyses, reporting, and rating practices would help companies identify important sustainability topics they have to address, best frameworks for benchmarking, and the key characteristics for indicators that reflect best practice. A benchmark based on a generally accepted framework, such as financial accounting, or the GRI would readily use key performance indicators such as environmental, social, economic and financial indicators in addition to other qualified information. As discussed in this chapter, sustainability reporting standards and guidelines provide a basis for independent third parties to verify, or assure, sustainability progress.

Case Study

Measuring Corporate-Wide Sustainability Performance

A leading financial services organization wished to maintain its market position by differentiating itself through its environmental and social leadership. After a review of its environmental and social performance and the development of a set of social and environmental policies, it decided to develop indicators for assessing and measuring its commitment to sustainability. The indicators development process involved the following four steps:

Step 1 – Identifying what is critical and relevant to the organization. What commitments does the organization need to support? How will it benchmark its performance? What do stakeholders expect of the company?

Step 2 – Creating a pool of indicators from a range of sources, including indicators used by peers in the same sector, those used by leaders in sustainability reporting, and those proposed by international agencies

Step 3 – Translating the explicit commitments in the organization's policy statements into potential indicators to be included in the primary list

Step 4 – Including metrics that the organization had already established

The organization then attempted to short list the indicator pool by identifying *indicators that meet the specific needs of the organization*, *indicators that are critically related to the core activities of the business*, and *indicators that are relevant to stakeholder concerns*.

From an original pool of over 500 potential indicators, the organization was able to establish nine key performance indicators that enabled it to enhance communication with its key stakeholders and also commit significantly to its societal obligations. Through this exercise, the organization was able to obtain the knowledge and information needed to further involve its stakeholders with company business decisions, inform them about the organization's business goals and objectives, and create the competitive advantage for which it aimed via changing the understanding, awareness, and expectations of the stakeholders. This case study provides insight into how an organization can develop indicators to measure corporate-wide sustainability performance.[25]

Notes

1. "Living Beyond Our Means: Natural Assets and Human Well-Being," 2005, The Millennium Eosystem Assessment Board Message, http://www.millenniumassessment.org/en/BoardStatement.aspx (accessed February 10, 2010).
2. Darrell Brown, Jesse Dillard, and R. Scott Marshall, "Triple Bottom Line: A Business Metaphor for a Social Construct," *Departament d'Economia de l'Empresa* 06/2 (March 2006).
3. "Strategic Interventions, Response Options, and DecisionMaking," 2005, The Millennium Eosystem Assessment, http://www.maweb.org/documents/document.306.aspx.pdf (accessed February 10, 2010).
4. Allen Hammond, Albert Adriaanse, Eric Rodenburg, Dirk Bryant, and Richard Woodward, "Environmental Indicators: A Systematic Approach to Measuring and Reporting on Environmental Policy Performance in the Context of Sustainable Development," *World Resources Institute* (May 1995).
5. Ibid., pp. 12-14.
6. A Guide Book to Environmental Indicators, www.csiro.au/csiro/envind/index.htm (accessed March 15, 2010).
7. Gerald J. Niemi and Michael E. McDonald, "Application of Ecological Indicators," *Annual Review of Ecology, Evolution, and Systematics* 35 (2004): 90.
8. "Environmental Sustainability Index, Benchmarking National Environmental Stewardship," 2005, Yale Center for Environmental Law and Policy,"Yale University Center for International Earth Science Information Network, Columbia University, 18, www.yale.edu/esi (accessed February 10, 2010).
9. Ibid., 29.
10. "Environmental Sustainability Index, Benchmarking National Environmental Stewardship," 2005, Yale Center for Environmental Law and Policy, Yale University

Center for International Earth Science Information Network, Columbia University, 39, www.yale.edu/esi (accessed February 10, 2010).

11. Gerald J. Niemi and Michael E. McDonald, "Application of Ecological Indicators," *Annual Review of Ecology, Evolution, and Systematics* 35 (2004): 89–111.
12. Ingeborg Fiala, "Eco-Efficiency Indicators as a Step to Indicators of Sustainable Development?" Austrian Ministry of Agriculture, Forestry, Environment, and Water Management, working paper 10 (October 2001): 7.
13. "Calculating Eco-Efficiency Indicators: A Workbook for Industry," 2001, IndEco Strategic Consulting, Inc. and Carole Burnham Consulting, The National Round Table on the Environment and the Economy, 22, http://indeco.ccm/www.nsf/papers/ee_wkbk (accessed February 12, 2010).
14. Ingeborg Fiala, "Eco-Efficiency Indicators as a Step to Indicators of Sustainable Development?" Austrian Ministry of Agriculture, Forestry, Environment and Water Management, working paper 10 (October 2001): 10.
15. "Calculating Eco-Efficiency Indicators: A Workbook for Industry," 2001, IndEco Strategic Consulting, Inc. and Carole Burnham Consulting, The National Round Table on the Environment and the Economy, 15, http://indeco.com/www.nsf/papers/ee_wkbk (accessed February 12, 2010).
16. Ibid., 22.
17. Frank Figge, Tobias Hahn, Stefan Schaltegger, and Marcus Wagner, "The Sustainability Balanced Scorecard—Linking Sustainability Management to Business Strategy," *Business Strategy and the Environment* 11 (2002): 272–75.
18. Timo W.M. van den Brink and Frans van der Woerd, "Industry Specific Sustainability Benchmarks: An ECSF Pilot Bridging Corporate Sustainability with Social Responsible Investments," *Journal of Business Ethics* 55 (2002): 269–84; Social Dimensions of Organizational Excellence: EFQM-EOQ Convention 2003 (Dec., 2004): 187–203. Published by Springer Stable, http://www.jstor.org/stable/25123382 (accessed May 15, 2010).
19. Giuseppe Munda, "A NAIADE Based Approach for Sustainability Benchmarking, " *International Journal of Environmental Technology and Management* 6 (2006): 65–78.
20. Calvin Cobs and Darlene Schuster, "Benchmarking Sustainability," *Chemical Engineering Progress* 103 (2007): 38–42.
21. Ibid., p. 41
22. Darrell Brown, Jesse Dillard, and R. Scott Marshall, "Triple Bottom Line: A Business Metaphor for a Social Construct," *Departament d'Economia de l'Empresa* 06/2 (March 2006): 23.
23. Philip Kimmet and Terry Boyd, "An Institutional Understanding of Triple Bottom Line Evaluations and the Use of Social and Environmental Metrics," Pacific Rim Real Estate Society conference (January 2004), Bangkok, http://eprints.qut.edu.au/27391/1/27391.pdf (accessed February 20, 2010).
24. Sustainability Reporting Guideline, Version 3.0, www.globalreporting.org (accessed February 18, 2010).
25. Justin J. Keeble, Sophie Topiol, and Simon Berkeley, "Using Indicators to Measure Sustainability Performance at a Corporate and Project Level," *Journal of Business Ethics* 44 (2003): 149–58.

CHAPTER 8

The Finance of Sustainability: New Trends, Opportunities, and Challenges

NASRIN R. KHALILI AND DEBBIE CERNAUSKAS

Corporate sustainability programs and strategies must balance opportunities and risks associated with sustainability in order to create long-term shareholder values. One of the major barriers to the adaptation of sustainability is the cost increase when sustainability is pursued over a business-as-usual approach. Sustainability, however, is moving beyond risk management to cost reduction and revenue generation. To minimize the risks and the liability, and in the absence of national regulations, many companies have developed voluntary sustainability initiatives and programs, some of which could and have achieved higher returns through higher worker productivity, healthier employees, and reduction in energy, material, and water usage. This chapter provides an overview of the critical and evolving field of sustainability financing and describes why it is crucial to develop clear policies that can attract investor support for sustainability projects. Also discussed are some of the hot-button issues in the finance of corporate sustainability and the financial instruments and potential avenues available for external financing of sustainability projects. Theories and practical applications that financial professionals can leverage to simultaneously earn a profit and positively impact the environment and society are presented and discussed.

Introduction

The financial implications of environmental opportunities and risk are becoming increasingly evident to organizations, financial institutions, and investors. The implications are also reflected in the world capital markets.

It has been demonstrated that financial markets that are equalized to environmental issues are able to create more permanent and powerful incentives for companies to improve their environmental performance while ensuring better returns for investors. The main concern, however, is whether the companies and the investors (for example, mainstream asset managers) can equally recognize the importance of the environmental issues, the sustainability factors, and their associated financial risks and values.

To address this concern, environmental information, including pollution sources, pollution characteristics, impacted environment, expected severity of the impact, and costs and liabilities associated with impact management, must be incorporated into the overall financial analytical frameworks. This approach would provide the sufficient information and drive for both companies and investors to adequately assess the impact of environmental considerations using sustainability approaches on a company or project risk and return trade-off. The most critical element is the truthful quantification of the financial implications of environmental risks and opportunities, and policies and programs that can facilitate the comprehensive disclosure of environmental risks and data by both companies and regulators.

However, when dealing with environmental risks, it is necessary to balance the benefits that occur with certainty, with losses that are uncertain, delayed, or might occur elsewhere. We should remember that many environmental problems have long-term consequences. Some have both immediate and long-term negative effects, for instance, urban air pollution from traffic may cause immediate odor annoyance as well as long-term health problems, while other environmental problems, such as the increase of atmospheric greenhouse gas concentrations or the depletion of natural resources (e.g., oil, water, minerals), do not have severe immediate effects, but in the long term such risks may have catastrophic consequences. In such cases, in which it may take decades or centuries before the negative effects will occur, temporal discounting can be expected. Heavy discounting, for example, that considers losses as not serious, must be avoided since it may result in decisions and behaviors that are incompatible with environmental sustainability.[1]

Markets that discount the environmental implications on the "risk" and the "return" will ultimately facilitate "capital allocations" to companies with sound "environmental strategies" due to reduced financial risks associated with managing their "externalities" by a third party.

For example, product manufacturing often has negative effects on the environment due to its air and water pollution, waste disposal issues, limitations with recycling its waste, high insurance policies, and its image and public relations. The company and the upper management, as the main legally and financially responsible entities, are accountable for their pollution and as such are required to develop or adopt sustainability programs and strategies for reducing or eliminating these pollutants before they are discharged to the environment. In other words, a company must internalize its externalities via adopting an effective sustainability (environmental management) strategy. This new financial responsibility is commonly considered as a cost and is incorporated into the traditional capital budgeting process. The result could be higher cost of production. This cost must be financed either internally or via external financing avenues. It is evident that the costs and liabilities faced by business due to the environmental concerns is in fact an economic issue that must be addressed through proper management strategies and financing. The following sections discuss programs, options, opportunities, and financing in support of sustainability projects at global, regional, and corporate levels.

Financing Sustainability Projects

Financing sustainability initiatives is an important issue for all companies with a sustainability focus. The type of financing, short term versus long term and internal versus external, will depend on the cash flow characteristics of the project. For example, an up-front investment may be required if abatement (pollution control) oriented sustainability projects require a new system or a new technology. In the case of reducing greenhouse gas emissions (GHGs), this cost may be recouped through the sale of emissions credits. A portion of the required capital investment may be internally financed through retained earnings.

Large capital investments, however, will necessitate external financing. Sources of external funding vary by country. In the United States and United Kingdom, companies frequently "raise funds" from the "capital markets" through the issuance of "negotiable securities," while in continental Europe and Japan, companies favor "bank borrowing" or "nonmarketable loans" through financial intermediaries.

Debt financing, the money that is borrowed either for the company assets (equipments, buildings) or for day-to-day operations of the business (purchasing inventory and supplies, or paying wages) can be either on the balance sheet (corporate financing) or off the balance sheet (project financing). The funding of large infrastructure projects under a project finance structure commonly includes several equity investors or sponsors and a syndicate of banks. The loans are generally nonrecourse, and loan repayment is secured primarily by the "assets" and "cash flows" of the project rather than the "balance sheet" of the project sponsor. Project lenders are given a "lien" against the assets of the project and may assume "control of the project" under certain circumstances.

A Special Purpose Entity (SPE) may be created to segregate the "project assets" and "liabilities" from the other assets owned by the project sponsor. The complexity of the contractual agreements for off-balance-sheet loans (project loans) makes them very costly, and hence they are generally used only for large projects. Alternatively, on-balance-sheet financing provides the lender more security. General corporate assets are security for the loan and the expected financial outcome of the project (i.e., marketability of the emissions credits generated by the project).

A key element of project finance is the identification and mitigation of economic, political, and technical risks. Without risk mitigation, the project may be deemed unfinanceable.

Capital Budgeting as Part of Strategic Decision Making for Sustainability Projects

Sustainability projects could initially be financed by the company via allocation of internal capital. If the business case developed for the project (see chapter 4 for business case development methods) justifies the need and addresses the new opportunities associated with the proposed project, the allocation of capital is warranted. Financial models used to assess a sustainability project could include Net Present Value (NPV), Internal Rate of Return (IRR), Return on Investment (ROI), Simple Payback Period (SPP), Discounted Cash Flow (DCF), and Profitability Index. Since the analysis effort can be significant, options are usually prescreened to ensure strategic fit and feasibility first via the development of a business case for the sustainability project, then ranking options using one of the above financial measures and choosing the option that adds the most value to the company.

Environmental concerns, costs, and liabilities faced by business today are an economic issue that can not be ignored and must be included in the managerial decision making. The traditional capital budgeting process of Awareness, Identification, Selection, and Monitoring must address environmental issues (Figure 8.1). For example, during the awareness stage of capital budgeting, management must develop an understanding for the environmental issues as a variable in the planning process. As such, it must assess if there is a risk due to environmental impacts (see chapter 2 for environmental management strategies) and evaluate how those potential risks can affect corporate goals and objectives. The economic life of a project must be evaluated according to the environmental costs, as they could surpass the project's life. For example, "cleanup" costs could pressure the company for years after completion of the actual project. The useful life of projects should be expanded to adapt to this consideration.

Cash flows are also affected by environmental issues as they alter direct and indirect costs, in addition to presenting hidden costs and contingent liability costs. The traditional NPV method of capital budgeting that uses cost of capital or weighted average cost of capital as the discount rate must be revisited and adjusted according to the environmental risks.[2]

Venture Capital for Sustainability

Venture Capital (VC) can be defined as a type of private equity capital funded by institutional investors and high-net-worth individuals invested in early-stage companies or projects.

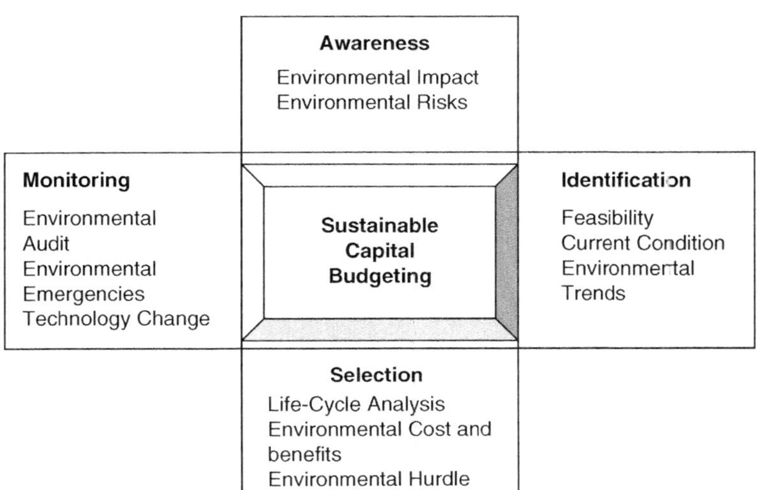

Figure 8.1 Sustainable capital budgeting.

VC financing of sustainability projects and companies started with the realization that financial returns are possible even when societal issues and benefits are factored into corporate strategic planning. Venture Capital for Sustainability is defined as a specific area within private equity financing in which profit objectives are supplemented by sustainability missions. Attempting to combine profit objectives with sustainability criteria, the venture capital fund is focused on the products, targeted economic impact, and processes and internal operations and their link and impact on sustainability. An example is investing in clean technology.[3]

Sustainable Small and Medium Enterprises: The Future for Emerging Economies

Small and medium enterprises (SMEs) play a critical role in both developing and industrialized economies. According to the World Business Council for Sustainable Development, in Organisation for Economic Co-operation and Development (OECD) countries, SMEs and microenterprises comprise 95% of firms, 60% of employment, and 55% of the gross domestic product (GDP). Sustainable SMEs are those that manufacture and market environmentally friendly products or serve low-income communities and generate additional benefits for society and the environment. Financing such value-added businesses in emerging economies makes sense for both business growth and sustainable development. In developing countries, however, sustainable SMEs face major barriers to growth and success, most notably access to finance and business development support.

Along with the rising interest in green investment, clean technology industries, and market-based approaches to poverty reduction and sustainable development, during the past 10 years international financial institutions, some not-for-profit investment communities, and private investors who see value in sustainable enterprises moved toward providing finance and business development support to sustainable SMEs in developing countries.

Effective sustainable SME investment requires understanding how the sector can best be supported and expanded, the financial gaps, the players, and the challenges involved with fundraising and coordination of capital, as well as providing technical assistance needed and monitoring progress and success.[4]

International Programs for Financing Sustainability

The most critical elements of financing sustainability projects are (a) identifying a set of environmental, governmental, social, and sustainability assumptions and factors that are most agreeable to both financial and corporate sectors, and (b) defining practices and guiding principles to effectively communicate these factors to the capital markets.

The World Bank, through its administration of the Climate Investment Funds (CIFs), provides funding for country-led sustainability projects such as climate change programs in developing countries. In September 2008, two CIFs (*Clean Technology Fund* and *Strategic Climate Fund*) were established by donor country pledges of over $6.1 billion. CIF funds are distributed through the World Bank and four regional development banks collectively termed *Multilateral Development Banks (MDBs)*. Sustainable economic development being a core mission of the MDBs, funds such as CIFs are available through MDBs to provide financing for projects focused on mitigation or strengthening resilience to climate change impacts. As mentioned, such financing is provided through long-term loans and grants.

The *International Finance Corporation (IFC)* of World Bank Group has developed policies and procedures for environmental assessment and management since the 1990s. In June 2003, after extensive advice and guidance from the IFC, ten major international banks adopted the *Equator Principles*, a voluntary set of guidelines based on the environmental and social guidelines and safeguard policies of the IFC. Starting in 2004, the IFC's *Environmental and Social Review Unit* developed a procedure for examining potential projects for their potential effects on the environment and the people in the project area. Any project that exhibits significant environmental effects is required to develop environmental impact assessments (EIAs) and environmental management plans.

To support micro, small, and medium enterprises working on global environmental issues, such as renewable energy and energy efficiency, ecotourism, sustainable agriculture, and agroforestry, in June 2004 the IFC established the *Environmental Business Finance Program (EBFP)* with $20 million in funds from the *Global Environment Facility*. The Environmental Projects Unit (EPU) at the IFC is responsible for developing innovative private-sector projects with environmental benefits and mainstreams those investments within the private sector and the IFC. The EPU collaborates with the Global Environment Facility (GEF) and other institutions to finance the projects.[5]

In 2008 the World Business Council on Sustainable Development (WBCSD) and the United Nations Environmental Program Finance Initiative published the key issues associated with translating environmental, social, and governance factors into sustainable business values.[6]

Microfinance and Sustainable Development

Microfinance refers to financial services for the poor, and as such is identified as a financial instrument that can support sustainable development. Microfinance is operational via donations that are used to lend microcredits. The demand for this type of financial services is large, but the supply of funds and donations is limited. So the question is, how can microfinance stay sustainable in order to assist environmental sustainability?

Financially sustainable microfinance institutions (MFIs) can become a permanent part of the financial system, if and when they can continue to operate even after grants or soft loans are no longer available. The most efficient financial model for MFIs is the ability to cover their costs through interest and other incomes paid by their clients and commercial funding sources. Most donor microfinanced projects fall into one of four types: retail MFIs that provide direct services to poor clients, for instance, a state-owned bank; wholesale "apex" funds that finance various retail MFIs, such as NGOs or private commercial banks; components of social funds or community development projects that provide "revolving credit funds" for local community organizations; or "technical implementers," such as an international NGO or consulting firm that conducts institutional capacity building, industry infrastructure, and policy work.

In the United States, the *National Credit Council*, an interagency body under the *Department of Finance*, has developed policies for involvement and active participation of the private sector in providing financial services to the poor The *National Strategy for Microfinance* suggests formation of a viable and sustainable private microfinancial market that is supported by government and an appropriate policy environment and institutional framework (an intervention of public and private sector).[7]

Financing and Investing in Climate Change

Need for Clear Policies

Addressing climate change requires mutual involvement of the investors and the businesses, and policies that can enable necessary flows of private capital at national, regional, and international levels. As expected, investors can play a significant role in supporting initiatives and programs targeted at climate challenge. But in order to attract their involvement, governments must develop clear and ambitious policy signals that can support and encourage their participation.[8]

Example policies to promote investing in efforts toward climate change include the following:

- ***Price signal on carbon.*** The development of policies and programs on clear and appropriate long-term price signals for carbon is essential in order for investors to integrate climate change considerations into decision-making processes and as such become effectively engaged with the companies on their climate strategies. A price on carbon emissions would establish the critical long-term price signal necessary to cause businesses and investors to reassess value, redirect their investments, and accelerate the transformation to a low-carbon economy. Those signals could, for example, demonstrate how investments in carbon-intensive projects may yield lower returns, how new and established zero- or low-carbon technologies can be deployed profitably, and whether investment in clean energy infrastructure will yield sound returns. A well-designed carbon market also plays a significant role in providing a cost-effective way to achieve emissions reductions.
- ***Attracting private sector investment.*** The requisite level of climate investment cannot be met through both public and private finance. Private-sector investment at a much larger scale will be essential to deliver the needed capital flows. The deployment of new finance mechanisms can incentivize unprecedented levels of private-sector investment and facilitate wider, more open markets for climate investment and carbon trading globally, especially in developing countries. The World Bank estimates that $140–175 billion annually is needed by 2030 to mitigate climate change on a 2°C trajectory, and $75–100 billion is needed annually for adaptation through 2050. Institutional investors could provide a significant portion of the required capital, if they could earn adequate risk-adjusted returns. According to United Nations Framework Convention on Climate Change (UNFCCC) estimates, private-sector investments constitute the largest share (up to 86%) of global investments and financial flows in response to climate change.[9]
- ***Development of public finance mechanisms.*** Public finance can play a key role in mobilizing private-sector investment in these markets on a much larger scale. It is imperative that public money allocated to address climate change be spent in a way that leverages private capital to the maximum extent possible by altering the risk-reward balance of private-sector investments. Research

shows that $1 of public investment spent through well-designed public finance mechanisms can leverage between $3 and $15 of private-sector money.

- ***Multilateral development banks and bilateral development institutions.*** Such institutions could play a key role in systematically deploying mechanisms that enable private sector institutions from both developed and developing countries to access packages of support that help reduce the risks faced by private investors, scale up the demand for low-carbon investment, and create commercially attractive investment opportunities.
- ***Disclosure of material climate-related risks.*** Disclosure must be part of mandatory filings by all publicly traded companies. All national regulators worldwide, including the U.S. Securities and Exchange Commission, must require companies to disclose to their investors material climate-related risks and the programs in place to manage those risks as a part of annual financial or risk reports submitted to investors and securities regulators.[10]

Global and Regional Financing Programs

Specialized regional private financing mechanisms have an important role in financing climate change mitigation and adaptation. While *mitigation* and *adaptation* are similar, they are different on some levels. The two involve different issues and need different financing schemes. *Mitigation* relates to a global public good, and *mitigative activities* have almost perfect global externalities. *Adaptation activities*, however, are limited to a smaller geographical area or population. Most adaptation measures relate to regional public goods, so they should be region or country specific.

Regional financing. Climate change is a global public good, but it has strong regional features, and as such it requires regional financing arrangements that have a very special and unique role in climate change adaptation. A regional financing arrangement refers to a financing facility or mechanism with two key features: (a) the activities it funds are limited to the region, and (b) the arrangement's member countries or governments from within the region have a substantial role in the decision making. Essentially, a regional private financing mechanism responds mainly to the specialized nature of the demand in a region.

An Adaptation Fund (financed through a 2% levy on revenue generated by the Clean Development Mechanism [CDM] and through voluntary contributions) is a key fund dedicated for adaptation to climate change and is estimated to be $80 million to $1 billion per annum by 2012. Other main adaptation funds include UNFCCC Special Funds (about $270 million) and a portion of the GEF Trust Fund ($50 million until 2010).[11]

Global financing. According to the UNFCCC, mitigation measures needed to return the global GHGs to current levels in 2030 require investment and financial flows of $200 billion to $210 billion per annum.[12] Investment needs for adaptation in developing countries in 2030 are estimated at $28 billion to $67 billion. As presented earlier in this chapter, the main dedicated sources of financing for mitigation at the global level include the Clean Development Mechanism (CDM) and various dedicated funds managed by the Global Environment Facility (GEF) and the World Bank. In 2007, the value of primary CDM transactions was $7.4 billion, which is estimated to have leveraged $36 billion of flows to developing countries. The GEF has about $250 million per annum in grants available for mitigation during 2006–2010. Example financial institutions that are most active in financing sustainability projects on regional and global scales include the following:

Regional:
Asian Development bank (ADB)
Greater Mekong Subregion (GMS)
Association of Southeast Asian Nations (ASEAN)
Central Asia Regional Economic Cooperation (CAREC)
South Asia Association for Regional Cooperation (SAARC)
Asia Pacific Carbon Fund (APCF)
Future Carbon Fund (FCF)
Climate Change Fund (CCF)
Clean Energy Financing Partnership Facility (CEFPF)
Water Financing Partnership Facility (WFPF)
Poverty and Environment Fund (PEF)
Global:
The Global Facility for Disaster Risk Reduction
Adaptation Fund
The Global Facility for Disaster Risk Reduction
Dedicated Funds
World Banks' Climate Investment Funds
European Commission's Global Climate Change Alliance (GCCA)
Consultative Group on International Agricultural Research (CGIAR)

World Health Organization (WHO)
United Nations Development Programme (UNDP)
World Meteorological Organization (WMO)

Governments in many countries have also started to provide financial support for climate change mitigation and adaptation activities within their territories. These are resulting in national programs and activities, which are the key building blocks of the global collective fight against climate change. However, national and global efforts alone are not sufficient to address the climate change challenges comprehensively. Regional institutions and regional financing arrangements also play a critical role, without which the collective global fight against climate change will not be complete.

An example regional project is the Renewable Energy Knowledge and Technology Transfer for Regional Innovation Strategies in the Malopolska region in Poland. This project was supported by the Integrated Regional Operational Program, and European Social Fund (ESF) provided 75% of the project cost. The aim of the project was to promote renewable energy in the Malopolska region. The 22 training sessions were organized by lecturers from various universities, and a database of renewable energy projects implemented in the region and a manual (1,000 copies) for the private sector interested in renewable energy were prepared. The project partners were the Polish Network Energie-Cities (PNEC), the University of Mining and Metallurgy in Krakow, and the Polish Association of Renewable Energy Sector and Environmental Protection Employers. The beneficiaries of the project are 22 counties in the Malopolska region including local authorities, SMEs, and graduate students. The success factors of the project were the cooperation among NGOs, universities, and the private sector and a relevant choice of funding. The project also provided new employment opportunities in private companies with salaries paid from the project for a half year, and new jobs were created for three graduate students. The difficulties that were faced during the implementation of the project were the changes involved with regulations and insurance policies that delayed paying the contractors. For those thinking of implementing a similar project, the project manager, Mrs. Maria Stankiewicz (PNEC), made suggestions not connected with financing: "You must organize a promotion campaign before providing regional training sessions, to have closer cooperation with the media and to try to overcome the passive attitude of most of the municipalities."[13,14]

Corporate Sustainability Initiatives and Reporting in the United States

Many U.S. corporations are actively pursuing corporate sustainability in the absence of national regulations. Sustainability activities include reporting of sustainability activities, green building construction and renovation, the use of alternative energy sources, and carbon trading.

Ceres, a national organization of investors and environmental and public interest groups to address sustainability issues, launched the Global Reporting Initiative (GRI) during the early 1990s. The GRI provides reporting guidelines designed to provide a framework for the reporting of economic, environmental, and social facets of a corporation. There are 20,000 stakeholders from 80 countries in the GRI network.[15] Bank of America produces an annual Sustainability Report utilizing the GRI Framework. In 2007, Bank of America announced a 10-year, $20 billion business initiative to advocate innovative lending and business strategies to address climate change. Proposed initiatives included the creation of new financial products and services and optimizing its own operations.[16]

While some companies have identified an economic benefit from measuring and reporting sustainability activities, others are waiting for national regulations. Some equity and bond investors are concerned that corporations are hiding the financial significance of environmental impacts including environmental liabilities and the risk associated with potential GHG[17] regulation. In the United States, the Securities and Exchange Commission (SEC) requires public corporations to disclose material environmental risks with regard to environmental costs, liabilities, and future risks. This reporting is still uneven across companies as Financial Accounting Standards Board (FASB) standards allow companies to report the lowest estimate of potential environmental costs. In 2007, a coalition of investors petitioned the SEC to require publicly traded companies to fully disclose their financial risk associated with potential GHG regulation.

Has the Sustainability Focus Moved Beyond Reducing Energy Costs?

Many corporations are pursuing green building and design initiatives to reduce energy consumption and increase employee productivity and health. Leading the effort in this area is the Green

Building Council (GBC), formed in 1993. The GBC developed the Leadership in Energy and Environmental Design (LEED) rating system to rate new construction and building renovations. LEED certification requires companies to address building performance in six categories: sustainability, water efficiency, indoor environmental quality, materials and resources, energy efficiency, and design innovation.

Toyota has one of the largest environmentally friendly building complexes in the United States at its Torrance, California, headquarters. The financial goals for Toyota were a rate of return greater than 10% and long-term operational savings. Toyota installed a solar rooftop system that reduced costs by $400,000 per year and a system to use reclaimed water that reduced potable water demand by 94%[18] (11 million gallons).

Another success story is a four-building renovation for the National Geographic Society (NGS) in Washington, DC. NGS's CFO estimated that the renovation increased the market value of the property by $4 for every $1 invested and reduced operating costs by 14%. The NGS achieved LEED Silver certification for these renovations.

Capital Markets: Carbon Credits and Carbon Trading

The United Nations Earth Summit in Rio de Janerio in 1992 led to the Framework Convention on Climate Change (UNFCCC), which had near universal membership and support of all major GHG emitting countries (including the United States). Country commitments under the UNFCCC were voluntary and no governmental reduction targets were established. A subsequent UNFCCC conference held in Kyoto Japan, in 1997 produced the Kyoto Protocol, which established firm emissions reduction targets for industrialized and developed economies. In order for the Kyoto Protocol to be binding it had to be ratified by at least 55 countries that account for 55% of GHG emissions from developed countries.[19] The Protocol established emission reductions for the United States at 7% from the 1990 level for each year in the 2008–2012 period.[20] Economists predicted this would result in a 3% decline in GDP.[21] The U.S. Senate, concerned about the cost implications of GHG emissions limits on the economy, and Australia refused to ratify the Kyoto Protocol, *but* the threshold was exceeded with the ratification by Russia in 2005.

Although the Kyoto calls for binding emission reductions, which vary by country during the 2008–2012 time frame, it does not prescribe how countries will meet their targets. Kyoto did propose three mechanisms to assist countries in meeting their targets: emissions trading schemes (ETSs), Joint Implementation (JI), and the Clean Development Mechanism (CDM). Countries adopting an ETS use a capital-markets-based mechanism generally referred to as a cap and trade system.

Governments place emission caps on industries (companies) and allow companies to find the least costly alternative to reducing emissions—abatement or emissions trading between companies. Joint Implementation mechanisms refer to emission reduction projects initiated by developed countries in another country (developed or developing) as a means of meeting their reduction targets established under Kyoto. The country earns emission reduction units (ERUs) only for projects that generate reductions in addition to business as usual.

The CDM allows developed countries to invest in an emission reduction project in a developing country to earn Certified Emission Reduction credits (CERs) as a means of meeting their emission reduction targets under Kyoto. CERs can be saved to meet emission reduction targets during the 2008–2012 time frame or they can be banked for later. CERs can only be granted for emission reductions that are in addition to business as usual.

Cap and Trade Programs

A cap and trade program sets a maximum or cap on GHG emissions from businesses or industries covered by regulations. Businesses are granted allowances by a regulatory agency that permits the holder to emit a specific amount of GHG emissions. An allowance generally represents the right to emit 1 ton of emissions. At the end of the year, if a company's emissions are higher than the allowances owned, the company must reduce emissions (e.g., by switching fuel or through conservation) or purchase allowances on the open market. If the company has less emissions than allowances, it can bank these allowances or sell them to the open market. GHG emitters covered by a cap must

- Measure, monitor, and report emissions
- Have enough allowances to cover their reported emissions at the end of every compliance period

Emitters may buy and sell allowances in order to comply with regulations. This enables emitters to determine the cheapest method of compliance, mitigation efforts, or allowance trading. Companies facing a high mitigation cost will choose to purchase allowances. This flexibility lowers the cost of compliance.

Regulation may be aimed at either upstream or downstream emitters. Upstream emitters include oil and gas companies, oil refineries, coal mining operations, etc. Downstream emitters are the end users. Whether regulation focuses on upstream or downstream emitters, the cost of GHG emissions will affect everyone. A cap and trade system creates a price for carbon emissions that will eventually show up in the price of every product whose life cycle produced carbon or GHG emissions. Companies that reduce their exposure to fossil fuels will have a competitive advantage.

Under a cap and trade system, allowances may be distributed by the government through an auction, generating revenue for the government. Most federal legislative proposals designate the U.S. Environmental Protection Agency (EPA) as being in charge of administering a cap and trade program for GHGs.

A cap and trade program is different from a carbon tax. They are similar in that both approaches create a price for carbon that provides companies with an incentive to reduce emissions. The difference lies in the way the price of carbon is established. A cap and trade program establishes a cap on the amount of emissions a company can generate. The carbon price is determined by market supply and demand for allowances in an emissions trading market. A carbon tax does not set a limit on emissions, but places an arbitrary price on carbon.

Currently, the United States does not have a national carbon cap and trade program due to the absence of regulations on carbon emissions. Regional programs do exist for some GHG emissions. In the Northeast United States, a regional cap and trade program exists to reduce nitrous oxide emissions. The Northeast Regional Greenhouse Gas Initiative (RGGI) covers electric power emitters of carbon in ten states. In Europe, the European Union Emissions Trading Scheme (EU-ETS) is a GHG cap and trade program regulating carbon emissions from 11,500 businesses in twenty-five countries.

Chicago Climate Exchange

The Chicago Climate Exchange (CCX) operates North America's only voluntary trading system for all six GHGs with independent third-party verification by the Financial Industry Regulatory

Authority (FINRA). CCX members enter into voluntary but legally binding commitments to reduce annual GHG emissions. Members whose reductions exceed their target earn surplus allowances that can be sold or banked. Conversely, members who are not able to meet their annual reduction targets can purchase credits (surplus allowances) from those who have exceeded their target reductions. Members can meet their emission targets by purchasing CCX Carbon Financial Instruments (CFI) contracts. Each CFI contract represents 100 metric tons of carbon equivalent.

U.S. Voluntary Initiatives

Although U.S. companies are not subject to climate change regulations such as limits on GHG emissions, many companies are preparing for the possibility that regulations will be enacted in the near future. Examples of voluntary corporate activity include the following:

- Wal-Mart has a goal of switching to 100% renewable energy to power its stores. Currently, Wal-Mart has installed solar panels on stores in California, and it has a contract with a West Texas wind farm to help power its stores.
- In 2007, PepsiCo headquarters switched to 100% green energy through renewable power brokers and the purchase of offset credits.
- Kohl's is one of the largest solar electricity users in the United States with solar panels installed on 60 stores.
- Dell reduced operating expenses by $3 million through increased energy efficiency while reducing GHG emissions.
- Johnson & Johnson generates electrical power from landfill gas and solar panels. Additionally, the company is a direct purchaser of wind and hydro power.

Sustainability Investment Risk Management

International Perspectives

A high degree of uncertainty is associated with the nature, extent, and timing of the impact of climate change, which creates a market for risk transfer and insurance products. The *Caribbean Catastrophe Risk Insurance Facility* is a good example of such a regional private financing mechanism. This facility provides short-term liquidity to the participating country governments in the aftermath of a natural disaster.

The World Bank in collaboration with ADB is developing a *Pacific Catastrophe Risk Pool Initiative*, which will ensure short-term liquidity to the Pacific Island states after a natural disaster. Although this facility is primarily focused on natural disasters, it is also directly related to climate change, which increasingly defines the frequency and severity of typhoons in the Pacific.

Another popular risk transfer mechanism is a *catastrophe (CAT) bond*, which has emerged as a useful instrument for dispersing catastrophic weather risk. The possible issuance of *region-specific CAT bonds* in the context of climate change is another interesting area to explore.

Government support to maintain the insurability of weather-related risks despite climate change include restricting development in vulnerable areas, investments in defensive infrastructure, and the provision of reliable and independent data on weather patterns. In some cases, tax and nontax incentives and other financial support (e.g., soft loans or grants) may also be required to make these mechanisms viable. Risk transfer and insurance products related to climate change are unlikely to succeed without suitable policy and regulatory support by the countries in the region.[22]

U.S. Perspectives

Investment managers are increasingly concerned about corporate exposure to climate-related risks and the sustainability initiatives, or lack thereof, of companies in their portfolios. For example, industries producing significant GHG emissions run the risk of potential governmental regulations that could significantly impact their profitability. There is some evidence supporting the notion that companies that manage environmental risk and pursue sustainability initiatives financially outperform those that do not follow such practices.[23]

U.S. corporations under SEC regulations are required to disclose material risks. Historically, this reporting has been weak at best, with uneven reporting across companies. There are perceived loopholes in SEC and FASB standards that allow companies to hide the financial significance of environmental impacts. Companies are allowed to report the cheapest estimate of environmental costs. The enactment of the Sarbanes Oxley Act (SOX) in 2002 may close this loophole as CEOs and CFOs are personally liable for the veracity of the financials. A coalition of investors filed a petition[24] in 2007 requesting that the SEC require publicly traded companies to fully disclose financial risk from climate change including the risk associated with GHG regulation.

The creation of the Dow Jones Sustainability Indexes (DJSI) is a manifestation of the concern of investment managers around environmental risks. The DJSI track the financial performance of sustainability-driven companies. The identification of companies for the indices is based on the Corporate Sustainability Assessment of SAM Research. Companies are selected for inclusion in the indices based on a defined set of criteria and factor weightings used to assess their sustainability opportunities and risks. The DJSI provide investors with a financial quantification of a company's sustainability opportunities and risks. According to the Government Accountability Office (GAO), "Environmental risks and liabilities are among conditions that, if undisclosed, could impair the public's ability to make sound investment decisions."[25]

The additional investment and financial flows needed in 2030 to cope with the adverse impacts of climate change in the Agriculture, Fishery and Forestry (AFF) sector is about US $14 billion. Slightly more than half of this amount will be needed for developing countries alone. It is estimated that approximately US $11 billion will be needed to purchase new capital, for example, to irrigate areas, adopt new practices, and move processing facilities. The additional financial flows needed in the AFF sector for research and extension activities to facilitate adaptation would be about US $3 billion.[26]

Summary

Specialized regional private financing mechanisms play an important role in financing climate change mitigation and adaptation. The financial implications of environmental opportunities and risk are becoming increasingly evident to organizations, financial institutions, and investors and are reflected in the world's capital markets. The financial markets that are equalized to environmental issues would be able to create permanent and powerful incentives for companies to improve their environmental performance, while also ensuring better returns for investors.

Investors are increasingly looking to invest in sustainable companies. Many investors believe companies pursuing sustainability initiatives will show superior performance and favorable risk-return profiles. Sustainability and climate risks are intangible liabilities that affect the market value of a corporation. In the absence of national regulations, many companies have developed voluntary sustainability initiatives to achieve higher returns through higher worker productivity, healthier employees, and a reduction in energy and water usage.

As explained previously, investors could play a critical role in the fight against climate change. To assist and direct their contribution, it is crucial for governments to develop clear and ambitious policy signals to attract international investment. On both the macro and micro scales, countries and private companies must take steps now if they are to attract the sizable amount of private investment needed to develop and make the transition to low-carbon technologies. The fight against climate change requires mutual involvement of investors and businesses. What is most needed today is the development of policies and programs on clear and appropriate long-term price signals for carbon, which is essential in order for investors to integrate climate change considerations into the decision-making processes and as such become effectively engaged with the companies on their climate strategies. A price on carbon emissions would establish the critical long-term price signal necessary to cause businesses and investors to reassess value, redirect their investments, and accelerate the transformation to a low-carbon economy.

Case Studies

Goldman Sachs Sustainability Programs

Goldman Sachs believes that a healthy environment is necessary for the well-being of society, its people, and its business, and it is the foundation for a sustainable and strong economy. It takes seriously its responsibility for environmental stewardship and believes that as a leading global financial institution it should play a constructive role in helping to address the challenges facing the environment. Goldman Sachs acknowledges the scientific consensus, led by the Intergovernmental Panel on Climate Change, that climate change is a reality and that human activities are largely responsible for increasing concentrations of greenhouse gases in the earth's atmosphere. It believes that climate change is one of the most significant environmental challenges of the twenty-first century and is linked to other important issues such as economic growth and development, poverty alleviation, access to clean water, and adequate energy supplies. Goldman Sachs also recognizes that an effective environmental policy must begin with a focus on minimizing the impact of its own operations. Accordingly, the company makes efforts to ensure that its facilities and business practices adopt leading-edge environmental safeguards. It has disclosed the environmental impact of its operations and reduced those impacts wherever practical. Its future sustainability efforts include the following:

- Reduce indirect greenhouse gas emissions by 7% from leased and owned offices by 2012, using a 2005 baseline.
- Increase use of recycled and environmentally certified wood, paper, and print products; use energy efficient equipment; and purchase more organic and sustainably harvested products and supplies.
- Purchase more products locally to reduce the environmental impact related to shipping, where practical.
- Develop uniform green building standards for use in the construction and major renovation of its facilities, with LEED Gold certification or other whole building standards as the ultimate goal.
- Develop environmentally sound procurement practices and incorporate environmental criteria into its supplier selection and review processes.
- Goldman Sachs is the owner of Cogentrix, a company that operates power plants in the United States. It reports the annual greenhouse gas emissions from these plants and will continue to work to reduce direct carbon emissions from them whenever practical.
- Continue to act as a market maker in emissions trading (CO_2, SO_2), weather derivatives, renewable energy credits, and other climate-related commodities, and look for ways to play a constructive role in promoting the development of these markets.
- Goldman Sachs intends to be a leading U.S. wind energy developer and generator through its recently acquired subsidiary, Horizon Wind Energy (f.k.a. Zilkha Renewable Energy).
- Plan to make available up to $1 billion to invest in renewable energy and energy efficiency projects.
- Evaluate the opportunities and, where appropriate, encourage the development of and participate in markets for water, biodiversity, forest management, forest-based ecosystems, and other ecosystem features and services.
- Continue to devise investment structures for renewable energy and invest alongside its energy clients, such as its wind energy

partnership with Shell Wind Energy and its solar energy fund with BP Solar.

- Explore investment opportunities in renewable and cleaner-burning alternative fuels such as renewable diesel (as its investment in Changing World Technologies), ethanol, and biomass.
- Seek to make investments in, and create financing structures to assist in the development and commercialization of, other environmentally friendly technologies.

Enhance Common Knowledge among Industry and Investors

To better inform investors about the impact of climate change on long-term growth, Goldman Sachs plans to support such initiatives as

- Broadening assessment of the impact of environmental and social issues to cover several more sectors, which it anticipates will help to establish the business case for sustainable development.
- Working to make environmental, social, and governance criteria a part of best-in-class investment research.
- Meeting with clients to discuss issues and trends, based on its research.
- Participating in and conveying meetings/seminars with clients, investors, and other experts to discuss strategic issues and identify market trends within industries and sectors.

Business Selection and Risk Management

Goldman Sachs believes that it is important to take the environmental impacts and practices of its clients and potential clients into consideration as it makes business selection decisions. It encourages clients conducting industrial and agricultural activity in environmentally sensitive areas to do so with the appropriate safeguards. The company adopts explicit prohibitions against financing or investing in industrial activity in certain limited areas that are so environmentally sensitive that they must be preserved in their present condition. Goldman Sachs will not finance any project or initiate loans where the specified use of proceeds would significantly convert or degrade a critical natural habitat. It will not finance projects that contravene any relevant international environmental agreement that has been enacted into the law of, or otherwise has the force of law in, the country in which the project is located.

Private Equity Investments Undertaken by the Firm's Merchant Banking Division

The company's private equity investment groups will continue to conduct an environmental review as part of their investment decision process for direct investments in companies in environmentally sensitive industries. The review process analyzes the company's prospective portfolio companies' compliance with applicable environmental laws and regulations.

The environmental review process is an integral part of its private equity investment groups' due diligence review of companies and their management. Once an investment is made, through its membership on a portfolio company's board of directors (where applicable), its private equity groups monitor its portfolio company's operations with respect to environmental compliance issues.[27]

Notes

1. Alexander Gattig and Laurie Hendrickx, "Judgmental Discounting and Environmental Risk Perception: Dimensional Similarities, Domain Differences, and Implications for Sustainability," *Journal of Social Issues* 63(1) (2007): 21–39.
2. D. Kite, "Capital Budgeting: Integrating Environmental Impact," *Journal of Cost Management* (1995): 11–14.
3. European Commission, "Venture Capital for Sustainability," *Eurosif* (2007).
4. Virginia Barreiro, Mareike Hussels, and Belinda Richards, "On the Frontiers of Finance, Scaling Up Investment in Sustainable Small and Medium Enterprises, in Developing Countries," *World Resources Institute*, August 2009.
5. World Bank Group, The International Finance Corporation (IFC), http://www.treas.gov/offices/international-affairs/intl/fy2006/ifc.pdf (accessed March 8, 2010).
6. "Translating Environmental, Social and Governance Factors into Sustainable Business Value, Key Insights for Companies and Investors." Report from an international workshop series of the WBCSD and UNEP, Geneva, April 26, 2010.
7. Consultative Group to Assist the Poorest, 1818 H Street, NW, Washington, DC 20433, Tel: (202) 473-9594, Fax: (202) 522-3744, E-mail: cgap@worldbank.org, Web: www.cgap.org.
8. "2009 Investor Statement on the Urgent Need for a Global Agreement on Climate Change," Institutional Investors Group on Climate Change, September 2009, http://www.ceres.org/Document.Doc?id=495 (accessed March 8, 2010).
9. Diwesh Sharan, "Financing Climate Change Mitigation and Adaptation. Role of Regional Financing Arrangements," *Asian Development Bank Sustainable Development Working Paper Series* 4 (December 2008).
10. "2009 Investor Statement on the Urgent Need for a Global Agreement on Climate Change," Institutional Investors Group on Climate Change, September 2009, http://www.ceres.org/Document.Doc?id=495 (accessed March 8, 2010).
11. Diwesh Sharan, "Financing Climate Change Mitigation and Adaptation Role of Regional Financing Arrangements," *Asian Development Bank Sustainable Development Working Paper Series* 4 (December 2008).

12. "Towards a Strategic framework on Climate Change and Development: Concept and Issue Paper", 2008, World Bank Group, http://www.org/DEVCOMMINT/Documentation/21928837/DC2008-0009(E)ClimateChange.pdf (accessed June 1, 2010), p. 20.
13. Ibid.
14. Financing Sustainable Energy Projects Trough the Structural Funds and the Cohesion Fund in 2007-2013", 2007, INTERREG IIIC, http://www.interreg3c.net/sixcms/media.php/5/Financing+sustainable+energy+through+Structural+Funds+2007-2013+(RUSE).pdf (accessed September 14, 2010).
15. H.S. Brown, M. deJong, and T. Lessidrenska, "The Rise of the Global Reporting Initiative (GRI) as a Case of Institutional Entrepreneurship," Corporate Social Responsibility Initiative, working paper 36, (May 2007).
16. Bank of America Sustainability Report, 2006, http://www.bankofamerica.com/environment/pdf/2006_Env_Report.pdf.
17. See chapters 1 and 11 for more information on climate change, GHG emissions, and associated regulatory requirements.
18. www.usgbc.org.
19. Kyoto Protocol to the United Nations Framework Convention on Climate Change, 1998, Article 25.
20. Ibid., Annex B.
21. Impacts of the Kyoto Protocol on U.S. Energy Markets and Economic Activity, Energy Information Administration, U.S. Department of Energy.
22. Diwesh Sharan, "Financing Climate Change Mitigation and Adaptation, Role of Regional Financing Arrangements," *Asian Development Bank Sustainable Development Working Paper Series* 4 (December 2008).
23. "Sec Issues Interpretive Guidance on Climate Risk Disclosure," 2010, *Client Alert, Thompson and Knight Attorneys and Counselors,* http://www.tklaw.com/resources/documents/Client%20Alert_SEC%20Issues%20Interpretive%20Guidance%20on%20Climate%20Risk%20Disclosure.pdf (accessed September 14, 2010).
24. Petition for Interpretive Guidance on Climate Risk Disclosure.
25. Stephen Taub, "SEC to Expand Environmental Disclosure," CFO.com, July 19, 2004, www.cfo.com/printable/articles.cfm/3015263 (accessed June 2, 2010).
26. United Nations Framework Convention on Climate Change, "Investment and Financial Flows to Address Climate Change," 2007, p. 104.
27. "Goldman Sachs Environmental Policy Framework," http://www2.goldmansachs.com/ideas/environment-and-energy/goldman-sachs/env-policy-pdf.pdf (accessed March 8, 2010).

CHAPTER 9

Sustainability Accounting and Reporting

CHARLES T. HAMILTON

The chapter discusses a number of accounting-related issues in terms of the overall concepts of environment and sustainability. The financial accounting focus of objectively measuring defined assets and liabilities often handles environmental costs as a part of the costing process and simply lumps these costs into the overhead cost pool. The financial accounting treatment of contingent liabilities is too rigid for environmental decision purposes. Environmental management should estimate the likelihood of an action being taken against the organization, and it should also estimate the potential liabilities related to cleanup costs and related fines if environmental pollution has occurred. The chapter also illustrates that several existing managerial methodological approaches are potentially very useful as environmental and sustainability tools.

Introduction

Formal accounting standards and reporting rules do not require sustainability and environmental detailed presentations in the preparation of financial statements. Generally Accepted Accounting Principles (GAAP) have never been formalized in a statement that addresses the disclosure needs related to sustainability and environmental issues. This chapter will introduce suggested guidance that has been proposed by various international groups, and it will discuss current accounting methodology and techniques that will allow these suggestions to become operational.

The discussions of current accounting tools will focus more on the concept of Environmental Cost Management. This concept is based on providing managers with sufficient and appropriate information that will allow them to consider this data when making decisions that are strategically necessary for proper conformity with the concept of sustainable accounting and reporting.

"Green Accounting" is still in its formative stages. In this chapter, two cases, Ontario Hydro and AT&T, will be discussed from the perspective of linking the case suggestions with current accounting methodology. The chapter will conclude with a discussion of the Green House Gas Protocols (GHS). The protocols are labeled as "A Corporate Accounting and Reporting Standard," but once again these protocols have nothing to do with financial statement accounting rules. They provide guidance and standards primarily related to record keeping and reporting of emission measurement results.

Corporate Sustainability

Maximizing financial performance in the short term can conflict with maximizing societal wealth. This conflict has caused the recognition of the broader concept of stakeholder versus classic shareholder value. Societal pressures create the need to properly manage the combination of environmental, social, and economic issues. Sustainable development considers the management of these issues as a key element in creating the proper environment for corporate survival. Socially responsible corporate behavior should guarantee survivability in the medium/long term and contribute toward the corporation's goals of increasing shareholder value.

This chapter is not directly concerned with the marketplace's stock selection and investing strategy. The focus is on the individual organization and how it can adapt its accounting system so that its managerial decisions will properly consider these sustainability issues. Multiple accounting concepts and methods will be discussed as a guide to the concept of "Financial Analysis and Sustainability."

Value Added

Stakeholder/shareholder value-added is a critical concept in terms of evaluating the existence of a sustainable environment. Typical corporate valuation and related valuation drivers are focused on sales growth, cash flow, working capital investment, fixed asset investment, and profitability related to the concept of return on capital. To enhance sustainability, environmental value drivers should be introduced into the environmental decision-making model.

Environmental value drivers should be considered in the structure of competitive strategy. Michael Porter introduced the framework for competitive strategy in the 1980s. In his text, he suggested three broad strategies that an organization needs to consider in its goal of achieving a competitive advantage in its industry group:

1. ***Low Cost*:** producing product of acceptable quality at the lowest cost.
2. ***Differentiation*:** producing a product that is unique in terms of quality or performance.
3. ***Focus*:** producing a product for a specific need in a defined region of the world. This strategy can be a combination of "low cost" and "differentiation."

Proposed environmental drivers are closely linked with the competitive strategy of differentiation. Chousa and Castro have proposed the following six financial drivers of sustainability. These drivers are linked to the management decision-making process that attempts to create a sustainable shareholder value.

1. ***Customer attraction*:** the ability to attract and retain customers because of the strengths in the product's life cycle; research and development through customer service.
2. ***Brand value and reputation*:** product quality and performance combined with environmental standards.
3. ***Human and intellectual capital*:** this is primarily a human resource investment issue that influences decisions related to the hiring, training, and education of employees and managerial groups, and also the creation of a work environment that encourages the use of these acquired skills to focus on innovation.
4. ***Risk profile*:** this is a concept related to the sustainability of the corporation's tangible and intangible assets. Financial statement accounting addresses this from the perspective of estimated useful lives and the intensity of asset use through methods of depreciation and amortization. Accounting does not consider the exposure risk of potential disasters. Clearly management

needs to consider these potential risks to preempt negative events and minimize damages when an event occurs.

5. ***Innovation***: this is directly related to Porter's competitive strategies. Will the company consistently design and produce new and improved products and services that allow it to maintain a competitive advantage?
6. ***License to operate***: this is a conceptual issue; it is not a governmental authority to operate in a certain environment. The level of acceptance of the corporation's functions by its stakeholders creates the basis for this driver. Basically, the company cannot allow financial, investing, and operational decisions to impair the value of this acceptance license.

The measurement of these six drivers is highly subjective. Clear and objective measures of accounting do not exist to attach value to these drivers, but this limitation does not change the necessity to evaluate these drivers as tools to improve decision making.

There is an organizational need to identify critical sustainable activities. The costs that can be assigned to these activities and the identification of cost drivers that provide a causal link with each activity are necessary steps to create the cost-benefit analysis that leads to proper decision making within a sustainable management system. This process will be addressed in more detail in the AT&T case discussion in which the accounting method of activity-based costing is introduced.

Capital Budgeting

Strategic investment decisions consistent with the concept of sustainability are critical for the long-term health of an organization. The capital budgeting model is primarily concerned with forecasting cash receipts and disbursements over a future period related to a specific investment decision. This cash flow is evaluated using the company's desired cost of capital. Cost of capital, as a concept, is the required return on an investment that will allow the company to maintain its perceived value in the market place. A company would not invest in a project if the financial returns were less than the cost of capital.

The capital budgeting methodology should be used in evaluating environmental investment decisions. For example, if an organization is evaluating the acquisition of new equipment for emissions control, it would need to estimate the cash receipts and disbursements over the anticipated life of the equipment.

Ratio Analysis

This tool allows the researcher to measure and evaluate corporate performance over time and trends, and to evaluate interrelationships and expectations based on the corporate data. It also allows for industry comparisons with comparable companies in the marketplace. The major limitation for the external use of this tool is the availability of the accounting data. The classification of accounting data for external use is structured around the needs of financial statement disclosure and presentation. This classification typically follows the DuPont Ratios Pyramid, which establishes the decomposition concept. The top of the pyramid begins with the summary measure of profitability called ROE (return on equity). This ratio is broken down as follows:

ROE = (Net Income/Total Assets) × (Total Assets/Common Equity)

The first component of this ratio is decomposed into ROA (return on assets) as follows:

ROA = (Net Income/Sales) × (Sales/Total Assets)

This decomposition of the ratios can continue until the limitation of available accounting classifications is reached.

The corporation will need to expand internal accounting classifications in order to properly use ratio analysis as a tool. The accounting limitation is based on the needs of external financial statement disclosure requirements. As an example, let's decompose the first component of ROA. The first component (Net Income/Sales) could be decomposed into the (Net Income/Operating Costs) × (Operating Costs/Sales) breakdown. Ratio analysis, as a tool, would be enhanced if the internal accounting data existed to further breakdown (Operating Costs/Sales) for sustainability issues. For example, the operating costs could be broken down into various cost classifications, but for this to be useful for sustainability measures, cost classifications would need to be created for environmental fines, emission costs, and energy consumption.

If the second component of ROA, (Sales/Total Assets), were decomposed, it would be useful if total asset classifications could be broken down into High Pollution Total Assets and Low Pollution

Total Assets. As another example, one of the many asset accounts that are part of total assets is inventory. Inventory could be broken down into raw material usage, work in process, and finished goods inventory. This would be possible with accounting classifications that currently exist in the accounting system. However, if the decomposition wanted to analyze waste and spoilage as a percentage of sales, the accounting system would need to be adjusted.

Accounting rules separate waste and spoilage into categories of normal and abnormal. Abnormal waste and spoilage is treated as a separate expense, and this information exists to facilitate the analysis of changes and trends in this category. However, accounting treats normal waste and spoilage as part of manufacturing overhead. The basic logic is that good units cannot be produced without incurring a certain level of waste and spoilage. Accordingly, accounting treats these costs as part of the normal production costs. It would be possible to reproduce these numbers using the internal data of an individual company, but this information is never disclosed in the external financial statements.

The external financial statement focus of accounting classifications is a severe limitation of the usefulness of ratio analysis for external stakeholders/shareholders. An individual corporation could create an internal accounting system that would increase the volume of accounting classifications. However, this would add to the complexity and cost of the accounting system. Management would need to consider these costs relative to the benefits of the more refined analysis relative to sustainability issues.

Balanced Scorecard

The basic concept of the Balanced Scorecard (BSC) is to provide critical success factors in one of four different dimensions. This scorecard provides measures of these factors, and it allows the company to create a benchmark for comparison with its competitive strategy. The following list consists of one financial and three nonfinancial dimensions:

1. ***Financial Performances:*** the accounting system provides measures of profitability and market value for shareholder evaluations.
2. ***Customer Satisfaction:*** measures of quality, service, cost, and functionality that indicate customer satisfaction.
3. ***Internal Business Process:*** measures the efficiency and effectiveness of the corporation's ability to produce product.

4. ***Innovation and Learning*:** measures the firm's ability to properly use its human resources strategically.

The above list of dimensions can easily be expanded to include the following environmental and social performance indicators[1]:

Environmental Performance Indicators (EPIs)

- Operational indicators measure potential stresses to the environment, for example, fossil fuel use, toxic and nontoxic waste, and pollutants.
- Management indicators measure efforts to reduce environmental effects, for example, hours of environmental training.
- Environmental indicators measure environmental quality, for example, ambient air pollution concentrations.

Social Performance Indicators (SPIs)

- Working conditions indicators measure worker safety and opportunity, for example, training hours and number of injuries.
- Community involvement indicators measure the firm's outreach to the local and broader community, for example, employee volunteering and participation in Habitat for Humanity.
- Philanthropy indicators measure the direct contribution by the firm and its employees to charitable organizations.

The role of the sustainable perspective of the BSC is to make the EPIs an integral part of management decision making, not only for regulatory compliance, but also for product design, purchasing, strategic planning, and other management functions. As for the BSC, there are a number of implementation issues, including measurement problems and confidentiality issues. For example, the Global Reporting Initiative (GRI; www.globalreporting.org), an independent global institution in partnership with the United Nations and other groups, has a goal of developing generally accepted standards of sustainability reporting.

Accounting Issues

Financial Accounting

Financial Accounting is mainly designed to satisfy the information needs of external stakeholders, such as investors, tax authorities, and creditors, all of who have a strong interest in receiving accurate, standardized information about an organization's financial performance. Financial reporting is regulated by national laws and international standards, which specify how different financial items should be treated.

In contrast, *Management Accounting* (MA) primarily focuses on satisfying the information needs of internal management. Although there are accepted good practices in the realm of MA, these practices are generally not regulated by law. Each organization can determine which MA practices and information are best suited to its organizational goals and culture.

Environmental Accounting

Environmental Accounting is a broad term used in a number of different contexts, such as

Assessment and disclosure of environment-related financial information in the context of financial accounting and reporting

Assessment and use of environment-related physical and monetary information in the context of Environmental Management Accounting

Estimation of external environmental impacts and costs, often referred to as Full Cost Accounting

Accounting for stocks and flows of natural resources in both physical and monetary terms, that is, Natural Resource Accounting

Aggregation and reporting of organizational-level accounting information, natural resource accounting information, and other information for national accounting purposes

Consideration of environment-related physical and monetary information in the broader context of sustainability accounting[2]

Sustainability Accounting

Sustainability Accounting is based on the prior presentation of Financial, Managerial, and Environmental Accounting concepts. A complicating issue is that all of these accounting models combine and allocate costs in a manner that sometimes makes sustainability decisions very difficult. An accounting methodology that is commonly used is the method of "joint costing." In the process of producing a group of products, all of the costs that are incurred are pooled into this joint cost until individual products can be clearly identified. This identification point is referred to as the split-off point. There are several accepted methods for allocating these joint costs to the identified products, but these methods are not a concern of this discussion. The joint processing of raw materials will include a combination of costs. These costs will consist of actual processing costs and environmental costs that are incurred to reach the split-off point.

The Financial Accounting model does not require that these costs are accounted for separately. They are simply grouped together as the cost of production and then allocated to the products when they can be identified. On the financial statements these costs will either be classified as inventory or cost of goods sold. Internally, management could set up more detailed classifications and track these cost separately, but these internal measurements would typically not be available for external evaluation purposes. A similar issue related to accounting for waste was discussed in the ratio analysis section of this chapter.

Materials Flow Accounting

Table 9.1 presents the structure for the concept of physical accounting. Environmental information systems should contain data that traces the inputs in physical units within the defined system boundary. As the boundary becomes more specific the tracing of the input data becomes the task of input technicians rather than accountants. As previously mentioned in this chapter, financial statement accounting usually treats a significant portion of waste and emissions as product cost, but that is not an issue in this situation. Physical flow leads to measures of efficiency and effectiveness related to environmental management.

These measures of physical flow are necessary to evaluate the environmental impact related to the consumption of natural resources. A broad framework could look at the organization's use of water as a resource from the perspective of total fresh water consumed and total wastewater generated. A goal of environmental management would be to narrow this framework down to water consumption and wastewater produced per unit of product manufactured. This would allow the organization to evaluate the performance of environmental changes in the process, and this would lead to environmental decisions made in conjunction with financial and managerial decisions in terms of continued production of certain products or the use of certain processes.

Table 9.1 System Boundaries for Material Flow Balances

Input	*System Boundaries*	*Output*
	Nations	
Materials	Regions	Products
Energy	Corporations	Waste
Water	Processes	Emissions
	Products	

Converting physical flow quantities into costs becomes more complicated because of the existence of internal and external costs. Internal costs are linked with financial statement accounting and would be the basis for the financial and managerial decisions referred to in the prior paragraph. However, external costs are typically excluded from these internal decisions. Environmental pollution is an example of an issue that contains both internal and external costs. Internal costs would typically consist of prevention measures, monitoring costs, and site cleanup costs. External costs are borne by the public and cover a wide range of issues (i.e., health costs, property value, regional and national cleanup costs, etc.).

Within an organization the physical accounting can be analyzed as strictly an input-output concept. Table 9.2 excludes the system boundaries and expands the input and output categories. Inputs and outputs are based on materials and production and do not include capital items such as equipment, buildings, land, etc. Financial Accounting uses depreciation methods to reflect the use and aging of certain fixed assets. Although land is not depreciated, the flow of mineral resources in the land can be accounted for using depletion methods. Depletion methodology is not an environmental approach, but rather a financial approach that matches the costs of the product with the revenue generated from the sale of the product.

Table 9.2 is not a presentation of volume or costs. It is simply a description of the various inputs and outputs in the production process. This information could be incorporated in the accounting system as accounting classifications. Measures of volume and costs could be inserted in these classifications by following the formal mechanics of the accounting system. Environmental management decisions need to establish appropriate classifications and measurements in this context of physical flow accounting.

Table 9.2 Physical Materials Accounting: Input and Output Types

Materials Inputs	*Product Outputs*
Raw and auxiliary materials	Products (including packaging)
Packaging materials	By-products (including packaging)
Merchandise	Nonproduct Options (Waste and Emissions)
Operating materials	Solid waste
Water	Hazardous waste
Energy	Waste water
	Air emissions

Cost Categories

Financial statement accounting begins this concept with two basic categories of cost: product costs and period costs. The accounting system has many accounting classifications, but these are grouped into these two costs in terms of the proper accounting treatment. Product costs consist of all costs that are incurred to manufacture the product or provide the service. The financial statements of a manufacturing company will funnel all of these product costs to the asset, which is inventory, or the expense, which is cost of goods sold. Period costs become direct line items on the income statement.

Environmental accounting can also allocate detailed data into broad cost categories. Table 9.3 presents an example of cost categories that will allow various stakeholders to analyze costs following a common language for discussion.

Two of the categories in Table 9.3 need to be discussed in terms of financial statement accounting issues. For item number 5, the current accounting treatment of research and development (R&D) costs is to expense rather than capitalize these costs as an asset. FASB Statement No. 2 requiring that R&D be expensed was issued in 1974.

Financial accounting rules consider R&D as a single classification, and it is presented in the financial statements as a period expense. Breaking down R&D into environmental and nonenvironmental research can certainly be accomplished at the organizational level. However, one would need to understand that some of these categorizations might not be perfectly objective. Issues of an environmental nature may not even be present in the initial stages of basic research, but the environmental issues become evident in later stages of the research process. The question then becomes, should a portion of these costs incurred in the basic stages be allocated to the environmental category?

Table 9.3 Environment-Related Cost Categories

1. Material Costs of Product Outputs Includes the purchase costs of natural resources such as water and other materials that are converted into products, by-products, and packaging
2. Materials Costs of Nonproduct Outputs Includes the purchase (and sometimes processing) costs of energy, water, and other materials that become Nonproduct Output (Waste and Emissions).
3. Waste and Emission Control Costs Includes costs for handling, treatment, and disposal of Waste and Emissions; remediation and compensation costs related to environmental damage; and any control-related regulatory compliance costs
4. Prevention and Other Environmental Management Costs Includes the costs of preventive environmental management activities such as cleaner production projects. Also includes costs for other environmental management activities such as environmental planning and systems, environmental measurement, environmental communication, and any other relevant activities
5. Research and Development Costs Includes the costs for Research and Development projects related to environmental issues
6. Less Tangible Costs Includes both internal and external costs related to less tangible issues. Examples include liability, future regulations, productivity, company image, stakeholder relations, and externalities

This allocation decision is similar to the joint costing issues discussed in the Sustainability Accounting section of the chapter. Clearly these allocations would be less than perfectly objective. This lack of objectivity was financial accounting's primary reason for requiring that R&D be expensed rather than capitalized as an asset. The old capitalization guidelines considered the likelihood that the R&D would result in successful product development and production. This portion of R&D was capitalized as an intangible asset.

Item number 6 contains several issues that require some discussion. The title of the category, less tangible costs, identifies the issue of objective measurement. Financial accounting is based on the Historical Cost Principle. Forecasts are not presented in external financial statements. However, from an environmental perspective, future changes in costs because of future regulations should be considered as part of environmental management.

In a similar vein, let's consider the concept of contingent liabilities. Financial accounting, FASB Statement No. 5, breaks down these contingent liabilities into three categories: the likelihood of loss, the ability to estimate the amount of loss, and the timing of the event that created the situation. The accounting treatments range from creating a formal liability to providing footnote disclosure to doing nothing. The financial accounting rules begin with the premise that a legal action has been initiated, or that a governmental organization has initiated the process where a fine or specific duty could be assessed. The auditors, with legal consultation, would evaluate the likelihood of loss as either probable, reasonably possible, or remote. For an actual liability to be recorded in the financial statements for the contingency, the loss must be evaluated as probable, the amount of loss would be subject to reasonable estimation, and the corporate event that led to the legal or governmental action must have occurred in the period covered by the audited financial statements. If no action is initiated, then financial accounting does not consider the existence of the contingency.

Environmental management should consider future costs when assessing contingent liabilities. The following are company activities that may create these contingencies and duties to rectify the situation[3]:

- Groundwater contamination (e.g., from working with solvent-containing substances)
- Surface water contamination (e.g., from spills and transport damage)
- Air emissions (e.g., sudden releases due to a breakdown of pollution treatment equipment)
- Energy emissions (e.g., radioactive emissions)
- Soil contamination (e.g., from containment surface water)

Duties may be required so that the company can fix the above problems:

- Duty to adapt the equipment and procedures to state of the art
- Duty to remove and recycle wastes
- Remediation and disposal duties
- Cleanup of contaminated sites

Environmental management does not believe that forecasting future violations and investigations is realistic. However, estimates of future costs to repair damage to the environment that has already occurred and has been investigated is a reasonable requirement.

Ontario Hydro Case Study

This case study introduces the concept of full cost accounting. Ontario Hydro is the largest utility in North America in terms of installed generating capacity. Ontario's definition of full cost accounting is as follows:

Full Cost Accounting (FCA) is a means by which environmental considerations can be integrated into business decisions. FCA incorporates environmental and other internal costs, with external impacts and cost/benefits of Ontario Hydro's activities on the environment and on human health. In cases where the external impacts cannot be monetized qualitative evaluations are used.[4]

Internal costs are the basic costs of performing business functions, and they are accounted for using the normal financial accounting model. External impacts relate to effects on the environment and human health that result from the organization's activity. The costs of the external impacts are borne by society, and they are not included in the costs of products and services using the traditional financial accounting model. When possible, Ontario Hydro has included monetized, external cost estimates, and impact costs into its performance reports.

Sustainable Development

Ontario Hydro believes that the use of FCA is a key component in its focus on sustainable development. Its chairman, Maurice F. Strong, made the following statement concerning the necessity of sustainable development:

Sustainable development is a matter of economic survival in a world of finite resources and unlimited desire for growth. For present and future generations to enjoy a good quality of life, government, industry, and individuals need to become ever more efficient in the use of materials and energy, minimizing wastes through recycling and reuse, and develop new disposal methods.[5]

Ontario Hydro has extended this concept to Sustainable Energy Development (SED). It believes that its strategic plan should stress SED actions that integrate environmental and economic decision making and adopt FCA. The company has articulated several reasons for supporting FCA[6]:

- ***Improved environmental cost management*** – improve identification, allocation, tracking, and management of environmental costs in each business unit.

- ***Cost avoidance*** – improve the ability of business units to anticipate future environmental liabilities and costs so that corrective action can be implemented earlier.
- ***Revenue enhancement*** – improve the ability of business units to identify revenue enhancement opportunities either through environmental technology innovations spurred by cost-cutting initiatives or by strategic alliances with companies that use waste products as material inputs in their own manufacturing.
- ***Improved decision making*** – aid business units to better integrate environment into decision analysis.
- ***Environmental quality improvement*** – establish an optimal level for reducing emissions/effluents/wastes with consideration for the least cost to society.
- ***Contribution to environmental policy*** – contribute effectively to the development of environmental regulation/standards and emission trading markets.
- ***Sustainable development*** – assist in the transition to a more sustainable energy future.

The above reasons were developed for their potential to assist Ontario Hydro in its decision-making efforts. The decisions surrounding these reasons are primarily related to the insurance of compliance with environmental regulations and environmental implications of various proposed projects. Questions that Ontario Hydro needed to consider are as follows[7]:

- What are the environmental implications of this proposal? What environmental approvals are required?
- Does this proposal comply with existing environmental regulations? Is there sufficient flexibility to respond to more stringent, future environmental regulations?
- Is this proposal consistent with existing corporate environmental initiatives?
- Will this proposal contribute to a policy of sustainable development; for example, will waste products be recycled? Has energy efficient equipment been incorporated?
- Will this proposal create a significant public concern—real or perceived? If so, then what measures are being considered to offset this effect?
- What are the environmental alternatives for/to this proposal? What are the relative merits of these alternatives?

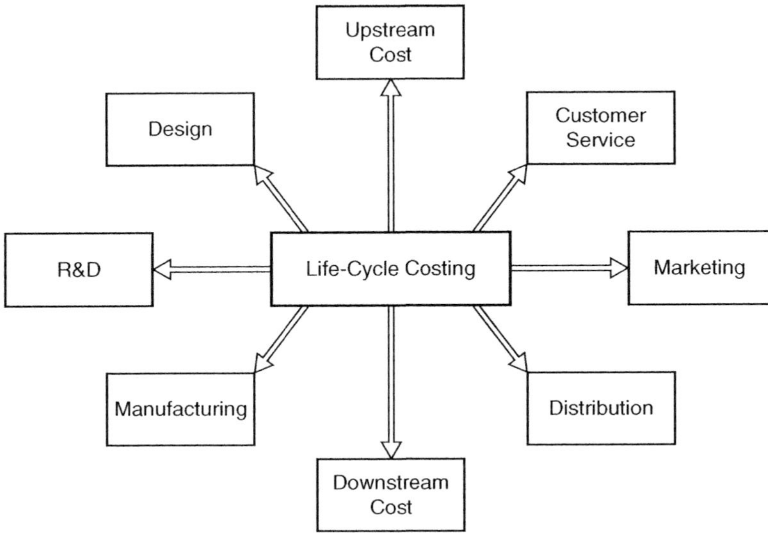

Figure 9.1 Life-Cycle Costing elements.

The combination of SED and FCA has moved Ontario Hydro towards the managerial concept of Life-Cycle Costing. This concept clearly relates to decision making rather than financial statement presentation. Figure 9.1 is a continuum of the Life-Cycle Costing concept.

The main concept with Life-Cycle Costing is that the system is not focused on determining manufacturing costs (i.e., financial statement accounting for the measurement of inventory costs), but rather the actual cost of delivering the product to the client, which is more consistent with a complete picture of the product in terms of decision making. The best way to explain the difference is that life cycle cost covers the continuum from research and development through customer service. In other words, the cost of a particular product or service is well beyond the actual costs attached to the production of inventory in the financial statement accounting context.

A brief summary of what Ontario Hydro has learned in combining these various concepts is that full costing has provided a picture that integrates environmental and business issues. Understanding costs of environmental impacts combined with business activities allows Ontario Hydro to make decisions that make "good business sense." The company understands that developing and implementing FCA will be a gradual process, but that this integration is necessary, and it will yield many environmental, economic, and competitiveness benefits.

The company also understands that it needs to have an understanding of the links between internal and external environmental costs. It also understands that these links are not static, but dynamic. As companies expand their internal cost domain this will lead to a corresponding reduction in the external cost domain. This control shift from external to internal impacts and costs is consistent with an organization that has made a serious commitment to sustainable development.

Green Accounting at AT&T: Case Study

The definition of "Green Accounting" is primarily based on environmental materials and activities. The concept of Green Accounting is primarily linked with environmental decision making. Basically, it has nothing to do with financial statement accounting. AT&T considers internal costs, which are labeled as "private costs." These are very similar to what Ontario Hydro labeled as internal environmental costs. At this stage AT&T is not considering "societal costs," which in prior discussions have been classified as externalities. AT&T's focus has been primarily related to customer expectations. Customers have been mainly concerned with three issues:

1. Measurement and control of chemical and material emissions
2. Environmental concerns of product packaging
3. Recycling of old products relative to new sales contracts

AT&T's primary goal has been to improve customer satisfaction by meeting or exceeding these environmental goals.

These goals are similar to the concept of Total Quality Management (TQM). The basic characteristic of TQM is focused on customer satisfaction. An organization tries to continually improve this relationship by fully involving the entire workforce. Both "bottom-up" and "top-down" focuses need to be considered. The "bottom-up" focus is primarily related to line employees providing inputs to manage and change company policies. The "top-down" focus needs the support and active involvement of top management to address potential changes.

In order for TQM to be functional, clear and objective measures of performance need to be established. Quality achievements need to be recognized in a periodic and timely manner. A critical overview of TQM is that employees and management must be continuously involved in the process of training and evaluation of TQM performance. AT&T has created a "Green Accounting" team that is

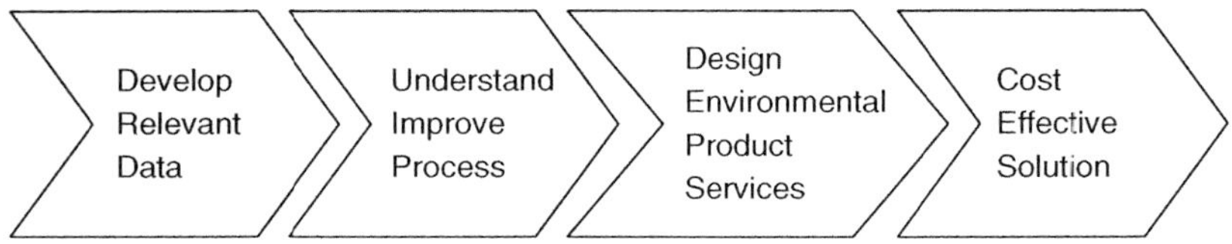

Figure 9.2 DfE flow of thoughts.

focused on the concept of customer satisfaction. As a subset of this overall goal of customer satisfaction, the team concluded that control and links to costs with green activities was necessary. Management and investment decisions related to current and future impacts in compliance with environmental standards were also necessary. As an overall concept, the linkage of customer desires needs to be considered in order to achieve sustainable profitable growth.

AT&T has recognized that "Green Accounting" needs to consider different functions and perspectives related to Design for Environment (DfE) (e.g., environmental, process/product design, research and development, and marketing). The DfE leads to economic considerations that lead to the flow of thought shown in Figure 9.2.

This flow structure attempts to consider the linkage with goals that minimize environmental harm, control costs, and avoid contingent liabilities. It also tries to provide evidence of compliance with voluntary and regulatory guidelines.

Activity-Based Costing

The AT&T case specifically addressed the issue of applying the "Activity-Based Costing/Management" approach to "Green Accounting." Activity-Based Costing is a management accounting technique that is concerned with the allocation of indirect manufacturing costs to product. Financial statement accounting principles have a basic rule that these indirect costs must be allocated in a "reasonable" manner. Traditional accounting overhead allocation allows for one large pool of indirect costs to be allocated based on the behavior of a single cost driver. The single cost driver traditionally is budgeted labor hours, labor dollars, or machine hours.

Activity-Based Costing has broken down this single overhead cost pool into multiple pool activities and used different cost drivers, based on the concept of causation, for each pool of activities. The AT&T case suggests identifying environmental pool activities as unique and separate activities. These activities could be allocated to specific plants or processes to evaluate the environmental impact of their performances.

AT&T has suggested activity drivers related to volume of waste, compliance procedures, inputs and outputs of materials, and performance measures (e.g., percent of recycled materials). Clearly, these allocations are subjective and based on estimates, but the primary concept is to develop a better sense of the costs of these various environmental activities. The selection of cost drivers must be linked with causation. If changes in the driver are not linked with actual changes in the underlying cost, then it is an inappropriate driver. Ideally the driver measurements would be objective and quantitative, but subjectivity and estimates will work as long as they are consistently created every period.

This is tied into the concept of Activity-Based Management. AT&T has identified several items as a management focus: evaluating product and process design, evaluating supplier qualifications in terms of environmental issues, evaluating process performance in terms of efficiency and waste, and environmental product disposal alternatives.

The AT&T Green Accounting team, in reviewing the actual information process at AT&T, concluded that the underlying data within the organization was not readily available to identify these environmental costs. The environmental costs were not separately identified. These costs were typically allocated to product overhead, research and development, or general and administrative overhead.

The Green Accounting team's basic conclusion assessed the AT&T plants' ability to learn how to identify and trace environmental costs and cost recoveries to specific products. A major project of the Green Accounting team was the development of its self-assessment tool. The tool consisted of the following items:

1. Status Survey – identify weaknesses in existing decision processes.
2. Environmental Activities Dictionary – definitions related to activities, resources, liabilities, residues, and wastes.
3. Activities/Resource Matrix – identify activities matched with related resources.
4. Protocols – sugg.estions and guidance on using the self-assessment tool.

This tool is still in the development stage, but the Green Accounting team believes that this will aid AT&T in creating environmental cost pools and assist it in identifying appropriate cost drivers that have objective measures that can be used in allocating costs in a causal manner.

The case specifically identifies that the next step beyond the design stage in the development of the assessment tool is the use of pilot locations for the detailed acquisition of environmental data, the development of guidelines for methods of assigning costs (appropriate cost drivers), the development of reporting standards by the financial division of AT&T, and the distribution of the package to AT&T business units for actual use.

Future goals involve estimates of contingent liabilities related to product life so that they can be predicted, allowing for the establishment of reserves in the environmental cost estimates. AT&T would also like to develop a better understanding of relevant versus nonrelevant data. The basic issue is to not waste critical resources trying to rectify nonrelevant events. Creating more precise definitions of inputs, outputs, and drivers will allow AT&T to have a better understanding of the relationship with Cost of Quality categories.

The Greenhouse Gas (GHG) Protocol

The protocol is a multinational effort to establish accounting and reporting standards for the measurement and disclosure of GHG emissions. The document's reference to accounting is entirely related to record keeping of the emission results. It has nothing to do with theoretical valuation concepts and the related financial statement preparations. However, the accounting structure was based on legitimate nonvaluation principles (i.e., relevance, completeness, consistency, transparency, and accuracy). These principles provided guidance to the construction of the GHG inventory.

The GHG Inventory

This inventory is basically a package of tools for measuring, evaluating, reporting, and controlling emissions. The use of the word inventory has nothing to do with the financial accounting concept of inventory. Financial accounting considers inventory as product held for resale. The inventory has guidelines for setting environmental targets and measuring progress towards business goals.

Organizations want their GHG inventory to assist in achieving multiple goals. The protocol presents the following framework to identify and describe these goals.

Business Goals Served by GHG Inventories[8]

Managing GHG Risks and Identifying Reduction Opportunities

- Identifying risks associated with GHG constraints in the future
- Identifying cost-effective reduction opportunities
- Setting GHG targets and measuring and reporting progress

Public Reporting and Participation in Voluntary GHG Programs

- Voluntary stakeholder reporting of GHG emissions and progress towards GHG targets
- Reporting to government and nongovernmental organizations' reporting programs, including GHG registries
- Eco-labeling and GHG certification

Participating in Mandatory Reporting Programs

- Participating in government reporting programs at the national, regional, or local level

Participating in GHG Markets

- Supporting internal GHG trading programs
- Participating in external cap and trade allowance trading programs
- Calculating carbon/GHG taxes

Recognition for Early Voluntary Action

- Providing information to support "baseline protection" and credit for early action

In addition to these goals, the accounting system related to this record keeping should clearly establish control in the meaning, recording, internal feedback, and reporting of these measured results. The organization should prepare and maintain a clear, methodological procedures manual that would be the initial underlying documentation that supports these accounting records. This manual would identify the required techniques, types of measurement, underlying assumptions, and defined inputs and outputs.

The documentation of the process and the existence of quality control are necessary to be in compliance with the accounting principles identified in the basic structure of the report. The results of the inventory tools must be measurable on a consistent and accurate basis, and they must be communicated in a similar manner. Internal or external stakeholders will not attach value to noncredible or poorly communicated results. Controls are also needed to assure that input data is appropriate and properly recorded. Data documentation needs to be reviewed so that assurances exist that the documentation template has been followed. Finally, the most important controls relate to the procedures methodology, the underlying calculations, and the recording and reporting of the results.

Summary

This chapter discussed a number of accounting-related issues in terms of the overall concepts of environment and sustainability. One finding is that the basic underlying financial accounting standards are occasionally in conflict with the needs of accounting for environment and sustainability. The financial accounting focus of objectively measuring defined assets and liabilities often handles environmental costs as simply a part of the costing process and lumps these costs into the overhead cost pool. AT&T's focus on activity-based costing would allow for identifying these environmental costs for internal reporting.

The financial accounting treatment of contingent liabilities is too rigid for environmental decision purposes. Environmental management should estimate the likelihood of an action being taken against the organization and also estimate the potential liabilities related to cleanup costs and related fines if environmental pollution occurs. Financial accounting does not recognize a contingency unless an action has been initiated and the process of determining a potential liability has begun.

Managerial accounting is more consistent with the goals of environmental management and sustainability accounting. The focus for all of these accounting environments is that accounting must compliment and improve management decisions. The most significant problem for environmental and sustainability accounting is lack of a consistent framework of accounting classifications that are consistent with related management decisions and goals. The chapter also illustrates that several existing managerial methodological approaches are potentially very useful as environmental and sustainability tools. Full costing, used by Ontario Hydro, and activity-based costing, used by AT&T, can be extremely useful if the underlying accounting classifications can be expanded to address the needs of environmental and sustainability goals.

Notes

1. E.J. Blocher, D.E. Stout, G. Cokins, and K.H. Chen, *Cost Management*, (McGraw Hill Irwin, 2008): 42–43.
2. "Environmental Management Accounting," *International Federation of Accountants* (August 2005): 12–14.
3. "Environmental Management Accounting Procedures and Principles," *Expert Working Group, United Nations Division for Sustainable Development* (2001): 23–24.
4. Ontario Hydro's Corporate Guidelines for Full Cost Accounting, September 1995.
5. Ontario Hydro's Case Study, ICF Incorporated (1996): 14.
6. Ibid., 20.
7. Ibid., 21–22.
8. Ibid., pp. 14.

CHAPTER 10

Promoting Sustainable Consumption

Nasrin R. Khalili, Whynde Melaragno, and Ghazale Haddadian

Consumption patterns could play a central role in promoting sustainability. Sustainable consumption is an umbrella that brings together a number of key issues, such as meeting society's needs, enhancing quality of life, improving product efficiency, minimizing waste, and taking a life cycle perspective, while taking into account the equity dimensions. Discussions on sustainable consumption are focused on the important role of businesses, particularly corporate strategies in developing sustainable consumption and production patterns. The terms, logistics, and factors impacting sustainable consumption are presented and the need for development of frameworks and policies that can enhance consumers' knowledge and behavior are discussed in this chapter. The emphasis has been placed on the role of government, education, and corporate strategies to promote sustainable consumption in support of sustainable development.

Introduction

Shifts in the scale and pattern of consumption are likely to be one of the most effective strategies for promoting sustainability. Meeting such an objective requires change in production efficiency, design of the products, and the expectations, choices, behavior, and life style of consumers. These factors are identified to be the main driving forces of the emerging concept of sustainable consumption.

The term sustainable consumption was first introduced by Agenda 21—the main policy document that emerged from the Rio Earth Summit in 1992. The United Nations Commission on

Sustainable Development (CSD) initiated an international work program for changing production and consumption patterns in 1995. At the "Rio plus 5" conference in 1997, governments identified sustainable consumption as an "overriding issue" and a "cross-cutting theme" in the sustainable development debate. Sustainable consumption was also given special attention at the 7th session of the CSD in 1999. In the same year, the Oxford Commission on Sustainable Consumption launched with the aim of formulating an "Action Plan" on sustainable consumption for the World Summit on Sustainable Development (WSSD). The United Nations Environment Programme (UNEP) launched a sustainable consumption network and incorporated sustainable consumption policies into the Consumer Protection Guidelines.

In 2001 a strategic document was published underlining the opportunities afforded by the new sustainable consumption focus. The following year, the UNEP also published a strategic review of progress towards sustainable consumption. By the time the WSSD assembled in 2002, "changing consumption and production patterns" had been recognized as one of three "overarching objectives" for sustainable development.[1]

What Is Sustainable Consumption?

Sustainable consumption is a balancing act. It is about consuming in such a way that the environment and quality of life are protected without compromising the lives of future consumers.[2] The special focus of sustainable consumption is on the economic activity of choosing, using, and disposing of goods and services and how this can be changed to bring social and environmental benefit. Sustainable consumption also supports the ability of current and future generations to meet their material and other needs, without causing irreversible damage to the environment or loss of function in natural systems. Sustainable consumption, however, is not about consuming differently; rather, it is about consuming efficiently and having an improved quality of life.[3]

According to the UNEP, sustainable consumption is an umbrella term that brings together a number of key issues, such as meeting the needs of society, enhancing quality of life, improving efficiency, minimizing waste, taking a life cycle perspective, and taking into account the equity dimension. The question is, however, how to integrate these components and develop policies that can provide for the basic requirements of life and the aspiration for improvements for both current and future generations while continually reducing environmental damage and the risk to human health.[4]

Sustainable consumption does not mean consuming less; it means consuming sustainably[5] by choosing sustainable products. Promoting sustainable consumption should emphasize both life style change and product development via the use of improved technologies, innovations in product design, and the supply of more eco-efficient products, services, and infrastructures when addressing sustainable consumption.

Why Sustainable Consumption?

Confronting consumption and seeking to influence consumer behavior and understand the process of lifestyle change are increasingly important topics for sustainable development.[6] There are distinct criticisms of conventional consumption patterns as they tend to create inequality and social and political tensions. This concern is mentioned in the UNEP's global status report, which discusses the "distorted" geography and demography of consumption. For example, it reported that meat consumption, water use, and electricity use per capita in the Northern Hemisphere are about 3.3, 3, and 10 times more, respectively, than those estimated in the Southern Hemisphere. Consumption is also closely associated to environmental pressure and resource use. OECD suggested that resource efficiency improvements are unlikely to be able to deliver the global factor of four-to-ten reductions in energy and material use that have been agreed upon as a condition for sustainability.[7] Also, the consumption habits of the average U.S. citizen require eighteen tons of natural resources per person per year and generate an even higher volume of wastes (including household, industrial, mining, and agricultural).[8] These trends do not indicate that consumption contributes to an improvement in human well-being as growing numbers of studies find that people in industrialized countries do not feel any happier or more satisfied as average income grows beyond the level to meet ba physical needs.

There are many potential opportunities to achieve sustair ity through sustainable consumption. Examples include sus energy consumption of households by replacing obsolete appliances with new ones, and building and renovati efficient housing using nontoxic materials. Renewable be more available for household use by establishing cooperation and networks among NGOs and partnerships with business and government.[9]

Although consumption plays a central role in sustainable global development, when we question consumption, we are judging living patterns and lifestyles, a notion that is difficult to suggest or carry out without categorizing factors that control or impact consumption patterns or formulating strategies that can justify and promote a sustainable consumption.

Consumption and Consumer Behavior

According to the theory of *evolution*, consumer behavior is conditioned, in part at least, by sexual competition, show-off, and status-seeking behaviors. Veblen's notion of *conspicuous consumption* and Hirsch's concept of *positional goods* both point to the importance of material goods in social positioning.[10] While "goods" communicate belongingness, affiliation, group identity, commitment to particular ideals, and distance from certain other ideals, ordinary everyday consumption is about *convenience, habit, practice, and individual responses to social and institutional norms.*

The main factors that influence consumer behavior and choice of products could be classified as those associated with the GDP index, business strategies used for product marketing, level of consumer education, government policies, cultural values, and product characteristics and specifications.

According to the 2008 World Bank development indicators, in 2005 the wealthiest 20% of the world accounted for 76.6% of total private consumption while the poorest one-fifth accounted for only 1.5%. Businesses spend millions of dollars each year to promote their products through various marketing campaigns. Ever-growing numbers of marketing consulting companies indicate that marketing plays a crucial role in product selection by customers. In fact, through advertising, business helps to set trends that influence consumer demand. According to Chad Holliday et al.,[11] it is logical to believe that marketing and advertising have the power to shift purchasing behavior that can enhance rather than hinder sustainability.

Education is a critical factor as well. The more educated customers are the more likely they are to make informed decisions about a product and to consider its life cycle assessment before choosing it. Hafstrom suggested that education will affect the expenditures of families differently for various categories of goods. For example, education of the father influences the expenditures of families, especially those for "future" goods.[12] Government policies, as mentioned, can play a pivotal role in changing consumer behaviors over time. The conventional view of sustainable consumption policy is based on one of two specific roles for government: The first role is one in which government tries to understand and control consumer behavior from the outside via setting regulations and standards, market instruments, and planning. For example, behavior in developed countries can be changed by limiting or regulating the consumption of nonseasonal food. The second role is one in which government seeks to influence consumers through information, education, and other psychological measures, for example, use of taxes and incentives.[13]

Culture is one of the external influences that impact the consumer. That is, culture represents influences that are imposed on the consumer by other individuals.[14] The characteristics of the product, the price, and the convenience also influence consumer selection significantly.[15]

Green Consumers? Do They Buy Sustainable Products?

As people become more concerned with their impact on the environment, the green consumer category will continue to grow. Businesses are also recognizing this phenomenon and are capitalizing on the emerging market for environmentally friendly goods and services. If the goal is to establish new and more sustainable ways of living, we should understand how consumers choose a products, who the green consumers are, and why they are green.[16] According to the 2010 State of Green Business Forum, only about 7% of consumers are motivated by altruism; the majority are motivated by the benefits of the product. For example, some people may buy energy efficient appliances to save money, while others may pay a premium for natural cosmetics because they are perceived as safer than conventional products. This highlights the importance of education and the role companies must play in educating costumers about green products and the company's impacts on the environment.[17]

A global survey of 7,751 consumers in eight major economies was conducted in 2007 by McKinsey & Company. The survey showed that 87% of consumers are concerned about the environmental and social impacts of the products they buy, but when it comes to actually buying green goods, only 33% of consumers said that they ready to buy green products or have already done so.

According to a 2007 Chain Store Age survey of 822 U.S. consumers, only 25% said they have purchased a green product other than organic food or energy efficient lighting. Organic foods, which consumers buy more for their own health than for the environment's, accounted for less than 3% of all food sales in 2006. In the same year, green laundry detergents and household cleaners made up less than 2% of sales in their categories. And despite their trendiness, hybrid cars made up little more than 2% of the U.S. auto market in 2007, according to a report by J.D. Power and Associates.

Role of Businesses?

According to a global survey, 61% of consumers say that corporations should take the lead in tackling the issue of climate change.[18] Businesses should consider the demographic characteristics of consumers who are interested in sustainable products. The major shift should not be to reduce consumption, but rather to promote consumption of sustainable products that can prosper within a strategy of sustainable development.[19] Trust and long-term thinking are critical elements for addressing sustainable behavior by businesses.[20]

The future leading companies will be those who, through their core businesses, help society manage its major challenges. For example, a company could create a sustainable product whose manufacturing, purchase, and use allows for economic development while still conserving resources for future generations and imposing minimal or no harm to the environment.

Consumption Opportunities

The consumption opportunities approach, which was first raised at the Rio Earth Summit, takes a broad strategic view of sustainable consumption and claims that green consumerism is a random and subjective act. It is ineffective in developed economies and often irrelevant in developing and transitional economies.

The consumption opportunities concept attempts to describe various problems with the concept of sustainable consumption since it was first raised at the Rio Earth Summit. For example, it presents reservations and so examines the link between sustainable consumption and sustainable development.

In practice, the consumption opportunities approach sets out a cycle of responsibility that links the actions of each stakeholder to other stakeholders in a strategic, positive, and mutually supportive way. The strategic elements of the approach include "Dematerialization" and "Optimization" of consumption patterns as presented in Figure 10.1. Dematerialization refers to efficient consumption of goods and services, in which the amount of resources used per unit of consumption is radically reduced. The Optimization of consumption patterns is, however, more involved and as such presents different terms for consumption and altered framework for economic and social choice.

Figure 10.1 presents the strategic elements of consumption opportunities and associated contributing agents. As shown, the consumption opportunities approach helps to divide up the responsibilities among various stakeholders. For example, Industry is primarily responsible for dematerialization leading to Efficient Consumption. The term "Conscious Consumption," however, refers to cases in which engaged consumers are searching for quality across a wide set of issues. "Appropriate Consumption" is perceived and described as consumption that is just one way to the high quality of life.[21]

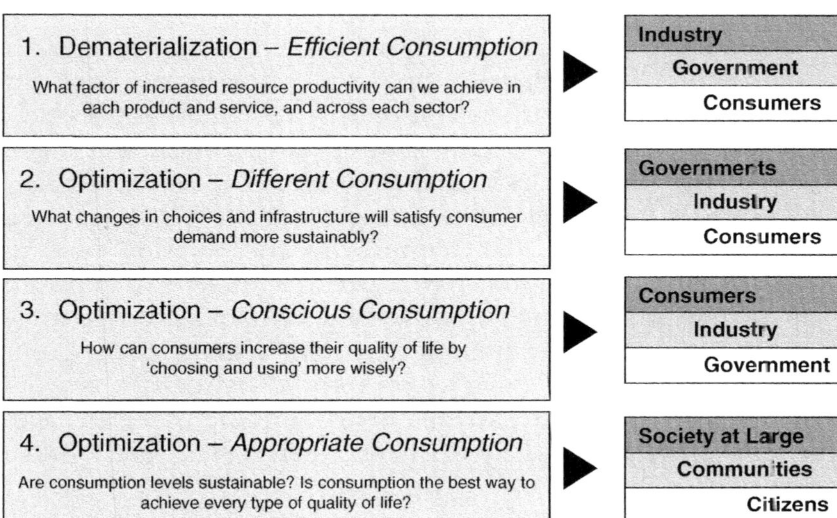

Figure 10.1 Sustainable consumption opportunities related to strategic elements and contributing major agents (adopted from UNEP, "Sustainable Consumption Opportunities," Ministry for Protection of Natural Resources and Environment, Republic of Serbia Belgrade, United Nations Environment Programme, March 21–22, 2002)

Shaping Consumption Patterns

Before suggesting any model or formulating a framework for changing consumption patterns, we must review and understand the most recognized corrective actions/policy suggestions targeting consumption and its current patterns. Tim Jackson proposed three main areas that sustainable consumption should target[22]: reducing the motivation for positional consumption, addressing social inequity, and promoting social and ethical "goods."

The drivers of the change could be socioeconomic factors, cultural values, product information (good and services), and political and institutional systems. For example, consumers could be locked into a process of unsustainable consumption over which they have very little control. The vital role of governments and businesses in this case is to make necessary institutional changes to assist consumers with their choices.

Diversity in consumption patterns could be by itself a force for change. The questions would then be whether diversity can be selected as a driver for changing consumption patterns and whether policies and trends should be developed with a focus on small groups. For example, policies could be put into place to promote sustainable consumption trends through the media, celebrities, businesses, governments, or other institutions.

Consumption patterns are also well correlated with every aspect of the culture. For example, in Britain a small minority of citizens makes considerable efforts to consume as sustainably as possible. A larger, growing minority is choosing ethical products. The majority is concerned about social and environmental issues, but places a low priority on them in their current consumption choices. Understanding the various "cultures of consumption" and the "values," "worldview," and "narratives" that underlie them would help the government and businesses in developing effective strategies for sustainable consumption in specific regions. Some groups would respond best to "market incentives," while others would respond best to "information and opportunities for engagement," and still others are unlikely to change their habits unless "forced by regulation."[23]

Promoting Sustainable Consumption

This section introduces some specific strategies for promoting sustainable consumption.

Use of Eco-Technologies to Produce Green Products. Consumption patterns, which are a dynamic system, will naturally change in the future by the forces of social, environmental, and economic factors such as global warming, increase or decrease in income, and welfare. For example, consumption patterns could change due to an increase in consumption as the three billion people with incomes of less than $3 per day, or 800 million people in developing and transition countries, earn enough to move into the high-consuming classes. The question becomes how we should frame future consumption in order to protect our natural environment. Eco-technologies such as energy efficiency, pollution controls, waste management, recycling, cradle-to-cradle products, and the zero-emissions industry have provided higher consumption with lower waste and environmental problems. The eco-technologies are now worth $600 billion per year, on par with the global car industry. There are big profits ahead for truly enterprising businesses.[24]

Some of the barriers to consumers selecting sustainable products is lack of awareness, the negative perceptions of their effectivness, distrust of green claims, and higher prices. Consumers have to be aware that a product exists before they buy it. However, due to the lack of correct marketing or inadequate communication, many don't even know about the green alternatives in many product categories. Consumers also must believe that a product will get the job done in order to buy it. Again, as a result of poor use of technology or communication, many believe that green products are of lower quality than their traditional counterparts. Price is also a very important driver. Consumers must decide whether a product is worth the cost and effort needed to purchase it. Businesses could significantly impact consumer behavior by making them aware of eco-friendly products and their benefits.

The importance of each barrier varies by product, industry, and geography. For instance, more than 90% of consumers who participated in the McKinsey global survey know about compact fluorescent light bulbs (CFLs), so lack of awareness is not a barrier to their purchasing them. But many customers think CFLs are too expensive and of dubious quality. Region, culture, and education also have a significant impact on the purchase of sustainable products. In the retail sector, for example, 14% of U.S. consumers say they are willing to pay a premium for green products, compared to 26% in Brazil. In the petroleum sector, 7% of French consumers are willing to pay a premium, compared to 26% in India.[25]

The 6-Step Approach to Promoting Sustainable Consumption

A "6-Step Solution" has been proposed to assist businesses with their journey toward promoting sustainable consumption and use of green products.[26]

Step 1: Educate Customers via Effective Green Advertising. According to the International Institute for Sustainable Development (IISD), understanding **the demographic characteristics of green consumers** would help businesses make more educated decisions while planning for their effective advertising practices.[27] For example, many young adults are influenced by their young children, women make choices for men, or consumers born before 1950 are the least green.

Through advertising, businesses can help to set trends that influence consumer demand. Green advertising campaigns by companies could be effective if businesses did the following:

- Educate consumers with marketing messages that connect environmental product attributes with desired consumer value (e.g., "pesticide-free produce is healthier," "energy efficiency saves money," or "solar power is convenient").
- Frame environmental product attributes as "solutions" for consumer needs, for example, "rechargeable batteries offer longer performance."
- Create engaging and educational websites about environmental products' desired value.
- Encourage positive word of mouth via consumers' social and Internet communication networks with compelling, interesting, or entertaining information about environmental products.[28]

Businesses must also tie product specifications and environmental attributes to the lifestyle of the consumers. For example, hikers care about the wetlands, while boaters are concerned about clean water. Effective marketing also requires that companies align their business with other eco-efficient businesses.

Step 2: Build Better Products. Consumers value performance, reliability, and durability much more than a product's ecological soundness. Indeed, to overcome their image problem, green products must often outperform their traditional counterparts. Toyota had to tackle early perceptions that the Prius had less power than nonhybrid cars by redesigning the Prius to meet the performance and style preferences of consumers. The carmaker increased the horsepower and conducted a campaign promoting the vehicle as "quick, roomy, and economical."

Step 3: Be Honest. To rebuild public trust, companies must report to the public about their true environmental impact, as well as about their efforts to reduce that impact. Many will need to identify and address specific historical concerns about their products or operations. Only then will consumers trust the company's earth-friendly claims. Telling consumers they should act green when the company itself is making little effort to improve its own operations would only lead to criticism. For example, the low-price airline Ryanair Ltd., which advertised itself as the industry leader in environmental efficiency, received significant negative press when CEO Michael O'Leary confessed that his claim that the airline had cut emissions of carbon dioxide by half over the past five years was an "error."

Step 4: Offer More and Show Environmental and Financial Benefits. Companies must make sure that consumers understand the returns, both financial and environmental, on their investment in order to increase sales of green products. When consumers find it easy to track their savings from using a product, they are more willing to try new green products, especially those that cost more. For example, the Prius's value goes well beyond functionality. The Prius caught consumers' attention because it had a unique and modern style that signaled the owners' commitment to the environment. Its dashboard communicates fuel consumption and energy efficiency, thereby broadcasting the car's environmental benefits.

Step 5: Bring Products to People. Companies cannot sell their products if consumers cannot find them. It sounds obvious, but many of today's green products are not widely available. Toyota has increased production of the Prius since 1999 by an average of 50% per year by communicating its intent to make the Prius widely available by running ads that say, "We've significantly increased production on the hard-to-find, easy-to-drive Toyota Prius."

Step 6: Make Sustainable Purchasing Easy. Companies must make green purchasing easy by communicating the product's environmental impact information in a very clear, simple, and easy to understand manner: consumers don't want to work hard, and more importantly, they don't want to be mini-scientists. For example, by selling only highly concentrated laundry detergent Wal-Mart makes it difficult to not make a green choice.[29]

Environmental Labeling versus Advertising

Eco-labels mainly rely on moral persuasion by influencing the customer's attitude toward protecting the environment and choosing eco-products or products with a reduced impact on the environment. Most eco-labels are based on the Life Cycle Assessment (LCA) of a product. An LCA educates the consumer about the environmental impact across the stages of a product's life cycle. According to the consumer study Eco Pulse 2009, by the Shelton Group, product labels are more important to helping consumers identify green products than advertising. Of course, untruthful labels can be illegal, by breaking Fair Trade Commission standards, or labels can be considered "green washing" by consumers, so creating an effective label can be challenging. The creation of standards is vital due to the lack of trust in the marketplace. The UL Environment is currently creating standards for green building products that will assist the LEED building certification process.[30]

The best eco-labels are seals or logos signifying that an independent organization has verified that a product meets a set of meaningful and consistent standards for environmental protection or social justice. The Consumers Union uses the following criteria to evaluate eco-labels:

***Meaningful and verifiable*:** Eco-labels should have a set of environmentally meaningful standards. These standards should be verifiable by the certifier.

***Consistent and clear*:** An eco-label used on one product should have the same meaning if used on other products.

***Transparent*:** The organization behind an eco-label should make information about organizational structure, funding, board of directors, and certification standards available to the public.

***Independent and protected from conflict of interest*:** Organizations establishing standards and deciding who can use a logo should not have any ties to, and should not receive any funding from the sale of, certified products or contributions from logo users beyond fees for certification. Employees of companies whose products are certified, or who are applying for certification should not be on the board of directors of the certifier (and no one affiliated with the certifier should be on the board of directors of the organization being certified).

All certification standards should be developed with input from multiple stakeholders including consumers, industry, environmentalists, and social representatives in a way that doesn't compromise the independence of the certifier.[31]

Lowering consumption under current market conditions would not motivate most businesses since, generally, consumption must increase for businesses to survive and profit.

However, businesses can reap multiple benefits by promoting green products and sustainable consumption by using innovative business strategies that focus on consumer education and awareness. The more educated the consumers are the more likely they are to choose a sustainable product over its traditional counterpart. Companies, however, could face a few challenges when attempting to promote sustainable consumption:

- Producing green/sustainable products could be more costly compared to their conventional counterparts.
- The market for green products may not exist, or may be much smaller than that for their counterparts.
- Human, technological, and capital resources needed to support sustainable consumption and development of green products may be constraints.

These challenges can be fully addressed through the development of effective management strategies that can maximize both internal and external resources in support of sustainability movements.

Although businesses should play a leading role in the green movement in order to shape market opportunities and manage potential regulation of their industries, they cannot achieve this goal alone. The involvement of government and NGOs is crucially important to achieving long-lasting changes in consumer behavior. For example, Americans recycled less than 10% of their waste in 1980. Today, they recycle more than 30%. This significant change in consumer behavior was created through the combined efforts of governments, businesses, and nonprofits. Governments are already involved in the education process of societies. Example projects and sustainable consumption programs that can be supported via green consumption policies include those initiatives that can result in offering green products at a reduced price.

Companies that pursue the development of a market for green products and also invest in promoting sustainable behavior must be supported by appropriate policies and financial instruments such as tax breaks, low-rate loans, and subsidies. Educating consumers could lead to the development of a green market, higher sales volume, and profitability. In fact, in the long term, if designed, managed, and executed properly, sustainability projects would pay for themselves.

The negative impact on a company's assets, if any, can be compensated by the development of short- and long-term policies that can provide and allow for the financial support of such initiatives by the government or appropriate financial institutions. Figure 10.2 presents a three-phase financial scenario in support of sustainable consumption initiatives.

Obstacles to Sustainable Consumption

The central problem to reaching more sustainable patterns of consumption and production is internalizing the cost of environmental impacts into prices. Further obstacles to sustainable consumption include overconsumption in some groups and corruption in various sectors. Governments need to take the lead at the policy level, but the overall approach must be both top-down and bottom-up. In terms of bottom-up, the needs are first for *education*, then for *personal*

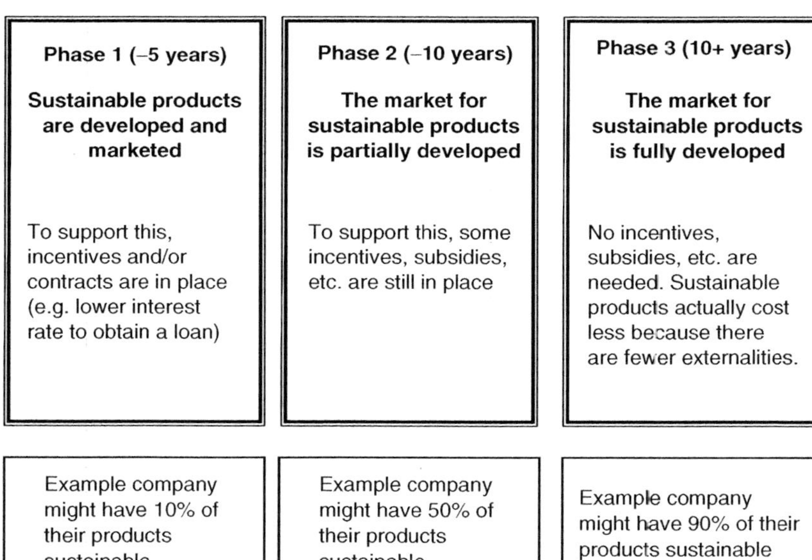

Figure 10.2 A three-phase financial scenario in support of sustainable consumption initiatives.

responsibility. Government could provide resources and substantial support to promote sustainable consumption. For example, governments could set up sectoral policy frameworks, establish model sustainable consumption programs in cities, and execute public awareness campaigns.[32]

Summary

The focus of this chapter is on effective communication practices and creating markets for sustainable products and services. Enhancing consumer, government, and financial institution knowledge and interest in sustainable product development and use eventually would benefit businesses, stakeholders, and more importantly, the environment that supports a sustainable future. Companies that invest in such efforts would benefit from revenues generated due to an increased market for sustainable products. In return, a well-developed market would allow them to reduce the price of green goods in such a way that it can benefit the consumers. Finally, the environment and society would benefit due to the low toxicity of green products and their minimal impact on resources. The aim here is to establish new and more sustainable ways of living, working, and producing " a new paradigm for life and happiness" and for these to become new habits. In fact, the leading companies of the future are those that, through their core businesses strategies, strive to help society manage the world's major challenges.

Case Studies

The Energy Star Success

This program, a joint effort launched by the EPA and the U.S. Department of Energy in 1992, educates consumers about how energy-efficient products can reduce energy use, save money, and protect the environment. Every product that meets government energy-efficiency standards can carry the Energy Star label, which has gained widespread consumer recognition and trust. Because federal regulations mandated energy labels on certain appliances, almost half of the air conditioners sold in the United States in 2005 carried the Energy Star label.[33]

Development of Index of Environmentally Sustainable Consumption

National Geographic has partnered with GlobeScan (www. GlobeScan.com) to develop an international research approach to measure and monitor consumer progress towards environmentally sustainable consumption. The key objectives of this survey were to provide regular quantitative measures of consumer behavior and to promote sustainable consumption. This research project focused on actual behavior and material lifestyles across 17 countries. Factors surveyed included household footprint, energy use, transportation habits, food consumption, and the relative penetration of green products versus traditional products. The results of this survey were used to develop a composite index of environmentally sustainable consumption called the Greendex. The Greendex will be used over time to monitor and report changes in consumer behavior. Each respondent earns a score that reflects the environmental impact of consumption patterns. Low scores signify greater environmental impacts and vice versa. Points are awarded or subtracted for specific forms of consumer behavior. Scoring does not provide any allowances according to the geography, climatic conditions where respondents live, culture, religion, or the relative availability of sustainable products.

Generally, Greendex scores in most countries have remained relatively stable since 2009 and often remain higher than the 2008 scores. However, Indians', Russians', and Americans' Greendex scores have increased notably. Greendex scores for Spanish, German, and South Korean consumers decreased modestly.[34]

Notes

1. Tim Jackson, "Motivating Sustainable Consumption: A Review of Evidence on Consumer Behavior and Behavioral Change," International Sustainability Workshop, May 19, 2005, pp. 4, 12.
2. Ibid., 2.
3. Sustainable Consumption & Production, Economic, regeneration Policies for Sustainable Consumption,"2003, a report to the Sustainable Development Commission, www.sd-commission.org.uk (accessed May 12, 2010), 14.
4. "Sustainable Consumption Opportunities",2002, Ministry for Protection of Natural Resources and Environment, Republic of Serbia, UNEP, http://postconflict.unep.ch/publications/scopeWeb.pdf (accessed September 16, 2010), 17.
5. Tim Jackson, Laurie Michaelis, "Policies for Sustainable Consumption." A report to the Sustainable Development Commission, May 20, 2003, p. 15.
6. Ibid., 5.

7. Ernst von Weizsäcker, A. Lovins, and L. Hunter Lovins, "Factor Four—Doubling Wealth, Halving Resource Use," *Earthscan* (March 15, 1997): 1–3.
8. Jonathan Harris, "Consumption and the Environment—Overview Essay," in *The Consumer Society*, eds. Neva R. Goodwin, Frank Ackerman, and David Kiron (Washington, DC: Island Press, 1997), 269.
9. UNEP, "Sustainable Consumption Opportunities," Ministry for Protection of Natural Resources and Environment, Republic of Serbia Belgrade, United Nations Environment Programme, March 21–22, 2002, p. 21.
10. Jeanne L. Hafstrom and Marilyn M. Dunsing, "Satisfaction and Education: A New Approach to Understanding Consumption Patterns," *Home Economics Research Journal* (September 1972): 3–5.
11. Chad Holliday, Stephan Schmidheiny, and Philip Watts, "Walking the Talk: The Business Case for Sustainable Development" (Sheffield: Greenleaf Publishing, 2002), 184.
12. Jeanne L. Hafstrom and Marilyn M. Dunsing, "Satisfaction and Education: A New Approach to Understanding Consumption Patterns," *Home Economics Research Journal* (September 1972): 1–3.
13. Tim Jackson and Laurie Michaelis, "Policies for Sustainable Consumption." A report to the Sustainable Development Commission, May 20, 2003, p. 61.
14. "Culture and Subculture" 2008, USC Marshal, University of South California, http://www.consumerpsychologist.com/cb_Culture.html (accessed September 16, 2010).
15. Laurie Demeritt, "What Makes a Green Consumer?" The Hartman Group, July 28, 2005, p. 2–4.
16. "Culture and Subculture" 2008, USC Marshal, University of South California, http://www.consumerpsychologist.com/cb_Culture.html (accessed September 16, 2010).
17. Sarah Lozanova, "Four Strategies for Green Marketing," *Triplepundit*, February 15, 2010, http://www.triplepundit.com/2010/02/4-strategies-for-green-marketing/ (accessed March 20, 2010).
18. Sheila Bonini and Jeremy Oppenheim, "Cultivating the Green Consumer," *Stanford Social Innovation Review*, September 27, 2008, p. 56.
19. Chad Holliday, Stephan Schmidheiny, and Philip Watts, "Walking the Talk: The Business Case for Sustainable Development" (Sheffield: Greenleaf Publishing, 2002), 191.
20. World Business Council for Sustainable Development, "Vision 2050, The New Agenda for Business," February 4, 2010, p. 5.
21. UNEP, "Sustainable Consumption Opportunities," Ministry for Protection of Natural Resources and Environment, Republic of Serbia Belgrade, United Nations Environment Programme, March 21–22, 2002, pp. 5, 9.
22. Tim Jackson, "Motivating Sustainable Consumption: A Review of Evidence on Consumer Behavior and Behavioral Change," International Sustainability Workshop, May 19, 2005, pp. 5–7.
23. Tim Jackson and Laurie Michaelis, "Sustainable Consumption and Production, Economic, Regeneration." A report to the Sustainable Development Commission, May 20, 2003, p. 7.
24. Norman Myers, "Sustainable Consumption" *Science, vol.* 287. no. 5462, (2000), 2419.
25. Sheila Bonini and Jeremy Oppenheim, "Cultivating the Green Consumer," *Stanford Social Innovation Review*, September 27, 2008, p. 58.
26. Ibid., 60.

27. "Green Consumers: *A Growing Market for Many Local Businesses* " 2006, UW EXTENSION, http://www.uwex.edu/ces/cced/downtowns/ltb/lets/LTB1106.pdf (accessed June 1, 2010)
28. Environmental Leader, "Successful Green Marketing Focuses on Consumer Needs," *Energy & Environmental News for Business*, June 20, 2007, http://www.environmental-leader.com/2007/06/20/successful-green-marketing-focuses-on-consumer-needs/ (accessed March 25, 2010).
29. Sarah Lozanova, "Four Strategies for Green Marketing," *Triplepundit*, February 15, 2010, http://www.triplepundit.com/2010/02/4-strategies-for-green-marketing/ (accessed March 20, 2010).
30. Ibid.
31. "What Makes a Good Eco-Label?" *Consumer Reports greenerchoices*, http://www.greenerchoices.org/eco-labels/eco-good.cfm (accessed June 1, 2010).
32. UNEP, "Sustainable Consumption Opportunities," Ministry for Protection of Natural Resources and Environment, Republic of Serbia Belgrade, United Nations Environment Programme, March 21–22, 2002, p. 11.
33. http://www.energystar.gov/
34. www.GlobeScan.com

CHAPTER 11

Approaches to Long-Term Global Sustainability Ecological, Carbon, and Water Footprints

NASRIN R. KHALILI

Human activities, industrial activities, production processes, transportation, disposal systems, and every product or service that humans consume has an impact on ecological systems. Greenhouse gas (GHG) emissions from the intensive use of coal-based energy has impacted climates and contributed to global warming and rises in the sea levels. The extensive use of water resources through industrial activities and consumption patterns has compromised the water resources. The concept of an ecological footprint is rooted in measuring how the human appropriation of the earth's resources relates to the carrying capacity of the earth. Prediction, forecasting, and projection, each with its own methods and outcomes, are common elements of ecological assessment approaches. Footprinting is another approach to estimating human impact on the climate, water resources, and ecosystem changes. The term footprint has been effectively used to design assessment frameworks and develop management strategies for addressing ecological impacts for which individuals, organizations, and nations are responsible. For example, the full carbon footprint encompasses a wide range of emission sources from the direct use of fuels to indirect impacts that can be attributed to an organization's disposition and practice. Accurate estimation of the "footprints" requires the development of well-structured and detailed assessment methodologies that can guarantee effective data collection, the proper selection of boundaries and scope of analysis, and disclosure of the results. This chapter discusses the "footprinting" approach and the key factors involved in the development of effective strategies and protocols for characterizing, measuring, and reporting carbon and water footprints, in particular.

Introduction

Human activities have significantly stressed ecosystems and negatively impacted natural resources and services that can be derived from the ecosystems. The pressures on ecosystems will intensify globally even more in coming decades if human attitudes, activities, and actions do not change. Although today's technology and knowledge could reduce the human impact on ecosystems considerably, they are unlikely to be deployed fully unless ecosystem services are perceived as limited and nonrenewable. For example, between 1950 and 1980 more land was converted to cropland than in the eighteenth and first half of the nineteenth centuries combined. Water taken from rivers and lakes to irrigate fields to meet the needs of industry and to supply households has doubled since 1960. The quantity of water impounded behind dams has quadrupled in the same period, and artificial reservoirs now hold much more water than free-flowing rivers do. As a result, the flow of some rivers has been substantially reduced. Globalization, human mobility, and plant and animal disposition, deliberately or by accident, have also impacted ecosystems. The Baltic Sea, for instance, contains 100 species from outside the region, a third of which are native to the North American Great Lakes. And a third of the 170 alien species in those lakes are native to the Baltic. A species introduced from outside can dramatically change the local system and the services it provides. For example, the arrival of the American comb jellyfish in the Black Sea has led to the destruction of 26 commercially viable systems.[1]

Ecological Footprints

The concept of ecological footprints was introduced in the 1990s in order to develop indicators of sustainable development and to measure how the human appropriation of the earth's resources relates to the carrying capacity of the earth. The aggregated use of land is seen as a good common denominator for expressing humans' impact on the earth's natural resources. Accordingly, the ecological footprint measures how much of nature, expressed in the common unit of "bioproductive space with world average productivity," is used exclusively for producing all the resources a given population consumes and absorbing the waste it produces. The ecological footprint can be calculated for individuals; a community, including villages, towns, cities, provinces, nations, or the global population as a whole; organizations; particular human activities; or specific goods or services.[2]

Framework for Ecological Impact Assessment

An analytical approach that consists of nine major tasks has been proposed to achieve the goals of the Millennium Ecosystem Assessment (MEA). Those tasks concentrate on the following:

- Identifying and categorizing ecosystems and their services
- Identifying links between human societies and ecosystem services
- Identifying the direct and indirect drivers of change
- Selecting indicators of ecosystem conditions, services, human well-being, and drivers
- Assessing historical trends and the current state of ecosystems, services, and drivers
- Evaluating the impact of a change in services on human well-being
- Developing scenarios of ecosystems, services, and drivers
- Evaluating response options to deal with ecosystem changes and human well-being
- Analyzing and communicating the uncertainty of assessment findings

The focal point of the MEA is to analyze interactions among the processes and systems; fill environmental, social, and economic data gaps; identify regions for collecting priority data; and synthesize the existing observations of the ecological changes. Commonly, the assessment consists of four or five scenarios that describe medium- to long-term changes in the ecosystems and their potential services. These scenarios are explicitly ecological perspectives and are built based on the global social and economic information.[3]

Although the MEA uses forecasts and other types of model projections where possible, additional methods of assessment can be used to provide more comprehensive coverage of future ecological changes in a format useful for decision making and policy developments. Since 1995, there has been widespread use of scenarios to assess the status of the global environment: World Business Council on Sustainable Development (WBCSD) scenarios aimed at helping corporate members reflect on the business risks and opportunities of the sustainable development challenge (FROG! GEOpolity, and Jazz: WBCSD 1997); World Water Vision's (WWV's) three global water scenarios were developed with a focus on water supply and demand including water requirements for ecosystems; IPCC Special Report on Emission Scenarios (SRES) and greenhouse gas emissions scenarios.[4]

Prediction, forecasting, and projection, each with its own methods for estimating ecological outcomes, are common elements of ecological assessment approaches. The following sections discuss "footprinting" as another approach to estimate human impact on climate and ecosystem changes. The concept of business ecological footprinting is introduced and is followed by a discussion of protocols for carbon footprinting and methods used to address the water footprints of organizations and nations.

Business Footprint Assessment

Businesses interact with ecosystems and ecosystem services in two important ways: they use services and they contribute to ecosystem change. The MEA showed that two-thirds of the ecosystem services examined in 2005 are degraded or used unsustainably. A reduction in ecosystem capacity and damaged capabilities would impact the global economy, businesses, and industry in three principal ways:

1. If current trends continue, ecosystem services that are freely available today will cease to be available or become more costly in the near future, and once internalized by primary industries, the additional costs that result will be passed downstream to secondary and tertiary industries and will transform the operating environment of all businesses.
2. Loss of ecosystem services will also affect the framework conditions within which businesses operate, influencing customer preferences, stockholder expectations, regulatory regimes, governmental policies, employee well-being, and the availability of finance and insurance.
3. Finally, new business opportunities will emerge as demand grows for more efficient or different ways to use ecosystem services for mitigating impacts or to track or trade services.[5,6]

In each case the net benefits from the more sustainably managed ecosystems are greater than those from converted ecosystems when measurements include both marketed and nonmarketed services, even though the private market benefits would be greater from the converted ecosystems.

Input-Output Analysis

The ecological footprints of a company can be estimated from input-output analysis (IOA), which is a top-down economic technique. This technique has also been used for the assessment of firms' environmental problems. For example, IOA is used in Life Cycle Assessment (LCA), which aims to calculate the total environmental burdens associated with a product.[7]

The boundary within which an organization accounts for its environmental, social, and economic effects is usually defined by the level of control on the operation or equity, although the level of influence and control will vary from organization to organization and from year to year. Extending the boundary beyond the immediate control of the organization still poses the question of exactly where to draw the line. Accordingly, it is important that organizations establish a clear boundary for an analysis that is consistent across all indicators. The boundary can be defined through a full life cycle analysis that starts by identifying the structure of the economic system at a particular economic entity, and then stretches across upstream production layers, containing sectors at different production stages linked together by the supply chains (see chapter 5). A particular impact for a good or a service can then be assessed from primary industries producing raw materials via secondary (manufacturing) industries into the sector or company that delivers the final product to the consumer, covering the full supply chain.

The general decomposition approach "structural path analysis" can also be used to systematically determine environmentally important production chains. The structural path analysis covers the entire upstream supply chain, unravels a company's impacts into single contributing supply paths, provides extensive detail of the impact of a sector's or company's activities, and allows for the investigation of the location of impacts within the supply chain. In the case of a company, the control over the input procurement process then provides the possibility of substituting impact-intensive suppliers with more sustainable suppliers.[8]

Climate Change and GHG Emission Management

Carbon Footprint

Climate change refers to a change in the state of the climate that can be identified by changes in the mean or the variability of its properties that persists for an extended period, typically decades or longer, whether due to natural variability or as a result of human activity. The United Nations Framework Convention on Climate Change (UNFCCC) refers to climate change as a change of climate that is attributed directly or indirectly to human activity that alters the composition of the global atmosphere and that is, in addition to natural climate variability, observed over comparable time periods.[9] In either definition, climate change is considered to be one of the most serious threats to sustainable development, with adverse impacts expected on the environment, human health, food security, economic activity, natural resources, and physical infrastructure.

Rising concentrations of anthropogenically produced GHGs in the earth's atmosphere are found to be the main reason for the observed and expected further changes in the climate. These increasing GHG emissions are caused or influenced by factors such as economic growth, technology, population, and governance. Among other factors, businesses have been recognized as significant producers of GHG emissions. The main sources of GHG emissions include energy supply and use, transport, agriculture, industrial processes, waste, solvents and other products, and international bunkers.[10] Increasingly, the business community is also being recognized as important for identifying business-led solutions to climate change challenges. For example, a growing number of corporations acknowledge the importance of corporate social responsibility, risk mitigation, and performance dimensions associated with the sustainable production and use of energy. As a result, issues relating to clean technology, carbon markets, energy efficiency and demand-side management, sectoral approaches, voluntary emission reduction commitments, adaptation, and forestry are of increasing interest to the business community.

The economic costs and risks of climate change could have a severe impact on economic growth and development, and as such, companies that are active in a wide variety of sectors and countries. Climate change is not only an environmental issue, as it is closely linked to concerns about energy security due to dependence on fossil fuels, and oil in particular, and to energy efficiency in relation to economic activity in general. Over the years, the impact of climate change has been surrounded with great uncertainty. This has, for example, included uncertainty about the type, magnitude, and timing of the physical impact; the best technological options to address the issue; and the materialization of public policies.[11]

To fight climate change and its impact on the global economy, many national and international panels have focused on mitigation strategies for GHG emissions that involve energy efficiency, zero-carbon technologies, large-scale carbon control, and clarity in climate policies. Business communities have supported these efforts and requested the development of a global climate change policy framework, valid beyond 2012, that promotes urgent and sustained mitigation and adaptation plans to prevent climate change from becoming the biggest challenge for future generations. The Bali Action Plan, which charted the course for a new negotiating process was designed to tackle climate change with business capability and initiatives in areas of energy efficiency; demand-side management; technology development; carbon markets and financing utilizing instruments such as sectoral approaches.[12,13]

GHG emission projections are widely used in the assessment of future climate change, and the underlying assumptions with respect to socioeconomic, demographic, and technological changes serve as inputs to many recent climate change vulnerability and impact assessments. Climatic changes can be derived from socio-economic and emission information. Understanding of the linkage between the two enable us to evaluate possible development pathways and global emissions constraints that would reduce the risk of future impacts that society may wish to avoid.

In the case of GHG emissions, global emissions constraints can be identified via measuring carbon footprints of human activities. Example barriers, enablers, and solutions to global climate management in the areas of investment, technology, and development could be identified as the lack of a price on carbon, risk, costs and complexity of current market arrangements, lack of capacity, lack of investment on a large scale, and lack of regulatory framework and governance structures to attract large-scale investments. Effective strategies could focus on capacity building, government regulation, risk management tools, public-private partnerships, and multistakeholder involvement in a technology platform. The best solutions proposed today call for the development of a stable regulatory framework; the development of finance packages for technology transfer to reduce underlying investment risks; transparency and clarity on funding mechanisms; consumer education; the development of an energy efficiency platform to exchange best practices and a technology research and development database on carbon and energy management; carbon pricing that reflects true costs; support to small and medium enterprises and best practices; and the development of minimum global efficiency standards and of more sectoral agreements and initiatives.[14]

Economics has played a visible role in climate policy debates in the United States and elsewhere, and a more prominent role than it has played in some other environmental problems. An economic approach to analyzing, understanding, and developing solutions to the problem of climate change is complex and at a minimum requires an understanding of the physical and technological dimensions of the climate change problem; estimates of the costs and benefits of controlling emissions of pollution leading to climate change; reviewing the fundamental economics of the problem via the use of analytic models that can capture an economic approach to the problem; designing climate policy instruments; and viable international climate agreements to address climate change problems.[15]

Understanding a company's GHG emissions by compiling a GHG inventory makes good business sense. Companies frequently cite the following five business goals as reasons for compiling a GHG inventory: (a) managing GHG risks and identifying reduction opportunities; (b) public reporting and participation in voluntary GHG programs; (c) participating in mandatory reporting programs; (d) participating in GHG markets; and (e) recognition for early voluntary action.

Managing GHG Emissions

An overview of the GHG management and carbon footprint assessment guidelines proposed by leading organizations such as the U.S. EPA Climate Leaders Offset Project and Carbon Reporting Rules and WRI-WBCSD frameworks are provided. The Climate Leaders GHG Inventory Guidance provides standards for companies to follow as they decide to account for their emissions. The guidance was inspired by an existing protocol developed by the World Resources Institute (WRI) and the World Business Council for Sustainable Development (WBCSD). The Climate Leaders GHG Inventory Guidance is a modification of the WRI/WBCSD GHG Protocol that fits the needs of Climate Leaders more precisely. GHG accounting concerns GHG emissions from operations that a company controls or owns. Accordingly, data collection would be specific to the operations, sites, geographic locations, business processes, and also the ownership. GHG reporting, on the other hand, concerns the presentation of GHG data in formats tailored to the needs of various reporting uses and users.

The WRI/WBCSD GHG Protocol. The goal and objective of the WRI/WBCSD Corporate Accounting and Reporting Standard are to help companies prepare a GHG inventory that represents a true and fair account of their emissions through the use of standardized approaches and principles. The goals and objectives then are to simply reduce the costs of compiling a GHG inventory; to provide businesses with information that can be used to build an effective strategy to manage and reduce GHG emissions; to facilitate participation in voluntary and mandatory GHG programs; and to increase consistency and transparency in GHG accounting and reporting among various companies and GHG programs.

Both businesses and other stakeholders benefit from converging on a common standard. For businesses, it reduces costs of their GHG inventory and is capable of meeting different internal and external information requirements. For others, it improves the consistency, transparency, and understandability of reported information, making it easier to track and compare progress over time.

Business operations vary in their legal and organizational structures; they include wholly owned operations, incorporated and nonincorporated, joint ventures, subsidiaries, and others. For the purposes of financial accounting, they are treated according to established rules that depend on the structure of the organization and the relationships among the parties involved. In setting organizational boundaries, a company selects an approach for consolidating GHG emissions and then consistently applies the selected approach to define those businesses and operations that constitute the company for the purpose of accounting and reporting GHG emissions. For corporate reporting, two distinct approaches can be used to consolidate GHG emissions: the "equity share" and "control" approaches.

Under the equity share approach, a company accounts for GHG emissions from operations according to its share of equity in the operation. The equity share reflects economic interest, which is the extent of rights a company has to the risks and rewards flowing from an operation. Typically, the share of economic risks and rewards in an operation is aligned with the company's percentage of ownership of that operation, and equity share will normally be the same as the ownership percentage.

Under the control approach, a company accounts for 100% of the GHG emissions from operations over which it has control, but it does not account for GHG emissions from operations in which it owns an interest but has no control over (control can be defined in either financial or operational terms). When using the control approach to consolidate GHG emissions, companies shall choose between either the operational control or financial control criteria.

The choice of the inventory boundary is dependent on the characteristics of the company, the intended purpose of information, and the needs of the users. When choosing the inventory boundary, a number of factors should be considered:

- Organizational structures: control (operational and financial), ownership, legal agreements, joint ventures, etc.
- Operational boundaries: on-site and off-site activities, processes, services, and impacts
- Business context: nature of activities, geographic locations, industry sector(s), purposes of information, and users of information

An operational boundary defines the scope of direct and indirect emissions for operations that fall within a company's established organizational boundary.

The operational boundary (scope 1, scope 2, scope 3) is decided at the corporate level after setting the organizational boundary. The selected operational boundary is then uniformly applied to identify and categorize direct and indirect emissions at each operational level. Companies report GHG emissions from sources they own or control as scope 1.

Scope 1: Direct Emissions. Direct GHG emissions are principally the result of the following types of activities undertaken by the company: generation of electricity, heat, or steam. These emissions result from combustion of fuels in stationary sources (e.g., boilers, furnaces, and turbines).

Scope 2: Indirect Emissions. For many companies, purchased electricity represents one of the largest sources of GHG emissions and the most significant opportunity to reduce these emissions. Accounting for scope 2 emissions allows companies to assess the risks and opportunities associated with changing electricity and GHG emissions costs. Another important reason for companies to track these emissions is that the information may be needed for some GHG programs.

Scope 3: Indirect Category 2 Emissions. Scope 3 is optional, but it provides an opportunity to be innovative in GHG management. Companies may want to focus on accounting for and reporting those activities that are relevant to their business and goals, and for which they have reliable information. Since companies have discretion over which categories they choose to report, scope 3 may not lend itself well to comparisons across companies. Some of these activities will be included under scope 1 if the pertinent emission sources are owned or controlled by the company (e.g., if the transportation of products is done in vehicles owned or controlled by the company). To determine if an activity falls within scope 1 or scope 3, the company should refer to the selected consolidation approach (equity or control) used in setting its organizational boundaries.[16,17]

Reporting Project-Based Reductions

A public GHG emissions report that is in accordance with the *GHG Protocol Corporate Standard* shall include a description of the company and inventory boundary; information about emissions including total scope 1 and 2 emissions, independent of any GHG trades such as sales, purchases, transfers, or banking of allowance; emissions data separately for each scope; emissions data for all GHGs separately; year chosen as the base year; an emissions profile over time that is consistent with and clarifies the chosen policy for making base-year emissions recalculations; an appropriate context for any significant emissions changes that trigger base-year emissions recalculation; emissions data for direct CO_2 emissions from biologically sequestered carbon; and methodologies used to calculate or measure emissions. Optional information could be provided, which includes emissions data from relevant scope 3 emissions activities for which reliable data can be obtained, a description of performance measured against internal and external benchmarks, relevant ratio performance indicators (e.g., emissions per kilowatt-hour generated, ton of material production, or sales), and GHG management and reduction programs or strategies.

It is important for companies to report their physical inventory emissions for their chosen inventory boundaries. GHG trades should, however, be reported in the company's public GHG report along with information on the credibility of the purchased or sold carbon offsets or credits. The reduced GHGs from operations usually are identified in inventory reports, unless they are sold, traded externally, or otherwise used as an offset or credit. Substituting fossil fuel with waste-derived fuel may have no direct effect on or may even increase a company's emissions, but it is important and has to be reported since it could result in emissions reductions elsewhere. Also installing an on-site power generation plant that can provide surplus electricity to other companies may increase a company's direct emissions, while displacing the consumption of grid electricity by the companies supplied.[18]

Other GHG Management Programs

It is important to distinguish between the GHG Protocol initiative and other GHG programs. The *GHG Protocol Corporate Standard* focuses only on the accounting and reporting of emissions. It does not require emissions information to be reported to WRI or WBCSD. In addition, though this standard is designed to develop a verifiable inventory, it does not provide a standard for how the verification process should be conducted. Many other existing GHG programs have used and referred to the WRI protocol for their own accounting and reporting requirements. Examples include most voluntary GHG reduction programs (e.g., the World Wildlife Fund (WWF), Climate Savers, the U.S. Environmental Protection Agency (EPA) Climate Leaders, GHG trading programs, such as the UK Emissions Trading Scheme (UK ETS), Chicago Climate Exchange (CCX), and the European Union Greenhouse Gas Emissions Allowance Trading Scheme (EU ETS).[19,20] The following section provides an overview of the Climate Leader Program for comparison.

U.S. EPA Climate Leaders Offset Project and Carbon Reporting Rules

Under the business-as-usual path, total gross U.S. GHG emissions are expected to rise 30% between 2000 and 2020. Implementation of *Climate Programs and Measures* could, however, reduce this growth by about 11%. Increased efforts to use cleaner fuels, more efficient technologies, and better management methods across all main sectors such as agriculture, forestry, mines, and landfills are projected to keep the growth of GHG emissions below the current growth of the U.S. economy.[21]

In its Fiscal Year 2008 Consolidated Appropriations Act (H.R. 2764; Public Law 110–161), Congress directed the EPA to publish a mandatory GHG reporting rule using the agency's existing authority under the Clean Air Act. The rule requires "mandatory reporting of GHGs at appropriate thresholds in all sectors of the economy." The EPA is responsible for determining those thresholds, as well as the frequency of reporting.[22]

In order to meet national emission reduction goals and to ensure positive impacts on climate change, companies must take forwarding actions toward the development of effective programs for both accurate estimation and effective reduction of their GHG emissions. The accurate estimation of GHG emissions and carbon footprint requires the development of well-structured emission monitoring and reduction protocols highlighting detailed assessment methodologies. Such a protocol guarantees effective data collection, proper selection of boundaries and scope of the coverage within which emissions are identified, and proper data analysis and disclosure of the results.[23]

GHG emission management should at a minimum include the development of a company strategic planning framework (top-down approach), assessment of the values at risk, development of emission inventory, assessment of the internal and external options for emission reduction, consideration of the product line operations, and development of an integrated environmental management strategy using provided information through the use of the framework.[24]

The EPA Climate Leaders program provides a company-wide GHG reduction guideline that includes techniques to be used for source identification within sectors and company boundaries, strategies and techniques for emission inventory development, methods for inventory management, and elements of effective reduction goal setting. Benchmarking has been used less frequently to evaluate corporate GHG performance.[25,26]

The Climate Leaders program was launched by the EPA in 2002 as an industry-government partnership that works with companies to develop *long-term climate change strategies*. The program has identified three key components central to a robust GHG management strategy:

- Inventory corporate-wide emissions of the six major GHGs from direct sources including stationary combustion, mobile combustion, and process and fugitive emissions, and from indirect sources such as electricity and steam purchases.
- Develop an Inventory Management Plan (IMP) that describes the process for completing and maintaining a high-quality, corporate-wide inventory.
- Set a long-term, forward-looking GHG emissions reduction goal and Inventory Management Plan to ensure credibility and consistency in emissions data, both of which are essential to tracking progress towards meeting a GHG reduction goal.[27]

An overview of the steps involved in the EPA Climate Leaders program for company-wide GHG reduction is provided in Figure 11.1 for the "Low Emitters" and "Small Businesses" with less than 10,000 tons/year emissions, and also the "Core Emitters" with GHG emissions of more than 10,000 tons/year.

Components of an effective GHG management strategy for core emitters. The presented guideline follows procedures highlighted in the EPA Climate Leaders Program, which is a comprehensive approach to goal setting, monitoring, evaluating, and mitigating GHG emissions. The guideline primarily calls for (a) the creation of a company-wide GHG inventory program, (b) the development of an IMP, and (c) setting goals and targets for GHG emission reductions.[28]

Companies must develop GHG reduction goals (Figure 11.1) customized according to the specifications of the companies (i.e., considering the uniqueness of their GHG emission [types, quantity], emission sources, and capabilities to reduce emissions). The criteria for setting GHG reduction goals include (a) goals must be set corporate-wide, and as such they are applicable to all operations in the United States; (b) the reduction plans must be based on the most recent base year for which emission data are available; (c) the goals must be set to be achieved

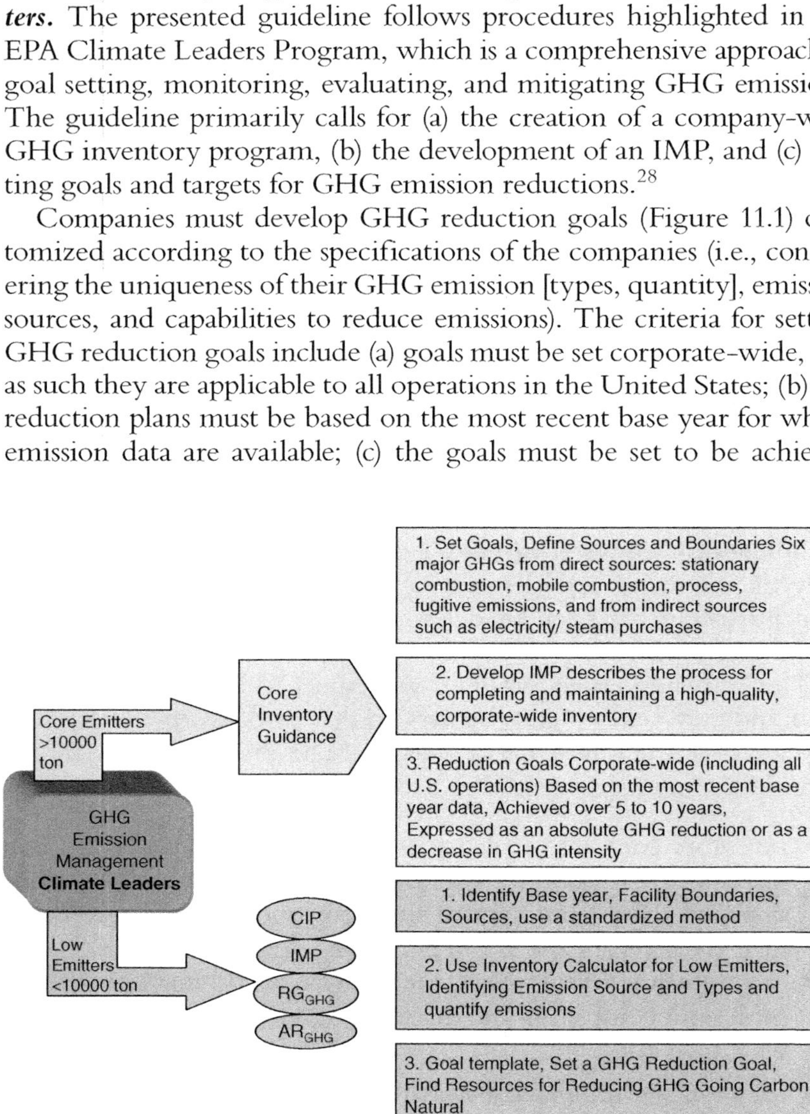

Figure 11.1 An overview of the steps involved with Getting Started, Calculating GHG Emissions, Creating IMP, and Setting Reduction Goals.

over five- to ten-year periods; (d) the reduction must be expressed as an absolute GHG reduction or as a decrease in GHG intensity.[29] The reduction goals and intensity may also vary depending on the source of emissions. For example, GHG emission intensity could decrease with respect to the sectors (energy generation sources, energy use from outside producers, potentials for technology advancements, renewing equipment or process modifications) or company demographics.

Estimating carbon footprint. Once the inventory boundary has been established, companies generally calculate GHG as follows:

1. Identify GHG emissions sources
    - Identify *core direct* emissions sources
    - Identify *core indirect* emissions sources
    - Identify *optional* emissions sources to the extent desired
    - Identify both routine and nonroutine operations. Nonroutine operations might include maintenance activities (including turnarounds) and upset conditions. *In some cases, nonroutine operations may be a significant source of emissions.*
2. Select an emissions calculation approach
    - For a particular source category, emissions calculations will generally rely on emission factors and other parameters (e.g., utilization factors, oxidation rates, and methane conversion factors). These factors and parameters may be published. Otherwise use default factors, based on company-specific data, site-specific data, or direct emission or other measurements.
    - Core direct emissions should be calculated based on the purchased quantities of commercial fuels (such as natural gas and heating oil) multiplied by relevant published emissions factors.
    - Core indirect emissions should typically be calculated from metered electricity consumption and supplier-specific, local grid, or other published emissions factors.
    - Optional emissions should be calculated from activity factors such as passenger miles and published or third-party emissions factors. In all of these cases, if source/facility-specific emissions factors are available, it is preferable that they be used. Climate Leaders provides source-specific guidelines to help facilitate the emissions estimation approach.
3. Collect activity data and choose emissions factors
    - Estimated emissions for a source category can be compared with historical data or other estimates to ensure that they fall within a reasonable range. Potentially unreasonable estimates

provide cause for checking emission factors or activity data and determining whether changes in methodology, market forces, or other events are sufficient reasons for the change. In situations where actual emission monitoring occurs (e.g., power plant CO_2 emissions), the data from monitors can be compared with estimated emissions using activity data and emission factors.

4. Apply quantification methodology to estimate GHG emissions
   - A GHG inventory is an accounting of the amount of GHGs emitted to or removed from the atmosphere over a specific period of time (e.g., one year). A GHG inventory also provides information on the activities that cause emissions and removals, as well as background on the methods used to make the calculations.
5. Record and analyze data, and develop emission reduction strategies
   - Emission reduction (or sequestration) opportunities generally fall into four main categories: Energy Efficiency, Low Carbon or No Carbon Energy Use, Process Optimization, and Carbon Sequestration. Additionally, emerging green power markets enable some companies to switch to less GHG-intensive electricity suppliers. Companies can also install an efficient cogeneration plant on site to replace the import of more GHG-intensive electricity from the grid. *Incorporating indirect emissions from electricity, heat, and steam usage into the core emissions reporting facilitates the transparent accounting of such choices.*

Components of an effective GHG management strategy for low emitters. As described previously, the GHG Protocol organizes sources into three categories (or "scopes"): direct emissions from sources that the company owns or controls, such as natural-gas-fired boilers or vehicle fleets; indirect emissions that are a consequence of the operations of the company but occur at sources owned or controlled by another company, most typically electricity, heat, or steam; and other indirect emissions such as employee travel and product transport (optional emissions).[30]

Since companies can use either an equity share approach or a control approach to define their organizational boundaries, the IMP should include a list of operations or facilities in the inventory based on the chosen organizational boundary, as well as procedures used to identify each operation or facility. A list of the GHGs emitted from each operation or facility should also be included.

Using well-documented methodologies that include verifiable quality assurance procedures and emission factors identified in data sources, companies are able to create an inventory for their GHG emissions. According to the Climate Leaders Program, participating companies must collect and report six major GHG emissions. As mentioned above, CO_2 equivalents, which are identified based on the global warming potential (GWP) value of each gas, is used for reporting procedures. A base calendar year can be chosen for the emissions inventory. This base year echoes emissions data for the most recent year the company joined the carbon emission monitoring and reduction program. In the event of a significant change in operation, structure, or emissions, the company must retroactively recalculate its base year emissions.

The IMP should also include corporate policies for adjusting base-year emissions in the event of structural changes. The GHG Protocol must mirror five principles:

1. Ensure that the GHG inventory technique and methodologies applied could appropriately reflect emissions so it is RELEVANT.
2. The protocol should account for all GHG emissions so it must be COMPLETE.
3. Methodologies used for the estimation are consistent within the company's chosen boundary so it is CONSISTENT.
4. All relevant issues are presented in a very clear and coherent manner and all assumptions and references used in the estimation pathway are stated, so the protocol includes TRANSPARENT data.
5. Quantification of GHG emissions are performed using acceptable measurement techniques and estimation procedures and uncertainty in the measurement is reduced as far as practicable, so efficient ACCURACY is warranted.[31]

Identifying GHG Reduction Opportunities

The company must evaluate emission reduction opportunities and consider establishing evaluation criteria to prioritize the reduction options and associated activities. The evaluation criteria could include, but not be limited to, the following:

- Evaluating the environmental, social, and economic impacts of the project

- Cost to implement the project
- Secured benefits and impact of the reduction on the firm, the environment, and the community
- Estimate of the net return on investment when made to reduce GHG emissions
- Time to implement
- Contribution to core business values and brand image
- Evaluation of the obstacles to implementation

With an evaluation protocol in place, the company can then best evaluate its top preferences for emission reduction activities over the five- to ten-year time horizon and construct a defensible, credible, achievable GHG reduction goal. Table 11.1, which was constructed according to the EPA Climate Leader GHG Protocol, describes the typical steps involved in creating credible, realistic, measurable, and achievable GHG reduction goals.

Climate Change and Business Issues

Although found to be responsible for the climate change, increasing GHG emissions are caused or influenced by factors such as economic growth, technology, population, and governance. According to the 2007 report by the Intergovernmental Panel on Climate Change (IPCC), the effects of climate change are already being observed, and scientific findings indicate that prompt action is necessary. Certain sectors of the business community have long been recognized as significant producers of GHG emissions. Increasingly, the business community is also being recognized as important for identifying business-led solutions to climate change challenges.

A growing number of corporations acknowledge the importance of corporate social responsibility, risk mitigation, and performance dimensions associated with the sustainable production and use of energy. As a result, issues relating to clean technology, carbon markets, energy efficiency and demand-side management, sectoral approaches, voluntary emission reduction commitments, adaptation, and forestry are of increasing interest to the business community.

Private sectors and businesses must address climate change as a long-term goal. They must actively get engaged with specific sustainability-oriented projects and actions such as reducing emissions from deforestation and forest degradation in developing countries to quick-start immediate progress. Businesses must also actively participate in projects and efforts that can guarantee reducing their impact on climate change at local, regional, national, and

Table 11.1 Steps in Setting and Tracking Performance Toward a GHG Target

Obtain senior management commitment
Implementing a reduction target is likely to necessitate changes in behavior and decision making throughout the organization and requires establishing an internal accountability and incentive system, as well as adequate resources
Decide on the target type (absolute vs. intensity)
An absolute target is expressed in terms of a reduction over time in a specified quantity of GHG emissions to the atmosphere (i.e., tons of CO_2 equivalents), whereas an intensity target is expressed as a reduction in the ratio of GHG emissions relative to another business metric (i.e., tons of CO_2 equivalents per ton of product, per kWh, ton-mileage, etc.) or some other metric such as sales, revenues, or office space
Decide on the target boundary
Under the Climate Leaders program, targets must be for the reduction of CO_2 equivalents on an absolute or intensity basis, for a minimum of core direct and indirect emissions from U.S. operations
Choose the target base year
Under the Climate Leaders program, for the purpose of assessing a company's performance against its emission reduction goal, the most current year that a partner has data available should be its base year (fixed base year)
Define the target time period
Under the Climate Leaders program, the goals should be based on prospective reductions beginning with the base year and looking 5–10 years into the future
Decide on the use of project offsets or credits
A GHG target can be met from internal reductions at sources included in the target boundary, or through additionally using offsets that are generated from GHG reduction projects that reduce emissions at sources outside the target boundary. It is important to ensure the credibility of the offsets (see chapter 8), specify the origin and nature of the offsets when reporting, and check that the offsets have not also been counted toward another organization's target (i.e., via contract)
Establish a target double counting policy
The policy must ensure that a GHG offset is not counted toward the target by both the selling and purchasing organizations. For an internal reduction project, the missions need to be added back to the inventory if the reductions are subsequently "sold" as an offset to another company
Decide on the target level
In addition to the guidelines and requirements from steps 1 through 7, considerations include understanding key drivers affecting GHG emissions, developing reductions strategies, looking at the future of the company, factoring relevant growth factors, evaluating existing environmental plans or energy plans that will affect GHG emissions, and benchmarking GHG emissions with similar organizations
Track and report progress against the target

international levels. What is most important for businesses is to build their reputation as "a responsible entity of the society."

Business unusual. The focus of new businesses must be on the innovative business approaches and models. Examples include supporting the market for satellites, which is developing; calling for government assistance to enable innovation and provide practical tools to end users;

developing solutions for and solving the coal problem; and designing good regulations, models, and policies for carbon prices. In addition, since 40% of carbon emissions come from construction, businesses must call for new construction technologies.[32] Other specific actions for sustainable business operations are as follows:

- Development of outreach programs for rapid uptake and changes in stakeholder attitudes.
- Working in a collaborative environment to address supply chain issues for mutual advantage.
- Stop relying on governments for all solutions.
- Business transformation, a new carbon accounting infrastructure, and use of the context of climate change in order to foster changes and innovations.
- Avoid sectoral thinking as it is the biggest obstacle to widespread implementation of new concepts.
- Establish value chains and business models that are more effective for society.
- Demonstrate possibilities for future value when focusing on shareholder understanding that businesses have social values.

Public-private partnerships. Successful partnerships between legislators and business representatives are a must for developing economically and environmentally sound legislation. Ideal areas for partnerships could include technology development, energy-efficient buildings, adaptation in developing countries, and combined food and biofuel production.

Consumers. The win-win situation of getting a 200% return on every dollar invested in energy efficiency in California through retrofitting of buildings and other efficiency measures encouraged customers to switch from old technologies, so developing targets, legislation, and incentive schemes to encourage customers to participate in the green movement is a must. Sectoral approaches will not lead to a comprehensive outcome, but an increasing willingness of consumers in both developed and developing countries will change their behaviors. The challenge is innovating more rapidly to bring new goods to the market faster and at competitive prices.[33]

Climate Change Impact on Water Resources

Climate change is expected to exacerbate current stresses on water resources from population growth and economic and land-use changes, including urbanization. On a regional scale, mountain snow pack, glaciers, and small ice caps play a crucial role in freshwater availability. Widespread mass losses from glaciers and reductions in snow cover over recent decades are projected to accelerate throughout the twenty-first century, reducing water availability, hydropower potential, and changing seasonality of flows in regions supplied by melt water from major mountain ranges, where more than one-sixth of the world population currently lives. Changes in precipitation and temperature lead to changes in runoff and water availability.

Runoff is projected with high confidence to increase 10% to 40% by mid-century at higher latitudes and in some wet tropical areas, including populous areas in East and Southeast Asia, and decrease 10% to 30% over some dry regions at mid-latitudes and dry tropics, due to decreases in rainfall and higher rates of evapotranspiration. There is also high confidence that many semi-arid areas (e.g., the Mediterranean Basin, western United States, southern Africa, and northeastern Brazil) will suffer a decrease in water resources due to climate change. Drought-affected areas are projected to increase in extent, with the potential for adverse impacts on multiple sectors (e.g.. agriculture, water supply, energy production, and health). Regionally, large increases in irrigation water demand as a result of climate changes is projected.

The negative impacts of climate change on freshwater systems outweigh its benefits. Areas in which runoff is projected to decline face a reduction in the value of the services provided by water resources. The beneficial impacts of increased annual runoff in some areas are likely to be tempered by the negative effects of increased precipitation variability and seasonal runoff shifts on water supply, water quality, and flood risk. Available research suggests a significant future increase in heavy rainfall events in many regions, including some in which the mean rainfall is projected to decrease. The resulting increased flood risk poses challenges to society, physical infrastructure, and water quality.[34]

Human Activities, Industrialization, and Water Issues

Water withdrawals from rivers and lakes for irrigation, household, and industrial use doubled in the last forty years. Humans now use between 40% and 50% of the fresh water running off land to which the majority of the population has access. In some regions, such as the Middle East and North Africa, humans use 120% of renewable supplies (due to the reliance on groundwater that is not recharged). Between 1960 and 2000, reservoir storage capacity quadrupled and, as a result, the amount of water stored behind large dams is estimated to be three to six times the amount held by natural river channels (this excludes natural lakes).[35]

Sustainable Water Management

Water Footprints

Water is a multifunctional and multidimensional natural resource. Despite its highly diverse temporal and spatial frames, it is the origin of every form of life. Although water resources have played a critical role in the development and advancement of societies, unintended effects of humanity's attempts to use water have significantly impacted the capacity and the quality of natural water systems. Currently, while 40% of the world's population live in extreme poverty, they do not have access to water due to inequitable distribution of water among the users—a situation that is affecting many nations, and particularly poorer populations.

The UN has taken on a lead role in addressing this challenge through the setting of the Millennium Development Goals, in which water has a crucial role to play. The critical challenges of these goals are to address and manage fresh water in such a way to enable poverty alleviation and socioeconomic development within an environmentally sound, integrated framework. International and global approaches and programs have been focusing on water issues. Examples include the Integrated Water Resource Management (IWRM), Development of Indicators and World Water Assessment, OECD programs, and the UNESCO initiatives including the Millennium Development Goals.

The IWRM program promotes cross-sectoral cooperation and coordinates the management and development of land, water (both surface water and groundwater), and other related resources. The main focus of this program is to maximize the resulting social and economic benefits in an equitable manner, without compromising ecosystem sustainability. This program addresses the watershed or basins, and adjacent coastal and marine environments,[36,37]

The indicator development and the World Water Assessment Program (WWAP) were established in 2000 under the auspices of the UN and were charged with the responsibility to monitor and report on water around the world. The focus of this program has been on the analysis of the availability, condition, and use of water systems around the word, and also to design reliable monitoring programs for assessing and reporting water management progress towards meeting the goals and targets of the WWAP.

Water Footprint

The main objective has been of the water footprint (WF) concept, which was developed analogously to the ecological footprint concept (as introduced in the 1990s) in 2002, has been to develop consumption-based indicators of water use. Due to their capabilities for demonstrating consumer and global dimensions of water use, water footprints and associated indicators can be used in the development of proper water governance.

Calculating a footprint: the item-by-item and balance-based approaches. Two calculation methods, "bottom-up" and "top-down," similar to those applied in ecological footprint analysis, are proposed for estimating water footprints. The bottom-up approach is an item-by-item approach used to estimate the WF by multiplying all goods and services consumed by their respective water needs. The top-down approach is, however, a balance-based compound calculation method. In this approach, the WF of a nation is calculated as the total use of water resources within the country plus the gross virtual water import minus the gross virtual water export.

Virtual water import refers to the volume of water used in other countries to make goods and services that are imported to and consumed within the country considered. Virtual-water export refers to the volume of water used domestically for making export products, which are consumed elsewhere. For example, to produce 1 kg of grain, 1000–2000 kg of water is needed, which is equivalent to 1–2 m^3. Producing livestock products generally requires even more water per kilogram of product. If one country exports a water-intensive product to another country, it exports water in virtual form. In this way some countries support other countries in their water needs. A water-scarce country might wish to import products that require a lot of water in their production (water-intensive products) and export products or services that require less water (water extensive products). This implies a net import of "virtual water" (as opposed to the import of real water, which is generally too expensive) and will relieve the pressure on the nation's own water resources.[38]

The balance-based (compound, top-down) calculation method is considered to be most practical for a rapid assessment of footprints of nations. The item-by-item (component-based, bottom-up) approach can be used for estimating a national footprint as well, but it is considered more suitable for the assessment of the footprint of an individual, business, or subnational community for which import-export data are not available. Calculation schemes based on the item-by-item approach can be translated into simple educational or awareness-raising tools.[39]

Water footprints show the extent of water use in relation to the consumption, and as such can be estimated for nations, businesses, and individuals. The WF is generally expressed in terms of the volume of freshwater use per year (fresh water on earth is only 2.5% of the total amount of available water to humans). For example, the water footprint of a nation can be estimated from both the internal water footprint (IWFP, the volume of water used for the production of the goods and services consumed by the country using domestic water resources) and external water footprint (EWFP, water used in other countries to produce goods and services imported). Hoekstra and Chapagain (2007) reported average water footprints for the period of 1997–2007 for the United States and China to be about 2480 m^3/cap/year and 700 m^3/cap/year, respectively.[40]

Water Footprint of Businesses

The water footprint of a business (corporate water footprint) refers to the total volume of fresh water that is used directly and indirectly to run and support the business. It consists of two components: the operational water footprint (i.e., the direct water use by the business in its own operations) and the supply-chain water footprint (i.e., the water use in the business's supply chain). Many businesses have a supply-chain water footprint that is much larger than the operational water footprint, for example, when a company does not have agricultural activity itself but is partly based on the intake of agricultural products (crop products, meat, milk, eggs, leather, cotton, wood/paper). When consumers use the products from a business, there can also be a water footprint in the end-use stage.[41]

The operational water footprint includes water incorporated into the product as an ingredient; water consumed, such as water not returned to the water system from where it was withdrawn during the production process, labeling, or packing; and water polluted as a result of the production process. The overhead operational water footprint is the water consumed or polluted because of water consumption by employees, including drinking water and water used in toilets and kitchens, for washing working clothes of the employees, for cleaning activities in the factory, and for gardening. The supply-chain water footprint related to product inputs consists of, for example, the water footprint of product ingredients other than water and the water footprint of other inputs used in production. The overhead supply-chain water footprint originates from all goods and services used in the factory that are not directly used in or for the production process of one particular product produced in the factory. Three different types of freshwater are considered for the analysis: blue, green, and grey. The *blue* water footprint is the volume of freshwater that evaporated from the global blue water resources (surface water and ground water); the *green* water footprint is the volume of water evaporated from the global green water resources (rainwater stored in the soil as soil moisture); and the *grey* water footprint is the volume of polluted water used in the production and use of goods and services.[42]

The efficient use of freshwater and control of pollution is often part of sustainability issues addressed by business. In the last ten years, initiatives were the foundation of the World Business Council for Sustainable Development (WBCSD 1997) and the Global Reporting Initiative (GRI 2000); the development of standards for environmental management systems, such as ISO and EMAS standards (OECD 2001); the development of Key Environmental Indicators (OECD 2001; Steg et al. 2001); and the introduction of the Global Water Tool (WBCSD 2007).[43]

In order to be able to assess its water footprint, a business should be clearly delineated. The boundaries of the business should be identified and schematized into a system of inputs and outputs. Water policies with respect to reducing and offsetting the impacts of the water footprints can be developed upon analysis of the operation system. The goals of a business with respect to reducing and offsetting the impacts of its water footprint can be prompted by the goal to reduce the business risks related to its freshwater appropriation. Alternatively, they can result from governmental regulations with respect to water use and pollution.

Business water footprint accounting can serve different purposes. For example, it can be used to identify the water-related impacts of the business on its social and natural environment; to create transparency to shareholders, business clients, consumers, and governments; to compare water use in similar business units (within a business or across businesses) and subsequent benchmarking and target setting; or to identify and support the development of policy to reduce business risks related to freshwater scarcity.

Summary

Human activities have significantly stressed the ecosystem and negatively impacted natural resources and services that can be derived from the ecosystems. It is anticipated that the pressures on ecosystems will intensify globally even more in coming decades if human attitudes, activities, and actions do not change. The concept of the ecological footprint was introduced in the 1990s in order to develop indicators of sustainable development and to measure how the human appropriation of the earth's resources relates to the carrying capacity of the earth. The aggregated use of land is used as a common denominator for expressing humans' impact on the earth's natural resources. The ecological footprint concept has been developed and used to measure how much of nature is used exclusively for producing all the resources a given population consumes and absorbing the waste it produces. The accurate estimation of a carbon footprint, on the other hand, requires the development of a well-structured and detailed assessment methodology that can guarantee effective data collection; proper selection of boundaries and scope of emissions; and proper data analysis and disclosure of the results (i.e., impact of industrial activities on the climate). The leading companies with a well-developed strategy for reducing their carbon footprint associated with GHG emissions have demonstrated that understanding emissions and energy data introduces opportunities to reduce risk to their reputation, insurance, and economic value.

Water is a commodity that is essential to human life. Due to their significant contribution to human life and the development of societies, water resources must be protected and used in the most sustainable manner. The export of a product from a water-efficient region (relatively low virtual water content of the product) to a water-inefficient region (relatively high virtual water content of the product) could save water globally. Whether trade of products from water-efficient to water-inefficient countries is beneficial from an economic point of view depends on a few additional factors, such as the character of the water saving (blue or green water saving) and the differences in productivity with respect to other relevant input factors such as land and labor.[44] The water footprint concept was developed in order to provide an indicator of human consumption of water. The water footprint concept is also used to develop prevention strategies and new technologies that can augment the existing natural water resources, reduce demand, and achieve higher efficiency.

Case Studies

Electric Power Research Institute GHG Emission Management

The Electric Power Research Institute's (EPRI's) Greenhouse Gas Risk Assessment identifies the steps involved in managing the GHG emissions reduction liabilities and financial risk at utilities. The EPRI's GHG Risk Assessment service is based on quantitative models and research analysis completed by EPRI's Program 103 "Greenhouse Gas Reduction Options." This program helps member companies to manage their financial and operational risks, reduce their costs, improve their image, and comply with climate policies. The EPRI project includes six activities:

1. Quantifying corporate GHG emissions
2. Setting boundaries
3. Developing an emissions baseline
4. Developing GHG reduction scenarios
5. Projecting GHG emissions reductions
6. Estimating the costs of emissions reductions

As shown, the six activities are modeled after steps identified by the EPA Climate Leader protocol. The deliverable of the program includes a GHG Emissions Inventory, GHG Emissions Baseline, GHG Emissions Reduction Scenarios through 2020, GHG Emissions and Financial Liabilities using pro-forma estimates of the expected annual cost of achieving the GHG emissions reductions identified and the net present value of these annual costs, and a Project Report that summarizes the GHG Risk Assessment approach and findings.[45]

Alcoa: Taking Advantage of Renewable Energy Certificates

Alcoa, a global manufacturer of aluminum, is implementing a variety of strategies to reduce its GHG emissions. One approach it to purchase renewable energy certificates, or RECs, to offset some of the company's GHG emissions. RECs, which represent the environmental benefits of renewable energy unbundled from the actual flow of electrons, are an innovative method of providing renewable energy to individual customers. RECs represent the unbundled environmental benefits, such as avoided CO_2 emissions, generated by producing electricity from renewable rather than fossil sources. RECs can be sold bundled with the electricity (as green power) or separately to customers interested in supporting renewable energy. Alcoa found that RECs offer a variety of advantages, including direct access to the benefits of renewable energy for facilities that may have limited renewable energy procurement options. In October 2003, Alcoa began purchasing RECs equivalent to 100% of the electricity used annually at four corporate offices in Tennessee, Pennsylvania, and New York. The RECs Alcoa is purchasing effectively mean that the four corporate centers are now operating on electricity generated by projects that produce electricity from landfill gas, avoiding the emission of more than 6.3 million kilograms (13.9 million pounds) of carbon dioxide annually. Alcoa chose RECs in part because the supplier was able to provide RECs to all four facilities through one contract. This flexibility lowered the administrative cost of purchasing renewable energy for multiple facilities that are served by different utilities. For more information on RECs, see the Green Power Market Development Group's Corporate Guide to Green Power Markets: Installment #5 (WRI 2003).[46]

Notes

1. "Living Beyond Our Means: Natural Assets and Human Well-Being," Statement from the Board, *Millennium Ecosystem Assessment*, March 2005, http://www.millenniumassessment.org (accessed June 2, 2010).
2. A.Y. Hoekstra, "Human Appropriation of Natural Capital: A Comparison of Ecological Footprint and Water Footprint Analysis," *Ecological Economics* (2009): 1964.
3. Millennium Ecosystem Assessment, *Ecosystems and Human Well-Being, A Framework for Assessment* (Washington, DC: Island Press, 2005), 147–50, http://pdf.wri.org/ecosystems_human_wellbeing.pdf (accessed June 4, 2010).
4. Ibid., 168–72.
5. "Ecosystems and Human Well-being, Opportunities and Challenges for Business and Industry." A Report of the *Millennium Ecosystem Assessment*, http://www.millenniumassessment.org/documents/document.305.aspx.pdf (accessed June 4, 2010). 5
6. Ibid., 27
7. Thomas Wiedmann, Manfred Lenzen, and John Barrett, "Companies on the Scale, Comparing and Benchmarking the Ecological Footprint of Businesses," *Journal of Industrial Ecology* 13 (May 3, 2009): 361–83.
8. T. Wiedmann, and M. Lenzen, "Sharing Responsibility along Supply Chains - A New Life-Cycle Approach and Software Tool for Triple-Bottom-Line Accounting," The Corporate Responsibility Research Conference, Trinity College Dublin, Ireland (September 2006). pp. 7-10.

9. "Investment and Financial Flows to Address Climate Change," United Nations Framework Convention on Climate Change, October 2007, http://unfccc.int/cooperation_and_support/financial_mechanism/items/4053.php (accessed June 5, 2010).
10. "Greenhouse Gas Emission Trends and Projections in Europe 2009, Tracking Progress towards Kyoto Targets," *EEA Report* 9 (2009): 143.
11. A. Kolk and J. Pinks, "Business and Climate Change: Key Strategic and Policy Challenges," *Amsterdam Law Forum* 2 (2010): 41–50.
12. "Summary of Copenhagen Business Day," *Business Day Bulletin* 160 (December 13, 2009), http://www.iisd.ca/climate/cop15/bd/ (accessed June 4, 2010).
13. "Investment and Financial Flows to Address Climate Change," United Nations Framework Convention on Climate Change, October 2007, http://unfccc.int/cooperation_and_support/financial_mechanism/items/4053.php (accessed June 5, 2010).
14. R.K. Pachauri and A. Reisinger, Fourth Assessment Report of the Intergovernmental Panel on Climate Change (IPCC), 2007, http://www.ipcc.ch/publications_and_data/ar4/syr/en/contents.html (accessed June 2, 2010).
15. Charles D. Kolstad and Michael Toman, "The Economics of Climate Policy," *Resources for the Future* Discussion Paper 00–40REV, June 2001, http://www.rff.org/documents/RFF-DP-00–40.pdf (accessed June 4, 2010).
16. Pankaj Bhatia and Janet Ranganathan, "The Greenhouse Gas Protocol: A Corporate Accounting and Reporting Standard," World Resources Institute and World Business Council for Sustainable Development, March 2004, http://www.wri.org/publication/greenhouse-gas-protocol-corporate-accounting-and-reporting-standard-revised-edition (accessed June 4, 2010).
17. Florence Daviet and Janet Ranganathan, "The Greenhouse Gas Protocol: The GHG Protocol for Project Accounting," WBCSD/WRI, November 2005, http://www.wri.org/publication/greenhouse-gas-protocol-ghg-protocol-project-accounting (accessed June 4, 2010).
18. Pankaj Bhatia and Janet Ranganathan, "The Greenhouse Gas Protocol: A Corporate Accounting and Reporting Standard," WBCSD/WRI, March 2004, http://www.wri.org/publication/greenhouse-gas-protocol-corporate-accounting-and-reporting-standard-revised-edition (accessed June 4, 2010): 63–66.
19. Pankaj Bhatia and Janet Ranganathan, "The Greenhouse Gas Protocol: A Corporate Accounting and Reporting Standard," WBCSD/WRI, March 2004, http://www.wri.org/publication/greenhouse-gas-protocol-corporate-accounting-and-reporting-standard-revised-edition (accessed June 4, 2010).
20. Florence Daviet and Janet Ranganathan, "The Greenhouse Gas Protocol: The GHG Protocol for Project Accounting," WBCSD/WRI, November 2005, http://www.wri.org/publication/greenhouse-gas-protocol-ghg-protocol-project-accounting (accessed June 4, 2010).
21. "Greenhouse Gas Projections," *U.S. Climate Action Report,* Chapter 5, 2010, http://www.state.gov/g/oes/rls/rpts/car/90324.htm (accessed June 2010): 76–85.
22. Ibid.
23. "Carbon Foot Printing, An Introduction for Organizations," Carbon Trust, August 2007 http://teenet.tei.or.th/Knowledge/Paper/carbonfootprint.pdf (accessed June 6, 2010).
24. "Green House Gas Emission Management," ICF International, www.icfi.com/Markets/Energy/doc_files/GHG_Emis_Mngmt.pdf (accessed June 2010).

25. "Climate Change, Green House Gas Emissions," EPA Climate Leader Program, http://epa.gov/climatechange/emissions/index.html (accessed June 2010).
26. Bella Tonkonogy, Jim Sullivan, and Gregory A. Norris, "Evaluating Corporate Climate Performance: A Model for Benchmarking GHG Reductions," US EPA Climate Leader Program, 2007, www.epa.gov/climateleaders/documents/resources/tonkonogy_published_aceee_paper.pdf (accessed June 2010).
27. Ibid.
28. Thomass M. Kerr Esq., Cynthia Cummis, Vincent Camobreco, and Bella Tonkonogy, "Managing Corporate Carbon Risk: Elements of an Effective Strategy," US EPA Climate Leader Program, 2006, www.epa.gov/climateleaders/resources/papers.html (accessed June 4, 2010).
29. Bella Tonkonogy, Jim Sullivan, and Gregory A. Norris, "Evaluating Corporate Climate Performance: A Model for Benchmarking GHG Reductions," US EPA Climate Leader Program, 2007, www.epa.gov/climateleaders/documents/resources/tonkonogy_published_aceee_paper.pdf (accessed June 2010).
30. Low emitter guidance, USEPA Climate Leaders, Office of Air and Radiation EPA 43-R-08-007, www.epa.gov/climateleaders (accessed March 2009).
31. Ibid.
32. "Summary of Copenhagen Business Day," *Business Day Bulletin* 160 (December 13, 2009), http://www.iisd.ca/climate/cop15/bd/ (accessed June 4, 2010).
33. Ibid.
34. R.K. Pachauri and A. Reisinger, Fourth Assessment Report of the Intergovernmental Panel on Climate Change (IPCC), 2007, http://www.ipcc.ch/publications_and_data/ar4/syr/en/contents.html (accessed June 2, 2010).
35. "Living Beyond Our Means: Natural Assets and Human Well-Being." Statement from the Board, Millennium Ecosystem Assessment, March 2005, http://www.millenniumassessment.org (accessed June 2, 2010).
36. D.J. Merrey, P. Drechsel, F.W.T. Penning de Vries, and H. Sally, International Water Management Institute (IWMI), Africa Regional Office, Private Bag X813, 0127 Silverton, Pretoria, South Africa.
37. "Integrated Water Resources Management (IWRM): A Way to Sustainability," InfoResources, 2003, http://www.inforesources.ch/pdf/focus1_e.pdf (accessed June 4, 2010).
38. A.K. Chapagain, A.Y. Hoekstra, and H.H.G. Savenije, "Saving Water through Global Trade," *Research Report Series, UNESCO-IHE* 17 (September 2005), http://www.waterfootprint.org/Reports/Report17.pdf (accessed June 2010).
39. A.Y. Hoekstra, "Human Appropriation of Natural Capital: A Comparison of Ecological Footprint and Water Footprint Analysis," *Ecological Economics* (2009): 1963–74, 1966.
40. A.Y. Hoekstra and A.K. Chapagain, "Water Footprints of Nations: Water Use by People as a Function of Their Consumption Pattern," *Water Resource Management* 21 (2007): 35–48.
41. A.E. Ercin, M.M. Aldaya, and A.Y. Hoekstra, "A Pilot in Corporate Water Footprint Accounting and Impact Assessment: The Water Footprint of Sugar-Containing Carbonated Beverage," *Value of Water Research Report Series, UNESCO-IHE* 39 (2009): 7.
42. Ibid., 10–15.
43. P.W. Gerbens-Leenes and A.Y. Hoekstra, "Business Water Footprint Accounting: A Tool to Assess How Production of Goods and Services Impact on Freshwater

Resources Worldwide," *The Value of Water Research Report Series UNESCO-IHE* (March 2008): 3, 9.

44. A.K. Chapagain, A.Y. Hoekstra, and H.H.G. Savenije, "Saving Water through Global Trade," *Research Report Series, UNESCO-IHE* 17 (September 2005), http://www.waterfootprint.org/Reports/Report17.pdf (accessed June 2010).
45. "Greenhouse Gas Risk Assessment," Electric Power Research Institute, August 2006, mydocs.epri.com/docs/public/000000000001014368.pdf (accessed March 2009).
46. Pankaj Bhatia and Janet Ranganathan, "The Greenhouse Gas Protocol: A Corporate Accounting and Reporting Standard," *WBCSD/WRI*, March 2004, http://www.wri.org/publication/greenhouse-gas-protocol-corporate-accounting-and-reporting-standard-revised-edition (accessed June 4, 2010): 64.

CONTRIBUTORS

Roya Ayman is a professor and the director of the Industrial and Organizational Psychology program of the Institute of Psychology, and a fellow of the Leadership Trust, U.K. Among her research contributions, Dr. Ayman was the coeditor of a book titled *Leadership Theory and Research: Perspectives and Directions*. She is an associate editor of the *Journal of Management and Organizations* and is on the editorial board of the *Leadership Quarterly* and *International Cross-Cultural Journal of Management*. Her numerous articles and chapters are on topics of leadership, culture, and diversity. As an active practitioner nationally and internationally, she has designed and conducted diversity training, cross-cultural interaction, and leadership development programs in private and public sectors.

Siva K. Balasubramanian's career as a manager, educator, and academic administrator spans three decades. He previously taught at the University of Iowa, University of Alberta, and Maastricht School of Management. Recently, he served as the Henry J. Rehn Professor at the College of Business, Southern Illinois University, Carbondale. Dr. Balasubramanian is the recipient of the prestigious Fulbright Research Chair award, in addition to several competitive research grants. He serves as a member of the editorial board at leading journals, is the website editor for the *Journal of Marketing*, and is the regional editor for North America for the *British Food Journal*. Dr. Balasubramanian's research interests focus on marketing communications (with an emphasis on product placements and public policy issues), diffusion of new product innovations, and advanced research/measurement tools in marketing. He is the author or coauthor of over thirty publications in leading marketing journals. His research reflects an interdisciplinary/empirical character. His stint in academia spans over two decades and includes multiple administrative roles (director of MBA program, director of Ph.D. program, and acting dean of the SIUC College of Business). He is listed in a variety of directories including Who's Who in Business Higher Education.

Debbie Cernauskas is a risk management consultant and an adjunct professor of finance at Northern Illinois University. She is also a board member for the Center for Risk Management and Quantitative Finance at the University of California (Santa Cruz) and a senior advisor for the Center for Business Innovation and Finance at Santa Clara University (Santa Clara, California). She has taught graduate and undergraduate courses in finance at several other Chicago-area universities including the Illinois Institute of Technology and DePaul University. Dr. Cernauskas is a financial professional and thought leader with risk management, operational management, decision sciences, business development, strategic and financial planning, and financial modeling expertise. She recently worked for IBM as a Senior Advisor for Risk Management for financial services firms and has experience in Basel II and Solvency II issues. As an industry professional, Deborah has worked in several industries including transportation, communications, and market research. She recently worked with the Operational Risk Data Exchange, a global loss data consortium that provides guidance on operational risk modeling and risk management for Basel II compliance and internal management. She is a coauthor with Anthony Tarantino of John Wiley and Son's *Financial Risk Management: Six Sigma and Other Next Generation Techniques* (April 2009). She has written peer reviewed articles for the *Journal of Internal Money and Finance*, *Journal of Operational Risk*, *Cost Engineering*, and *Journal of Equipment Lease Financing*. She received her B.S. and M.S. in Applied Probability and Statistics, her MBA with a concentration in financial management, and her Ph.D. in Management Science with a concentration in finance.

Ghazale Haddadian is an Environmental Management and Sustainability Masters Candidate at the Illinois Institute of Technology, Stuart School of Business, in Chicago, Illinois. Ms. Haddadian has a B.S. degree in Computer Science with a concentration in data mining and relational data analysis, and an MBA in Finance and International Business from Wright State University in Dayton, Ohio. Her professional and academic experience includes implementation of RFID solutions for resource time tracking and the design of sustainable economic development strategies in small towns.

Charles T. Hamilton is a clinical associate professor at the Stuart School of Business. Prof. Hamilton teaches auditing, financial accounting, and managerial accounting. His professional experience includes auditing for an international public accounting firm and providing independent audit and consulting services. His primary research interest is in accounting education and the behavioral factors that influence audit judgment. He served as an Audit Standards Discussion Leader for the Illinois CPA Society. He writes about the teaching of accounting, including the chapter "The Auditor and Legal Liability" in *Great Ideas for Teaching Accounting*. Dr. Hamilton's research interest is in accounting education and behavioral factors in audit judgment.

Erica L. Hartman is a Project Manager at APT where she provides services in the areas of organizational surveys, job analysis, selection, performance management, and multisource feedback. Erica received her master's degree and Ph.D. from the Illinois Institute of Technology (IIT) Industrial and Organizational Psychology Program. In addition to her formal academic training, Dr. Hartman has written various publications including a book chapter titled "Leadership Development in Higher Institutions: A Present and Future Perspective," which is included in *The Future of Leadership Development*. She has also published a chapter on Situational Leadership Theory in the Encyclopedia of Leadership series and has made several presentations at the Society for Industrial/Organizational Psychology (SIOP).

Gaurav Jain is pursuing a master's degree in finance at the Stuart School of Business, Illinois Institute of Technology at Chicago. After receiving a degree in mechanical engineering from the Indian Institute of Technology (IIT) Bombay, he worked as a Senior Research Associate at a leading Indian firm that specializes in niche markets. Gaurav is also the recipient of the prestigious National Talent Search (NTS) scholarship awarded by the government of India. Gaurav is passionately committed to green marketing practices and nurturing the environment.

Nasrin R. Khalili is Associate Professor of Environmental Management at Illinois Institute of Technology Stuart School of Business. Dr. Khalili's research focus and teaching expertise are in the areas of environmental management, sustainability, and managerial decision-making. Her areas of specialization range from synthesis and development of catalysts and adsorbents for removal of pollutants from industrial waste streams to analysis of environmental economics and cost valuations for sustainability projects. Her most recent research is focused on the development of sustainable energy portfolio models for developing nations. Dr. Khalili holds two patents for the design of new processes for converting waste sludge to activated carbon and a catalyst for NOx removal. Her recent research resulted in the development of an award-winning water purification system called "KlarAqua." In collaboration with her graduate student, she designed and copyrighted a computer program in 2007 titled "Environmental Attribute Calculator" (EAC). This program can be used to design energy management programs with application in a wide range of industrial and commercial buildings. Professor Khalili holds a B.S. in Chemistry and M.Sc. and Ph.D. in Environmental Engineering.

Whynde Melaragno is a business consultant, primarily focused on business strategy development and execution mainly for Fortune 500 companies. She is a recognized expert in the emerging discipline of "business architecture," which serves a critical link between strategy and its successful execution across departments within large organizations. Whynde has a master's degree in environmental management and sustainability from the Illinois Institute of Technology, Stuart School of Business, in Chicago, Illinois, and an undergraduate degree in biology and chemistry. Through her unique combination of academic and professional experience, she brings business and sustainability together with a solid, real-life understanding of what it really takes for business to achieve sustainable practices while staying competitive in the new economy.

Navid Sabbaghi is an Assistant Professor of Management Science at the Illinois Institute of Technology, Stuart School of Business. He conducts research in the areas of mathematical modeling and optimization, incentives and supply contracts, green supply chain management, and energy and emissions management. He teaches MBA courses on modeling and decision making and Ph.D. courses on optimization.

Omid Sabbaghi is an Assistant Professor of Finance at the University of Detroit Mercy, College of Business Administration. He conducts research in the areas of socially responsible investments, risk management, corporate finance, and asset pricing. He teaches MBA courses on investments and corporate finance and has lectured and consulted with financial firms in the United States. He received the Standard & Poor's Best Paper Award in Investments: Asset Pricing. Dr. Sabbaghi has also received the Academy of Finance Best Paper Award in Investments for his work on socially responsible investments. Dr. Sabbaghi has a B.A. in economics, statistics, and applied mathematics from University of California at Berkeley, and MBA and Ph.D. in business from the University of Chicago.

INDEX

Printed by Printforce, the Netherlands